Digital Innovation for Pandemics

A pandemic does not only bring health concerns for society but also significantly affects individuals and government and business operations. Recently, COVID-19 has substantially hampered conventional businesses and organizations worldwide. Digital technology can help achieve business continuity and overcome challenges caused by pandemic situations. Digital innovation is the application of digital technology to existing business problems. Ideas such as digital transformation and digitization are closely related to digital innovation. In this pandemic period, many businesses recognize that they need to transform, innovate, and adopt new technologies to stay competitive. However, digital transformation is an inherently complex process, and the time pressure to adopt quickly may result in further complexities for organizations in fostering digital technologies.

Digital Innovations for Pandemics: Concepts, Challenges, Constraints, and Opportunities presents the potential of digital responses to the COVID-19 pandemic. It explores new digital concepts for learning and teaching, provides an overview of organizational responses to the crisis through digital technologies, and examines digital solutions developed to manage the crisis. Examining how information systems researchers can contribute to these global efforts, this book seeks to showcase how consumers, citizens, entrepreneurs, organizations, institutions, and governments are leveraging new and emerging digital innovations to disrupt and transform value creation in the pandemic era. It captures the breadth of digital innovations carried out to handle the pandemic and looks at the use of digital technologies to strengthen various processes. The book features the following:

- Solutions on how digital technologies enable responses to a global crisis
- An analysis of information systems used during the management of the COVID-19 pandemic
- New concepts for digital business and innovative content models for different sectors

This book is written for advanced undergraduate students, postgraduate students, researchers, and scholars in the field of digital business, education, and healthcare. It includes theoretical chapters and case studies from leading scholars and practitioners on the technology-adoption practices of non-government organizations (NGOs), government, and business.

Digital Innovation for Pandemics

Concepts, Challenges, Constraints, and Opportunities

Edited by
Jasleen Kaur & Navjot Sidhu

CRC Press
Taylor & Francis Group
Boca Raton London New York

CRC Press is an imprint of the
Taylor & Francis Group, an **informa** business

AN AUERBACH BOOK

First Edition published 2023
by CRC Press
6000 Broken Sound Parkway NW, Suite 300, Boca Raton, FL 33487-2742

and by CRC Press
2 Park Square, Milton Park, Abingdon, Oxon, OX14 4RN

© 2023 Taylor & Francis Group, LLC

CRC Press is an imprint of Taylor & Francis Group, LLC

ISBN: 978-1-032-20772-8 (hbk)
ISBN: 978-1-032-35761-4 (pbk)
ISBN: 978-1-003-32843-8 (ebk)

DOI: 10.1201/9781003328438

Typeset in Garamond
by Apex CoVantage, LLC

Contents

Contributors

Nadiah Yan Abdullah is a language teacher at the Centre for Languages and General Studies, Universiti Pendidikan Sultan Idris. She has more than thirty years of experience in teaching English language in primary, secondary, and tertiary levels. Currently, she is teaching proficiency courses to undergraduates and international students. Her research interests include teaching vocabulary, curriculum change, teaching phonics, and higher education.

Mazhar Shamsi Ansary completed his Graduation in Education honors from JK College, Purulia, West Bengal, in 2012. After graduating, he went to Sidho-Kanho-Birsha University for a master's degree (Department of Education) and completed it in 2014. Then he qualified for the NET (National Eligibility Test) in December 2016. He is presently working as an assistant professor in the Department of Education at Netaji Nagar College for Women, Netaji Nagar, Kolkata, as well as pursuing his PhD at Sidho-Kanho-Birsha University on the topic of "Attitude of Post Graduate Students towards Mobile Learning in West Bengal and Jharkhand: A Comparative Study." He has published more than 10 research articles in various reputed national and international journals and edited books. He has presented many research papers in national and international seminars and conferences. His research interests are educational technology, peace education, women education, minority education, sustainable development, indigenous knowledge, etc.

Dr. Sudin Bag is presently an assistant professor of business administration in Vidyasagar University, West Bengal, India. Dr. Bag has more than 10 years of working experience, which is inclusive of corporate exposure and teaching in management in colleges and university. His areas of interest include marketing management, services marketing, research methodology, consumer behavior, and entrepreneurship, to name a few. He has published over 25 research papers in reputed national and international journals, contributed a good number of research papers in edited volumes, including *Springer Nature*, and also authored two books (including one edited volume) of high repute. Dr. Bag is associated with various academic institutions and professional bodies. He is the recipient of IARA Best Faculty Award—2019 in the field of management.

Moumita Banerjee is a faculty of Economics at South Calcutta Girls' College, affiliated with University of Calcutta, India. She received her master's degree in economics from the University of Calcutta in 2016. She began her teaching career in 2018. She teaches microeconomics, macroeconomics, econometrics, international economics, money and financial markets, and public economics in undergraduate courses. Her primary research goals are directed toward understanding financial markets by engaging in theoretical and empirical studies. Her future plans are aimed toward the formulation of new concepts and developing models on blockchain technology for digital assets that go beyond traditional financial instruments.

Dr. Santosh Kumar Behera is presently working as an associate professor in the Department of Education, Kazi Nazrul University, Asansol, Paschim Bardhaman, West Bengal-713340, India. After completing his graduate degree from Fakir Mohan University, Odisha, he got himself admitted to the MA in Education program at Vinaya Bhavana, Visva Bharati (a central university in India) and then did research work leading to his PhD paper titled "An Investigation into the Attitude of SC and ST Children of Southern Orissa towards Education" at Vinaya Bhavana, Visva-Bharati, Santiniketan. He has 11 years' teaching experience. His research interests are SC and ST education/tribal education, educational technology, philosophy of education, peace education, teacher education, comparative education, curriculum studies, higher education, and measurement and evaluation in education. He has contributed lot of articles and edited volumes in the educational fields. He is the editor in chief of *EDUQUEST*, an international refereed journal in education (ISSN: 2277-3614, printed version).

Mr. Alamgir Biswas Mr. Alamgir Biswas is an assistant librarian at Adamas University, Kolkata, West Bengal, India. He has completed his MLISc, MA (English), and he is about to submit his doctoral thesis in massive open online courses. He has over 10 years of teaching and administrative experience. He has published seven research papers in different UGC Care, SCOPUS, and Web of Science Journals and presented in three national and eight international conferences/seminars.

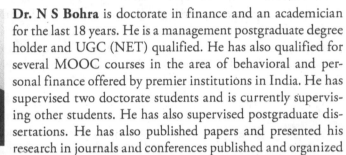

Dr. N S Bohra is doctorate in finance and an academician for the last 18 years. He is a management postgraduate degree holder and UGC (NET) qualified. He has also qualified for several MOOC courses in the area of behavioral and personal finance offered by premier institutions in India. He has supervised two doctorate students and is currently supervising other students. He has also supervised postgraduate dissertations. He has also published papers and presented his research in journals and conferences published and organized by reputed publishers and institutions across the globe. Dr. Bohra is also associated with CDSL and SEBI as resource person for spreading financial literacy in India.

Rajashree Chaurasia received her BTech (IT) and MTech (IT) degrees from Guru Gobind Singh Indraprastha University, Delhi, India, in 2009 and 2014, respectively. She is a gold medalist in both B.Tech. and M.Tech. and UGC NET qualified. She was with Infosys Technologies Ltd. from 2009 to 2011 and thereafter taught at Guru Tegh Bahadur Institute of Technology for a year. She has been serving as Assistant Professor in the Department of Computer Engineering at Directorate of Training and Technical Education, Delhi (Government of NCT of Delhi), since 2012. She holds a Group 'A' Gazetted post in the institution mentioned. She is an active researcher in the fields of computer security, computer graphics, and computational biology.

Vikas S. Chomal holds a PhD, MPhil, and MCA. He is working as an assistant professor in the School of Engineering, P P Savani University at Kosamba, Surat in Gujarat, India. He has a number of publications in reputed journals and conferences to his credit. His papers have been indexed by Scopus and have been widely cited. His research interest lies in the area of software engineering. He has received best paper awards and has widely traveled in the country for research purposes.

Dr. Saheli Guha Neogi Ghatak is an assistant professor in the Department of Sociology, School of Liberal Arts and Culture Studies, Adamas University, West Bengal, India. She has completed her PhD, MA (sociology), MSW, and MLIS. She has eight years of teaching experience in UG, PG and five years of research experience and is presently guiding four research scholars. She has edited one book—*Digitalization of Economy and* Society—published by CRC Press, Taylor and Francis Group and contributed over 16 research papers to national and international peer-reviewed journals. She has also contributed book chapters and presented research papers in more than 30 national and international seminars/conferences. She was invited as a guest researcher at the University of Copenhagen, Denmark, in 2018 and invited as chairperson of the international conference in Bangladesh in 2019. Dr. Ghatak is a life member of the Indian Sociological Society.

Dr. Udayan Ghose is working as Professor in the University School of Information, Communication and Technology (Guru Gobind Singh Indraprastha University). He joined GGS Indraprastha University as Lecturer in 2002. Before undertaking an assignment at GGSIPU, he worked as a lecturer at Birla Institute of Technology, Mesra, Ranchi. He obtained his master's degree in physics with a specialization in solid state physics from Banaras Hindu University, Varanasi, and subsequently obtained an M.Tech degree in computer science from Birla Institute of Technology, Mesra, Ranchi. From GGS IP University, he obtained his PhD (information technology) degree in the area of "data analysis using ICA techniques."

Dr. Maumita Ghosh is Head, Department of Economics, South Calcutta Girls' College, Calcutta. She obtained her PhD in health economics from Burdwan University. She conducted a minor research project on health issues of Darjeeling Hills residents, financed by the UGC. She taught in the Loreto College, Darjeeling (presently known as Southfield College) in the capacity of Associate Professor. Presently she is associated with the South Calcutta Girls' College, Calcutta. Some of her recent major research interests lie in the areas of financial economics, digital currency system, etc.

Revathi Gopal is a senior lecturer at the Faculty of Languages and Communication, Universiti Pendidikan Sultan Idris. She received her PhD degree in TESL from the Universiti Pendidikan Sultan Idris, in 2019. Currently, she teaches poetry in English and approaches to teaching literature in ESL classrooms. Her academic interests are reading and literature in English.

Dr Rani Gul is Assistant Professor at the University of Malakand, KPK, Pakistan. She has been in the field of teaching for the last 13 years. She has served in different academic and administrative positions and has a vast teaching-learning experience at both the national and international level. Her research spans a wide range of issues covering different domains of educational psychology, linguistics, curriculum, pedagogy, teacher education, science education, etc. She has been engaged in teaching and supervision activities at the undergraduate and postgraduate levels at both private and public sector universities.

Dr. Gulab Khan Khilji is currently serving as Deputy Director-Curriculum at the Bureau of Curriculum Secondary Education Department Balochistan, Quetta. He earned his PhD in Curriculum and Instruction from the University of North Texas, USA, in 2016. He has been working in different capacities in the areas of teacher education, education policy, curriculum, and education assessment with measurable contributions on his credit. His research interests include curriculum studies, education policy, teacher education, sociocultural theory, and qualitative research.

Ketan Kotecha is an administrator and a teacher of deep learning. His interest areas are artificial intelligence, computer algorithms, machine learning, and deep learning. Dr. Kotecha has expertise and experience of cutting-edge research and projects in AI and deep learning for the last 25-plus years. He has published widely with 100-plus publications in several excellent peer-reviewed journals on various topics ranging from cutting-edge AI, education policies, teaching and learning practices, and AI for all. He is a recipient of two SPARC projects in AI and worth INR 166 lacs from MHRD, Government of India, in collaboration with Arizona State University, USA, and the University of Queensland, Australia.

He is also a recipient of numerous prestigious awards like the Erasmus+ faculty mobility grant to Poland; the DUO-India professors' fellowship for research in responsible AI, in collaboration with Brunel University, UK; the LEAP grant at Cambridge University UK; the UKIERI grant with Aston University, UK; and a grant from the Royal Academy of Engineering, UK under the Newton Bhabha Fund. Dr Kotecha has published three patents and delivered keynote speeches at various national and international forums, including at Machine Intelligence Labs, USA, IIT Bombay under the World Bank project; the International Indian Science Festival organized by the Department of Science and Technology, Government of India; and many more. He is currently the associate editor of the *IEEE Access* journal.

Mahendran Maniam is an associate professor at the Faculty of Languages and Communication, Universiti Pendidikan Sultan Idris. He obtained his PhD (TESL) from the International Islamic University of Malaysia in 2009. His research areas are mainly in applied linguistics. He currently conducts research and supervises doctoral and master students in the areas of second language acquisition and language learning strategies. He is also the deputy chief editor of *Journal of ELT and Education (JEE)*. He was recently appointed as a visiting professor at Bharath University (Chennai), India.

Sasigaran Moneyam is the director of Centre for Languages and General Studies (CEFLAGS), Universiti Pendidikan Sultan Idris. He has obtained both bachelor's and master's degrees in the field of TESL from (UPSI). He has many years of experience in teaching English at the tertiary level.

Mazura Mastura Muhammad is an associate professor and the dean of the Faculty of Languages and Communication, Universiti Pendidikan Sultan Idris. She obtained her PhD from Lancaster University, UK. Academically, she is interested in corpus linguistics, which is interrelated with language big data. Hence, most of her research interests are related to this area as well as teaching English as a second language (TESL), language testing and assessment, policy research, and historical linguistics.

Eng Tek Ong is currently a professor of science education at the Faculty of Social Sciences and Liberal Arts, UCSI University (Malaysia). He has taught in secondary schools and was seconded at SEAMEO RECSAM as a science education specialist and subsequently senior science education specialist as well as the head of the Science Division. Before joining the university, he was a senior assistant director at the School Inspectorate, Malaysian Ministry of Education.

Sodip Roy has been working as an assistant professor of political science at Bangladesh Open University (BOU) since 2012. Prior to this, he served as a BCS (Education) cadre from the 28th BCS in A H Z Government College, Madarganj, Jamalpur. He studied at University of Dhaka, Durham University and University of Nottingham (Malaysia). He is an awardee of the Commonwealth Shared Scholarship (UK) and Tilburg University Alumni Scholarship (Netherlands). His areas of interest are refugee and migration, ethnic conflicts, and open and distance learning (ODL). He has published many articles and book chapters in the national and international arenas since his academic career started. He is the author of two book chapters in *Bangladesh: Rastro o Rajniti* (Songbed publication) and *Bangladeshe Nirbachon* (Prothoma Prokashon). There are four more textbooks written by him for different levels of learners of BOU. His forthcoming book is translations (in Bengali) of Giorgio Agamben's *Homo Sacer: Sovereign Power and Bare Life*.

Jatinderkumar R. Saini received a PhD degree in 2009. He secured gold medals and a first rank at the university level in all years of postgraduation, preceded by a silver medal in the final year of graduation. He is recipient of DAAD Fellowship (Germany). He has an h-index of 16, i10 index of 30, and 200-plus research publications in various journals and conferences. Ten candidates have been awarded a PhD degree under his supervision. He has reviewed 500-plus papers, with 50-plus papers for journals of ACM Transactions and IEEE Transactions. He has been included in top 1% of computer science reviewers in the world by WoS. He has completed more than 50 physical or MOOC certifications from different organizations, including IBM, Google, Massachusetts Institute of Technology, Stanford University, University of Texas, Johns Hopkins University, Cambridge University, Pennsylvania State University, Rice University, Vanderbilt University, and University of California. He is Jt. Secretary and Executive Committee Member of ISRS, Pune Chapter. Formerly, he was an active executive committee member in various capacities with the chapters of different professional bodies like CSI, IETE, and ISG. He is working as Professor and Director at SICSR, Symbiosis International (Deemed University), Pune, India. Formerly, he also worked at one of only four licensed Certifying Authorities of Ministry of Information Technology, Government of India.

Amiya Kumar Sarkar has a BA degree (political science) from Netaji Subhas Open University and an MA degree (public administration) from Shobit University. He is pursuing his PhD from Adamas University, Kolkata, in the area of tribal development in Jharkhand. Besides his academics, he is actively associated with different social welfare activities and plays an active role in different cultural, political, and social activities.

Ms. Mahak Sethi is working as an Assistant Professor at Graphic Era Deemed to be University, Dehradun, Uttarakhand, India. She completed her master's degree in business administration with a specialization in finance and marketing and is currently pursuing her doctorate degree in the field of finance, where her key research areas are general finance, financial literacy, and digital payments. Ms. Sethi has also counseled many candidates for higher education as an admission counselor at Graphic Era University, Dehradun. She has presented her literary texts at various national and international conferences.

Charanjit Kaur Swaran Singh is an associate professor at the Faculty of Languages and Communication, Universiti Pendidikan Sultan Idris. She received a PhD degree in TESL from the Universiti Putra Malaysia in 2014. She has more than 15 years of teaching experience. Her research interests include teaching English as a second language, language assessment, and teacher education.

Tarsame Singh Masa Singh is a member of the International Literacy Association and a Penang Chapter executive member for the Malaysian English Language Teaching Association. He often works as a conference secretary and judge for poster presentations. He is actively involved as a reviewer for local peer-reviewed journals and conference proceedings. He has a keen interest in the area of oral communication strategies and language learning strategies among second language learners. He plays a major role in planning and implementing highly immersive activities at the institute and regional levels to sustain learners' interest in the English language.

Dr. Abhijit Sinha, presently an associate professor in commerce at Vidyasagar University, West Bengal (India), has been in academics for seventeen years. He secured his first and second positions in M.Com and MBA examinations, respectively. He holds interest in the areas of finance, banking, and corporate governance, to name a few. Dr. Sinha is a prolific researcher who has published more than seventy research articles, presented papers in more than sixty occasions in different national and international conferences, and successfully guided scholars for the awarding of doctorate and M.Phil. degrees. He has completed two projects, one sponsored by the UGC and the other by ICSSR. Dr. Sinha is an author of three books, two of which are published by international publishing houses, and is also the co-editor of four books published by national-level publishers.

Muhammad Fadzllah Zaini is a senior lecturer at the Department of Malay Language and Literature, Faculty of Languages and Communication, Sultan Idris University of Education. His areas of specialization are corpus linguistics, computer linguistics, and machine learning. He is active in industrial grant research and international associations related to digital humanities, the Learner Corpora Association, and the IEEE.

Chapter 1

Investigating the Factors That Facilitate the Acceptability of Digital-Based Education among Students of Higher Education during COVID-19

Dr. Sudin Bag and Dr. Abhijit Sinha

Content

DOI: 10.1201/9781003328438-1

1.1 Introduction

The innovations in different spheres of life have affected human orientation. The development around us has led to the unending development that is being brought about with knowledge creation and sharing and honing the hard and soft skills that individuals possess. In order to match with the changing circumstances, the basic prerequites required in this dynamic world include the ability to create and mix freely with others to generate innovative answers to existing problems and power to critically understand and assess the information offered regarding its trustworthiness so that it can be integrated into the current task (Aksyukhin et al., 2009). The world is slowly moving to the use of artificial intelligence, machine learning, Internet of Things, and cloud computing, to name a few, all of which fall under 4.0 technologies. This new generation of technology refers to digitalization, which is the era of managing big data. It should be noted that increased digitalization help to increase the volume and production efficiency through increased speed of operations and product quality and also reducing the defective rate (Jager et al., 2015). Kopotun et al. (2020) opined that with the fast changing and developing technologies, workplaces would require the need for latest technologies that disrupt industries and create new industries. Moreover, it is an urgent need for employers to employ the right staff who will help to keep pace with changing needs by being a good learner. Nowadays, the improvement of information culture is among the inescapable roles of an education system (Lauri et al., 2016).

The industry needs have forced students to change and upgrade themselves in terms of skills so that they fit the changed industry environment. Today's industry requires data analytics experts who possess the skills to crunch and handle big data and use them to generate solutions. The innovations that have taken place in the field of teaching and learning have helped to combat distance barriers and the problems emanating from teacher choice and the pace of following classes that students faced in the learning process. Thus, the problems of traditional teaching and learning processes have been mitigated with digitalization in education that the world has been experiencing since the beginning of the pandemic. However, it can be noted that this is made possible by the fast penetration of computers and the internet. The availability of broadband and connectivity in many parts of the country has made it possible to apply it in the educational sector. The researchers in this contribution focus on digital-based education and, more importantly, look at the perception of students toward adapting to this technology-driven education platform for continuous learning.

1.2. Theoretical Underpinning and Hypotheses of the Study

The developments during the last couple of decades point that there is a slow transformation from the traditional teaching-learning method to the online mode of education (Bisht et al., 2020). Though the practice has existed in India, it has been limited to a few institutes only. Till 2020, Indian higher educational institutions were not allowed to have more than one-fifth of their degrees offered online. Thus, the rate of transformation is yet to gain pace. However, the way pandemic affected different stakeholders changed the way education has been running in the country. The Indian experience has been a lot different from that of Western countries. The entire academic curriculum has been forced to shift to the tech-based mode of education, which is not so in Western countries, where many institutes have already been running several courses on online mode. Though education using the digital platform is the new practice, which has been contributing to continuing the education process despite the pandemic, this mode is not free from criticism. Online learning is not supportive of the two-way communication process and also does not allow observation over the learners (Jones & O'Shea, 2004). Similar such challenges are pointed by Taso and Chakraborty (2020) with respect to e-learning. The challenges in online education have also been studied from other perspectives, like the conduct of online examination (Sarrayrih & Ilyas, 2013), method of assessment (Ozden et al., 2004), and speed of assessment (Baleni, 2015). The study by Khan and Khan (2019) finds that the issues of technological incompetence and lack of trust on the ICT infrastructure for education are serious issues that hamper the success of online education.

The inclusion of education by the United Nations as one of the Sustainable Development Goals, e-learning will prove to be helpful in bringing inclusiveness in education. Though Ali (2020) finds that students in higher education have a relatively better knowledge about ICT, one should note that there are serious impediments in the process of online education that are faced by students, which include network issues and hardware-related problems. Though the issue of the understandability of shared resources is not that serious, getting access to resources is a problem for students. As per a study made by the Azim Premji Foundation, around three-fifths of school-going children do not have access to opportunities to learn online and only 15% of the rural Indian households have internet access, which is 42% in urban households (Das, 2020). This is in addition to the complaints about a nonconducive learning environment where there is less opportunity for interaction. There are other serious issues in this mode of education, which include loneliness, the inability to clarify doubts in time (Yusuf & Banawi, 2013; Abou et al., 2014), lack of access to the internet, poor infrastructure backup, and the inability to create an environment that promotes interaction (Aboagye et al., 2020). Despite the serious issues that confront the online form of education, there is evidence that points to several advantages associated with this mode, which include flexible methods (Abou et al., 2014; Dhawan, 2020), a platform for easy interaction in the form of chats (Marinoni et al., 2020; Anwar & Adnan, 2020), and easy distribution of content along with easy adoption as per requirement (Abou et al., 2014; Suresh et al., 2018).

It is therefore evident from extant literature that there are pros and cons connected with the system. However, the future of the mode of this type of education delivery will be a lot different from the present one. Hence, acceptability is an issue that has to be looked into by researchers. The present research therefore aims to recognize the factors that affect technology acceptance among the students of higher education, which can thereby help to identify the key focus areas that need to be included in the education-related decisions to be framed by the government.

The issue is relevant in the present circumstance where online education seems to be an inevitable option, so it is necessary to deeply explore the online form of education with special reference to the student community. According to Coman et al. (2020), it is vital to single out the key factors that play a vital role in the acceptance of technology-oriented teaching-learning. Despite several research papers being published during the pandemic, there is a paucity of research evidence in the global context that look into the effectiveness of this form of education (Hallgarten, 2020). The present study aims to address the inquiry by gaining insights about the impression of students toward online education in institutions engaged in higher studies in order to identify the factors that facilitate the acceptance of technology. The previous contributions mainly rely on the Technology Acceptance Model (TAM) developed by Davis in 1989, which considered the constructs that influenced the level of acceptance of technology (Park, 2009). The model is commonly used to assess the extent of the acceptance of new technology among users by establishing a causal relationship among external variables, beliefs, and attitudes toward technology and the use of the technology. This model developed by Davis considers three aspects, which include cognitive response, affective response, and behavioral response (Jones & Hubona, 2005). The two constructs of perceived usefulness and perceived easiness of use point to cognitive response. This cognitive response gives its manifestation in the form of affective response (as attitudes toward technology) and finally gets converted into a behavioral response (intention to use the new technology). A further look into the model shows that the independent dimensions that are considered include the perceived usefulness of technology and the perceived easiness of its use. The former dimension implies the belief that the new technology will give better outcomes (Lee et al., 2003). It means that if the users (in this case, students) think that online education will generate better outcomes, there is a higher chance of their using it (Yee et al., 2009). The second dimension of the original TAM is related to the extent of effort that will be necessary to learn and use new technology (Alrafi, 2009). From the general conception, it can be said that if the effort required for learning the new technology is less, more students will be accepting of the new technology. However, during the last three decades, researchers made changes to the model by considering new constructs (Kim et al., 2009; Shen et al., 2006). As per the model design of TAM, the path shows that higher levels of perceived usefulness and perceived ease of use leads to attitudes in favor of technology that get reflected in higher behavioral intention (Park, 2009). It is seen that a state of positive feeling generates positive thought whereas negative feelings attract negative thought, both of which impact the level of acceptance of new technology (Isen & Labroo, 2003; Forgas & George, 2001). For the purpose of this investigation, the researchers consider the construct "external variable," which refers to the consideration of several external forces like quality of content (Yuen & Park, 2012) and playfulness together with instant connectivity (Jang et al., 2016). The dependent variable in the original model is behavioral intention, which pertains to the intent of the user to use or not to use the online form of education (Ramayah & Ignatius, 2005; Li & Huang, 2009).

Based on the previous review of literature, the theoretical framework that is proposed for this study is presented in the form of a model in Figure 1.1, wherein the hypotheses are mentioned.

Based on the previous theoretical framework, the hypotheses of the study are as follows:

H1: External variables have a significant influence on the perceived benefits with the adaptation of technology.

H2: External variables have a significant influence on the perceived ease of use toward the adaptation of technology.

H3: Perceived ease of use has a significant impact on students' attitude.

H4: Perceived ease of use has a significant effect on the perceived benefits with the adaptation of technology.

H5: Perceived benefits have a significant influence on the attitude of students.

H6: Perceived benefits have a significant direct effect on adapting technology in education.

H7: Attitude has a significant mediating role in the connection between perceived benefits, perceived ease of use, and the adaptation of technology in higher education.

H8: Perceived ease of use has a significant direct impact on the adaptation of technology-oriented education.

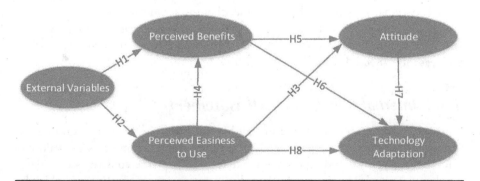

Figure 1.1   Theoretical framework.

1.3. Research Methodology

1.3.1 Sample and Data Collection

The data-based objective inquiry is based on a convenient sample of 868 higher education students studying in various institutes in the state of West Bengal (India). The online survey method is employed, in which a questionnaire is developed using a Google Forms link. The questionnaire link is shared with the students of different government undergraduate and postgraduate higher institutions with the help of their concerned teachers contacted over mobile or electronic mail. The researchers believe that in this present crisis scenario due to the pandemic, the research context has elements of homogeneity and generalizability due to two prominent justifications. Firstly, all the respondents belong to the same group, viz higher education, and secondly, the sample is exposed to the same stimuli (in this case, the pandemic). The research instrument for this exploratory study is well-structured for identifying the attitudes of students toward technology and their intention with respect to the online form of education. The extreme values (outliers) have been identified with the help of Z-score values for univariate cases and the Mahalanobis distance method for multivariate cases as recommended by Pallant (2011). It is a necessary step that is required to reduce error variance and increase the power of statistical testing. Also, if outliers are not removed in multivariate analysis, assumptions of sphericity and multivariate normality would be violated and give rise to Type-I and Type-II errors (Zimmerman, 1994). By applying the procedure, twelve outliers are identified (eight in univariate and four in multivariate cases) and thereby excluded from further analysis. Therefore, the actual sample size for the purpose of analysis 856. The analyses of data are done with the help of the SMART-PLS software version 3.3.3.

The demographic profile of the respondents collected through a sampling technique is presented in the following table.

From Table 1.1 and Figure 1.2, it is found that the ratio of male-female respondents is 3:2. Fifty-seven percent of the respondents are involved in undergraduate studies, whereas 43% are pursuing a posgraduate degree from a state-aided university in India. Regarding the discipline, there is a wide spectrum. Most of the students belong to the commerce stream, followed by the science discipline. It is further revealed that almost two-thirds of the respondents are from rural areas, whereas only 18% are from the urban belt.

1.3.2 Internal Consistency Measurement

The researchers use reliability and validity measures in order to examine the internal consistency of the proposal (Chin, 2010). Table 1.2 presents the values of Cronbach's alpha (α) and composite reliability (CR) for the constructs considered for the study. In this investigation, the value in each case exceeds the threshold value of 0.70 (Bag & Omrane, 2021; Nunnally & Bernstein, 1978). The value of average

Table 1.1   Profile of Student Respondents from Higher Educational Institutes

Characteristics	N	%	Characteristics	N	%
Gender			Course		
Male	512	60	Postgraduate	368	43
Female	344	40	Undergraduate	488	57
Discipline			Residence		
Arts	123	14	Urban	158	18
Commerce	486	57	Semi-urban	192	22
Science	247	29	Rural	506	60

Source: Primary survey

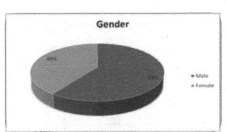

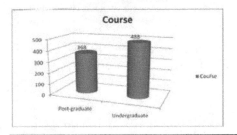

Figure 1.2   Profile of respondents.

variance extracted (AVE) is computed for assessing convergent validity. In this regard, the cutoff criterion of at least 0.50, as proposed by Fornell and Larcker (1981), is considered. The AVE score of minimum 0.5 indicates that there is convergent validity (Bag & Omrane, 2022). In other words, a construct is well capable of explaining the variability of its indicators (Gotz et al., 2010). The following table (no. 2) shows that the value of AVE lies between 0.596 and 0.678, thereby satisfying the given criterion. Hence, the reliability and validity of the research instrument is established.

Table 1.2 Measures of Reliability and Validity

Construct	No. of Indicators	A	CR	AVE	Q²
Attitude	6	0.862	0.897	0.593	0.357
External Variables	6	0.854	0.890	0.576	–
Perceived Benefits	7	0.906	0.925	0.640	0.447
Perceived Easiness to Use	6	0.853	0.891	0.577	0.249
Technology Adaptation	7	0.886	0.912	0.597	0.396

Source: Authors' calculation

'α' indicates Cronbach's alpha.

Table 1.3 Results of Discriminant Validity

	AT	EV	PB	PEU	TA
AT					
EV	0.645				
PB	0.848	0.813			
PEU	0.812	0.743	0.886		
TA	0.898	0.635	0.798	0.775	

Source: Authors' calculation

Note: AT—attitude; EV—external variables; PB—perceived benefits; PEU—perceived ease of use; TA—technology adaptation

The Heterotrait-Monotrait ratio (HTMT) is considered for testing discriminant validity. As per this criterion, the ratio should be less than the minimum value of 0.9 in order to establish a significant difference between two factors (Henseler et al., 2016; Ghorai et al., 2021). Table 1.3 in this study points that the criterion value is fulfilled for all cases, as evident from the values of correlation being less than the cutoff point. Hence, discriminant validity is established.

1.3.3 Evaluation of Inner Model and Hypotheses Testing

With the examination of the outer model and after testing for its basic requirements, the inner model is examined. It has to be done in order to know the explanatory power of the model and its predictive relevance. Path analysis is also done in order to understand the value of the path coefficients and their significance to understand whether the hypothesized relationships are accepted or rejected. The basic criterion to understand the strength of a model is the value of R-squared. The f^2 value denotes the effect size in the path model as given in Figure 1.2. The interpretation of the effect size depends on the value obtained. A value of 0.35 shows a large effect, whereas the values 0.15 and 0.02 represent medium and small effects, respectively (Bag & Omrane, 2021; Sawilowsky, 2009). In this examination, all the f^2 values are found to be nonnegative, thereby pointing that all the constructs are pertinent in explaining the attitudinal variance toward technology of the students toward online education. Thereafter, the redundancy analysis is done using the blindfolding method. It shows that the omission distance is eight, which lies within the criterion between five and ten (Bag et al., 2021; Hair et al., 2013). The Q^2 values are also calculated, which measure the effect of a latent variable at the structural level. In order to determine the statistical significance of the different paths in the model, the coefficients of these paths are computed using the bootstrapping method at a 5% significance level followed by a bias-correction technique.

1.4. Results of Analysis

After the consideration of the measurement of the outer model followed by the inner model, it is found that the coefficients of the different paths in the model are significant. Thus, all the hypothesized relationships get rejected, and the alternate hypotheses are accepted. The results of the direct relationship between perceived benefits, perceived ease of use, and technology adaptation toward higher education are presented in Figure 1.3 and Table 1.4. The outcome reveals a positive and significant relationship between external variables with perceived benefits (β=0.394) and perceived ease of use (β=0.662). This result confronts the findings in Unal and Uzun (2021), who stated that external variables such as perceived enjoyment, output quality, and playfulness (Wang et al., 2021) influence users' perception about the usefulness and ease of use of the digital-based form of education. The researchers further note that perceived ease of use has a positive influence on the perceived benefits' path (β=0.526) in a technology-oriented educational system. The analysis also divulges that both perceived benefit and perceived ease of use (β=0.319) have a positive and significant effect on technology adaptation. This result confirms the result in Buabeng-Andoh (2021), which stated that perceived benefits and ease of use are the two main constructs behind the acceptance of new technology by users. Furthermore, Saeed Al-Maroof et al. (2021) in their study opine that perceived usefulness and ease of use have a direct influence on the continuous intention to use technology.

Then, the study considers whether attitude acts a mediator in influencing the relationship between perceived benefits, perceived ease of use, and technology

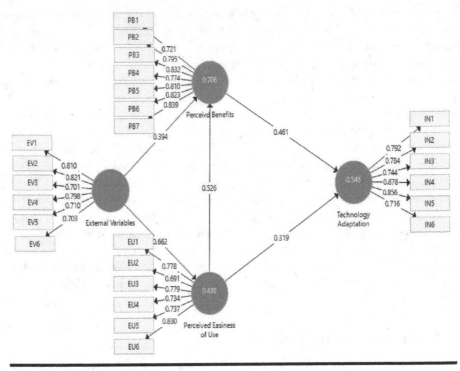

Figure 1.3 Path model showing direct relationships.

Table 1.4 Path Model Showing Direct Relationships

	Paths	β Value	t Value
H1	External Variables → Perceived Benefits	0.394	9.814**
H2	External Variables → Perceived easiness of use	0.662	23.560**
H4	Perceived easiness of use → Perceived Benefits	0.526	13.755**
H6	Perceived Benefits → Technology Adaptation	0.461	9.367*
H8	Perceived Easiness of use → Technology Adaptation	0.319	5.914**

Source: Authors' calculation

adaptation by learners in higher educational institutions for continuous learning during this pandemic. The findings of the relationship are given in Figure 1.4 and Table 1.5, which reveal that both perceived benefit (β=0.515) and perceived ease of use (β=0.311) have a positive and significant influence on students' attitudes toward technology-oriented education. This result is in agreement with the

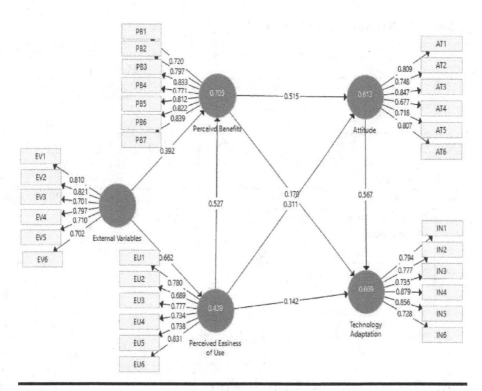

Figure 1.4 Path model including mediating variable.

findings in Goh and Wen (2021), where it was established that these two constructs are found to influence the attitudes of the hospitality management students toward using asynchronous online discussion boards as a platform to participate in tutorial question sessions. The present study also establishes that attitude has a significant influence on technology adaptation (β=0.567) in the case of using of digital teaching-learning platforms for continuous study during the pandemic. This result corroborates the findings in a recent study by Akour et al. (2021) that investigated the intention of people to learn using any mobile device and stated that a positive attitude a has significant influence on the adaptation of new technology.

Moreover, the result reveals that after introducing attitude as a mediating variable between perceived benefits and ease of use and technology adaptation, the value of the path coefficient slightly reduces, but the value of R^2 increases by 13%. The value of R^2 for technology adaptation is 0.669, which represents a strong relationship with the endogenous latent variable (Chin, 1998). Also, the result of the redundancy analysis shows that the Q^2 values (in Table 1.2) exceed 0.35, which reflects the sound effect in the relationship between endogenous and exogenous variables (Ringle et al., 2012; Bag & Omrane, 2022). The effect size is also calculated, whose results are presented in Table 1.5.

Table 1.5   Results of Path Model with Mediator

Paths		β Value	t Value	Effect Size (f2)
H1	External Variables → Perceived Benefits	0.393	9.817**	0.293
H2	External Variables → Perceived easiness of use	0.662	23.560**	0.781
H3	Perceived easiness of use → Attitudes	0.310	6.114**	0.452
H4	Perceived easiness of use → Perceived Benefits	0.526	13.755**	0.526
H5	Perceived Benefits → Attitudes	0.515	10.326**	0.262
H6	Perceived Benefits → Technology Adaptation	0.260	6.153*	0.286
H7	Attitudes → Technology Adaptation	0.603	15.309**	0.467
H8	Perceived easiness of use → Technology Adaptation	0.142	5.763*	0.221

Source: Computation by researchers

** significant at 1% level, * significant at 5% level.

1.5. Discussion and Conclusion

With the objective to identify perception of students of higher education toward a technology- oriented digital-based education system, it is noted from the study that students have a positive attitude toward the adaptation to a tech-based system, which supports the findings in Sheffield et al. (2015), Konwar (2017), Joo et al. (2018) and Osgerby (2013), which came out before COVID-19 came into the picture. But there are clear indications from previous studies that in a hybrid learning environment, the preference was more toward traditional face-to-face learning (Marriott et al., 2004; Osgerby, 2013). However, both online and offline systems were equally acceptable provided that the former was appropriately designed (Sinha & Bag, 2022). The result in this empirical contribution also supports the findings in Akour et al. (2021), who noted that the two key factors that created a positive attitude among the students toward an online teaching-learning method included perceived usefulness and ease of use, which ultimately have a positive impact on the intention to adapt technology for continuous education. In the same line, Han and Sa (2021) stated that perceived usefulness is positively impacted by perceived ease of use, and more importantly, both these factors have a positive effect on satisfaction, which positively impacted the intention of accepting online education during COVID-19 in Korea.

In order to check the internal consistency of the data collected, composite reliability (CR) and Cronbach's alpha are checked, which show that the CR values lie between 0.890 and 0.925, whereas Cronbach's alpha values exceed 0.70 (Islam & Bag, 2020). The computed values range between 0.805 and 0.906. Furthermore, the convergent validity of the latent variables is tested with the help of average variance extracted (AVE), which shows that the values range from 0.577 to 0.640 and hence are at an acceptable level, the cutoff value being 0.5 (Ray et al., 2021; Gotz et al., 2010). Thus, the unidimensionality of measurement scales is established. Regarding the discriminant validity, results show that the measurement scales reflect discriminant validity. The correlation value of the constructs is lower than the recommended threshold of 0.9, which thereby satisfies the condition of the HTMT ratio. Hence, from the discussion, the researchers opine that apart from internal consistency, convergent and divergent validities of the measurement model are well established, which are requirements for accepting the structural model. Moreover, the goodness of model fit, which is calculated using the SRMR value (0.061), is found to be acceptable as it is below the threshold value of 0.07.

The structural model (PLS-SEM) is therefore employed to find the relationship among the constructs considered for the study. The results of PLS-SEM (see Figure 1.4 and Table 1.5) show that the external variables have a bigger effect on perceived ease of use of digital-based education than the perceived benefits, though in both the cases, the effect is statistically significant. This result confirms the findings in earlier contributions of Sukendro et al. (2020) and Fauzi et al. (2021), who concluded that external variables have a significant influence on perceived usefulness and ease of use toward adapting technology-oriented education, which helped to continue with education during this pandemic. Similarly, it is noted that during the COVID-19 period, perceived benefits have a relatively higher impact on the attitude of students of higher education compared to perceived ease of use, which supports the result in Han and Sa (2021), who conducted the study during the pandemic, and Huang et al. (2019), who did the research prepandemic. It is therefore interesting to see that for making students more interested in engaging themselves more seriously in a digital education platform, it is necessary for experts and academics to highlight and project the advantages that the system gives to knowledge seekers. Moreover, the providers of such technology need to keep in mind the ease of use of the platform so that truly participative, more engaging, and lively interactions take place without hassle to the teachers and the learners. Thus, the connections that are drawn from the research framework for the study give interesting results and are worthy of being considered for designing policies and guidelines related to digital education in the country.

1.6. Implications of the Study

The pandemic is still continuing unabated. With newer strains of the virus coming into the picture, the digital form of education will seem to be continue for a long time. The present crisis and this experience for mankind have no precedence in recent years. In this background, with the education sector being seriously impacted, the present study is an effort to explore the intention of learners in higher education institutes in engaging with online education platforms through the lens of the TAM framework.

In this regard, external variables like quality of content, playfulness, and enjoyment during studies motivate students to move toward digital education. The research finds that students of higher education feel quite self-efficacious when it comes to the effects of perceived usefulness and ease of use toward the adaptation to an online platform for continuous learning. The results of this exploratory investigation indicate that external variables are important dimensions that have a say on the acceptance of an online-based system of education, which also mediates the effect of perceived usefulness and the intention to use regarding attitudes toward technology. This conclusion is in line with the findings in Wadie and Lanouar (2012) and Blessinger and Wankel (2013), which were done prior to the occurrence of COVID-19. In addition, this exploratory investigation establishes the positive and significant influence of both factors, viz perceived usefulness and perceived ease of use, on attitudes toward the intent to familiarize with digital-based education. These findings also find support from few earlier contributions like Bag et al. (2020). However, the research by Martinez-Lopez et al. (2020) finds the relatively stronger impact of perceived usefulness on attitudes toward technology compared to perceived ease of use. Thus, the result during the COVID-19 shows that students seriously engage and participate in digital-based education when they find that the system is useful to them in the long run and can contribute toward career building. The findings of this study have important implications for decision makers. It is necessary to ensure that students are well explained to about the possible benefits that they may get from their engagement in online education. Moreover, since ease of use is also an important element, there is a need to develop an environment where the teachers act as facilitators and not just mentors to the student community, which will create a learning atmosphere where students, mainly from rural areas, get acquainted with the online-based system. The time is ripe to ensure that the students develop a positive attitude toward such a tech-based education system, which is likely to continue with enough applications in the coming days.

1.7. Scope for Future Study

Like other research studies, this research work is also not free from limitations, which commonly opens various windows for future research. For instance, the study is based on single cross-sectional data; thus, it is hardly possible to measure the user intention over the advancement of technology and environmental changes. Moreover, the perception of students about usefulness and ease of use are explored to measure students' attitudes toward the intention to adapt technology. But future research work may explore other variables such as social norms, perceived behavioral control, etc. to produce more generalized results on this matter. In addition, future research studies can focus on the differences of user intention toward technology adaptation in higher education in terms of different sociodemographic profiles like gender, level of education, residential status, and so on.

Acknowledgment

This paper is largely an outcome of the research project sponsored by the Indian Council of Social Science Research (ICSSR). However, the responsibility for the facts stated, opinions expressed, and the conclusions drawn is entirely that of the authors.

References

Aboagye, E., Yawson, J. A., and Appiah, K. N. "COVID-19 and E-Learning: The Challenges of Students in Tertiary Institutions." *Social Educational Research* (2020): 1–8.

Abou El-Seoud, S., Seddiek, N., Taj-Eddin, I., Ghenghesh, P., Nosseir, A., and El-Khouly, M. "E-Learning and Students' Motivation: A Research Study on the Effect of E-Learning on Higher Education." *International Journal of Emerging Technological Learning* 9 (2014): 689–695.

Akour, I., Alshurideh, M., Al Kurdi, B., Al Ali, A., and Salloum, S. "Using Machine Learning Algorithms to Predict People's Intention to Use Mobile Learning Platforms During the COVID-19 Pandemic: Machine Learning Approach." *JMIR Medical Education* 7, No. 1 (2021): 240–252.

Aksyukhin, A. A., Vyzen, A. A., and Maksheneva, Z. V. "Information Technologies in Education and Science." *Modern High Technology* 11 (2009): 50–52.

Ali, W. "Online and Remote Learning in Higher Education Institutes: A Necessity in Light of COVID-19 Pandemic." *Higher Education Studies* 10, No. 3 (2020): 16–25.

Alrafi, A. "Technology Acceptance Model." In: A. Alrafi (Ed.), *Information Systems Adoption: A Study of the Technology Acceptance Model*, pp. 1–12. VDM Verlag, Germany; 2009.

Anwar, K., and Adnan, M. "Online learning Amid the COVID-19 Pandemic: Students Perspectives." *Journal of Pedagogical Research* 1 (2020): 45–51.

Azim Premji Foundation. *Myths of Online Education: Field Studies in Education, Research Group.* Azim Premji University; September, 2020. http://publications.azimpremji foundation.org/2429/1/Myths_of_online_education.pdf, accessed on January 20, 2022.

Bag, S., Aich, P., and Islam, M. A. "Behavioral Intention of 'Digital Natives' Toward Adapting the Online Education System in Higher Education." *Journal of Applied Research in Higher Education* 14, No. 1 (2020). http://doi.org/10.1108/JARHE-08-2020-0278.

Bag, S., and Omrane, A. "The Relationship Between the Personality Traits of Entrepreneurs and Their Decision-making Process: The Role of Manufacturing SMEs' Institutional Environment in India." *Forum Scientiae Oeconomia* 9, No. 3 (2021): 103–122.

Bag, S., and Omrane, A. "Corporate Social Responsibility and Its Overall Effects on Financial Performance: Empirical Evidence from Indian Companies." *Journal of African Business* 23, No. 1 (2022): 264–280.

Bag, S., Ray, N., and Banerjee, B. "Assessing the Effects of Experiential Quality on Behavioural Intention of Customers in Banking Services: The Moderating Role of Experiential Satisfaction." *FIIB Business Review* (2021): 1–14.

Baleni, Z. "Online Formative Assessment in Higher Education: Its Pros and Cons." *The Electronic Journal of e-Learning* 13, No. 4 (2015): 228–236.

Bisht, R. K., Jasola, S., and Bisht, I. P. "Acceptability and Challenges of Online Higher Education in the Era of COVID-19: A Study of Students' Perspective." *Asian Education and Development Studies* 11, No. 2 (2020). http://doi.org/10.1108/AEDS-05-2020-0119.

Blessinger, P., and Wankel, C. "Novel Approaches in Higher Education: An Introduction to Web 2.0 and Blended Learning Technologies." In: C. Wankel and P. Blessinger (Eds.), *Increasing Student Engagement and Retention in E-Learning Environments: Web 2.0 and Blended Learning Technologies*, pp. 3–16. Emerald Group Publishing, Bingley; 2013.

Buabeng-Andoh, C. "Exploring University Students' Intention to Use Mobile Learning: A Research Model Approach." *Education and Information Technologies* 26, No. 1 (2021): 241–256.

Chin, W. W. "The Partial Least Squares Approach to Structural Equation Modeling." *Modern Methods for Business Research* 295, No. 2 (1998): 295–336.

Chin, W. W. "How to Write up and Report PLS Analyses." In: *Handbook of Partial Least Squares*, pp. 655–690. Springer, Berlin, Heidelberg; 2010.

Coman, C., Tiru, L. G., Schmitz, L. M., Stanciu, C., and Bularca, M. C. "Online Teaching and Learning in Higher Education during the Coronavirus Pandemic: Students' Perspective." *Sustainability* 12, No. 24 (2020): 10367. http://doi.org/10.3390/su122410367.

Das, S. "Digital Divide Biggest Scourge in Online Study." *Daily Pioneer: Bhubaneshwar Edition*, 2020, August 06. Retrieved at www.dailypioneer.com/2020/state-editions/digital-divide-biggest-scourge-in-online-study.html, accessed on January 20, 2022.

Davis, F. D. "Perceived Usefulness, Perceived Ease of Use, and User Acceptance of Information Technology." *MIS Quarterly* (1989): 319–340.

Dhawan, S. "Online Learning: A Panacea in the Time of COVID-19 Crisis." *Journal of Educational Technological System* 49 (2020): 5–22.

Fauzi, A., Wandira, R., Sepri, D., and Hafid, A. "Exploring Students' Acceptance of Google Classroom during the Covid-19 Pandemic by Using the Technology Acceptance Model in West Sumatera Universities." *Electronic Journal of e-Learning* 19, No. 4 (2021): 233–240.

Forgas, J. P., and George, J. M. "Affective Influences on Judgments and Behavior in Organizations: An Information Processing Perspective." *Organizational Behavior & Human Decision Processes* 86, No. 1 (2001): 3–34

Fornell, C., and Larcker, D. F. "Evaluating Structural Equation Models with Unobservable Variables and Measurement Error." *Journal of Marketing Research* 18, No. 1 (1981): 39–50

Ghorai, S., Sinha, A., and Bag, S. "Exploring the Relationship between Attitude and Purchase Intention Towards Organic Food-does 'Willingness to Pay' Mediate the Effect?" *IITM Journal of Management and IT* 12, No. 2 (2021): 48–58.

Goh, E., and Wen, J. "Applying the Technology Acceptance Model to Understand Hospitality Management Students' Intentions to Use Electronic Discussion Boards as a Learning Tool." *Journal of Teaching in Travel & Tourism* 21, No. 2 (2021): 142–154.

Gotz, O., Liehr-Gobbers, K., and Krafft, M. "Evaluation of Structural Equation Models Using the Partial Least Squares (PLS) Approach." In *Handbook of Partial Least Squares*, pp. 691–711. Springer, Berlin, Heidelberg; 2010.

Hair, J. F., Ringle, C. M., and Sarstedt, M. "Partial Least Squares Structural Equation Modeling: Rigorous Applications, Better Results and Higher Acceptance." *Long Range Planning* 46, No. 1–2 (2013): 1–12.

Hallgarten, J. *Evidence on Efforts to Mitigate the Negative Educational Impact of Past Disease Outbreaks K4D Helpdesk Report 793.* Education Development Trust, Reading, UK; 2020.

Han, J. H., and Sa, H. J. "Acceptance of and Satisfaction with Online Educational Classes Through the Technology Acceptance Model (TAM): The COVID-19 Situation in Korea." *Asia Pacific Education Review* (2021): 1–13.

Henseler, J., Hubona, G., and Ray, P. A. "Using PLS Path Modeling in New Technology Research: Updated Guidelines." *Industrial Management & Data Systems* 116, No. 1 (2016): 2–20.

Huang, F., Teo, T., and Zhou, M. "Chinese Students' Intentions to Use the Internet for Learning." *Educational Technology Research and Development* 68, No. 2 (2019). http://doi.org/10.1007/s11423-019-09695-y.

Isen, A. M., and Labroo, A. A. "Some Ways in Which Positive Affect Facilitates Decision Making and Judgment." In: L. S. Schneider and J. Shanteau (Eds.), *Emerging Perspectives on Judgement and Decision Research*, pp. 365–393. Cambridge University Press, Cambridge, UK; 2003.

Islam, A., and Bag, S. "Assessing Service Quality in Higher Education: A Study in Indian Public Universities." *Shodh Sanchar Bulletin* 10, No. 38 (2020): 70–78.

Jager, A., Moll, C., Som, O., and Zanker, C. "Analysis of the Impact of Robotic Systems on Employment in the European Union." *Final Report.* Publications Office of the European Union, Luxembourg; 2015.

Jang, D. H., Yi, P., and Shin, I. S. "Examining the Effectiveness of Digital Textbook Use on Students' Learning Outcomes in South Korea: A Meta-analysis." *The Asia-Pacific Education Researcher* 25, No. 1 (2016): 57–68.

Jones, A., and Hubona, G. "The Mediation of External Variables in the Technology Acceptance Model." *Information & Management* 43, No. 6 (2005): 706–717.

Jones, N., and O'Shea, J. "Challenging Hierarchies: The Impact of E-learning." *Higher Education* 48 (2004): 379–395.

Joo, Y. J., So, H. J., and Kim, N. H. "Examination of Relationships Among Students' Self-determination, Technology Acceptance, Satisfaction, and Continuance Intention to Use K-MOOCs." *Computers & Education* 122 (2018): 260–272.

Khan, S., and Khan, R. A. "Online assessments: Exploring Perspectives of University Students." *Education and Information Technologies* 24, No. 1 (2019): 661–677.

Kim, Y.-J., Chun, J.-U., and Song, J. "Investigating the Role of Attitudes Toward Technology in Technology Acceptance from an Attitudes Toward Technology Strength Perspective." *International Journal of Information Management* 29 (2009): 67–77

Konwar, I. H. "A Study on Attitude of College Students Towards E-learning with Special Reference to North Lakhimpur of Lakhimpur District, Assam." *International Journal of Information Science and Education* 4, No. 1 (2017): 1–9

Kopotun, I. M., Durdynets, M. Y., Teremtsova, N. V., Markina, L. L., and Prisnyakova, L. M. "The Use of Smart Technologies in the Professional Training of Students of the Law Departments for the Development of Their Critical Thinking." *International Journal of Learning, Teaching and Educational Research* 19, No. 3 (2020): 174–187.

Lauri, L., Heidmets, M., and Virkus, S. "The Information Culture of Higher Education Institutions: The Estonian Case." *Information Research* 21, No. 3 (2016, September): 722. http://InformationR.net/ir/21-3/paper722.html.

Lee, Y., Kozar, K. A., and Larsen, K. R. "The Technology Acceptance Model: Past, Present, and Future." *Communications of the Association for Information Systems* 12, No. 1 (2003): 752–780.

Li, Y., and Huang, J. "Applying Theory of Perceived Risk and Technology Acceptance Model in the Online Shopping Channel." *World Academy of Science, Engineering and Technology* 53 (2009): 919–925.

Marinoni, G., Vant, L. H., and Jensen, T. (2020). *The Impact of COVID-19 on Higher Education Around the World. International Association of Universities*. www.iauaiu.net/IMG/pdf/iau_covid19_:///and_he_survey_report_final_may_2020.pdf (accessed on March 19, 2021).

Marriott, N., Marriott, P., and Selwyn, N. "Accounting Undergraduates' Changing Use of ICT and Their Views on Using the Internet in Higher Education—A Research Note." *Accounting Education* 13, No. 4 (2004): 117–130.

Martinez-Lopez, R., Yot-Domínguez, C., and Trigo, M. E. "Analysis of the Internet Use and Students' Web 2.0 Digital Competence in a Russian University." *International Journal of Technology Enhanced Learning* 12, No. 3 (2020): 316–342.

Nunnally, J. C., and Bernstein, I. H. "Psychometric Theory Mcgraw-Hill New York." *The Role of University in the Development of Entrepreneurial Vocations: A Spanish Study* (1978): 387–405.

Omrane, A., and Bag, S. "Determinants of Customer Buying Intention Towards Residential Property in Kolkata (India): An Exploratory Study Using PLS-SEM Approach." *International Journal of Business Innovation and Research* 28, No. 1 (2022): 119–139.

Osgerby, J. "Students' Perceptions of the Introduction of a Blended Learning Environment: An Exploratory Case Study." *Accounting Education* 22, No. 1 (2013): 85–99.

Ozden, M. Y., Erturk, I., and Sanli, R. "Students' Perceptions of Online Assessment: A Case Study." *Journal of Distance Education* (2004): 77–92.

Pallant, J. *SPSS Survival Manual: A Step by Step Guide to Data Analysis Using IBM SPSS*. Routledge, London; 2011.

Park, S. Y. "An Analysis of the Technology Acceptance Model in Understanding University Students' Behavioral Intention to Use e-Learning." *Educational Technology & Society* 12, No. 3 (2009): 150–162. https://library3.hud.ac.uk/summon/.

Ramayah, T., and Ignatius, J. "Impact of Perceived Usefulness, Perceived Easiness of Use and Perceived Enjoyment on Intention to Shop Online." *ICFAI Journal of Systems Management III*, No. 3 (2005): 36–51.

Ray, N., Mukherjee, T., and Bag, S. "Chaos and Complexity of Understanding Online Shopping Behaviour from Marketing Perspective." In: *Chaos, Complexity and Leadership 2021*, pp. 131–145. Springer, Cham; 2021.

Ringle, C. M., Sarstedt, M., and Straub, D. W. "Editor's Comments: A Critical Look at the Use of PLS-SEM." *MIS Quarterly* (2012): iii–xiv.

Saeed Al-Maroof, R., Alhumaid, K., and Salloum, S. "The Continuous Intention to Use E-learning, from Two Different Perspectives." *Education Sciences* 11, No. 1 (2021): 6–14.

Sarrayrih, M. A., and Ilyas, M. "Challenges of Online Exam, Performances and Problems for Online University Exam." *International Journal of Computer Science* 10, No. 1 (2013): 439–443.

Sawilowsky, S. S. "New Effect Size Rules of Thumb." *Journal of Modern Applied Statistical Methods* 8, No. 2 (2009): 26–30.

Sheffield, S. L. M., McSweeney, J. M., and Panych, A. "Exploring Future Teachers' Awareness, Competence, Confidence, and Attitudes Regarding Teaching Online: Incorporating Blended/Online Experience into the Teaching and Learning in Higher Education Course for Graduate Students." *The Canadian Journal of Higher Education* 45, No. 3 (2015): 1–14.

Shen, D., Laffey, J., Lin, Y., and Huang, X. "Social Influence for Perceived Usefulness and Ease-of-use of Course Delivery Systems." *Journal of Interactive Online Learning* 5, No. 3 (2006): 270–282.

Sinha, A., and Bag, S. "Intention of Postgraduate Students Towards the Online Education System: Application of Extended Technology Acceptance Model." *Journal of Applied Research in Higher Education* (2022). http://doi.org/10.1108/JARHE-06-2021-0233.

Sukendro, S., Habibi, A., Khaeruddin, K., Indrayana, B., Syahruddin, S., Makadada, F. A., and Hakim, H. "Using an Extended Technology Acceptance Model to Understand Students' Use of E-learning During Covid-19: Indonesian Sport Science Education Context." *Heliyon* 6, No. 11 (2020): 1–9. http://doi.org/10.1016/j.heliyon.2020.e05410.

Suresh, M., Priya, V. V., and Gayathri, R. "Effect of E-learning on Academic Performance of Undergraduate Students." *Drug Invention Today* 10 (2018): 1797–1800.

Taso, K., and Chakrabarty, A. "E-learning in Higher Education in India: Experiences and Challenges—an Exploratory Study." In: S. L. Peng, L. Son, G. Suseendran and D. Balaganesh (Eds.), *Intelligent Computing and Innovation on Data Science, Lecture Notes in Networks and Systems*, 118, 715–723. Springer, Singapore; 2020.

Unal, E., and Uzun, A. M. "Understanding University Students' Behavioral Intention to Use Edmodo Through the Lens of an Extended Technology Acceptance Model." *British Journal of Educational Technology* 52, No. 2 (2021): 619–637.

Wadie, N., and Lanouar, C. "Factors Affecting the Adoption of Internet Banking in Tunisia: An Integration Theory of Acceptance Model and Theory of Planned Behavior." *The Journal of High Technology Management Research* 23, No. 1 (2012): 1–14.

Wang, S., Tlili, A., Zhu, L., and Yang, J. "Do Playfulness and University Support Facilitate the Adoption of Online Education in a Crisis? COVID-19 as a Case Study Based on the Technology Acceptance Model." *Sustainability* 13, No. 16 (2021): 9104–9112.

Yee, H. T. K., Luan, W. S., Ayub, A. F., and Mahmud, R. "A Review of the Literature: Determinants of Online Learning Among Students." *European Journal of Social Sciences* 8, No. 2 (2009): 246–252.

Yuen, H. K., and Park, J. H. "The Digital Divide in Education and Students' Home Use of ICT." In *Proceedings of the 2nd International Conference on The Future of Education*, 1–4. Simonelli Editore University Press, Italy; 2012.

Yusuf, N., and Al-Banawi, N. "The Impact of Changing Technology: The Case of E-Learning." *Contemporary Issues Educational Research* 6 (2013): 173–180.

Zimmerman, D. W. "A Note on the Influence of Outliers on Parametric and Nonparametric Tests." *Journal of General Psychology* 121, No. 4 (1994): 391–401.

Chapter 2

The Readiness of Schools for an Online System of Education amid the COVID-19 Pandemic in Quetta, Balochistan

Rani Gul and Gulab Khan Khilji

Contents

DOI: 10.1201/9781003328438-2

2.1 Introduction

The unprecedented outbreak of the infectious coronavirus disease (COVID-19) has rapidly affected the global economy by shutting down all businesses and disrupting world trade and movements. This pandemic has also badly struck the education sector by closing all the educational institutions across the world and pushing them to migrate to online learning. Online learning is the use of digital devices and technologies in developing learning materials, instructional delivery, and assessment (Gul & Khilji 2021).

Like in other developing countries, initiating an online system of education in Pakistan is inevitable due to the prolonged closure of educational institutes since March 2020. Seeing this situation, in June 2020, the Higher Education Commission (HEC) of Pakistan immediately issued directives to all universities to utilize their existing infrastructure and capabilities and start online classes. At present, universities across the country are running their graduate and postgraduate programs online, but at the school level, no initiative has been taken by the federal or provincial government to provide an alternate learning platform to 1.47 million students (National Education Statistics 2018) who are enrolled in these public schools.

2.2 State of Education in Quetta, Balochistan

Quetta District is the capital city of the province Balochistan (Gul, Tahir, & Ishfaq 2020) and has a very low literacy rate of 46 % among all the other provinces of the country. The state of education in Quetta is considered better compared to other districts of the province but cannot be rated as good because major issues exist in the access to education and its quality. These issues include availability of schools, lack of basic facilities, teaching-learning quality, out-of-school children, etc. The reported male literacy rate is 66%, and female literacy is 46% (Ayub, Gul, Ali, & Maroof 2021; PSLM 2019–2020).

2.2.1 School Availability

Access to education is hindered by the availability of schools from primary to elementary and the secondary level to higher secondary. There are a total 358 primary schools, but for the elementary level, the number of schools is only 89 elementary schools, and at the secondary and higher secondary level, it further goes down to 77 secondary schools and 5 higher secondary schools. The overall ratio of primary to elementary schools is 4:1; for boys it is 7:1 and for girls it is 2:1 (BEMIS 2018). Among these 358 primary schools, there are 63 primary schools with a single room and 50 (14%) primary schools with a single teacher (Pakistan Economic Survey 2019).

2.2.2 Teaching-Learning Quality

The teaching-learning quality is a major concern in quality education in Quetta District. The 2018 Annual Status Report of Education indicates that the lack of professional development trainings for in-service teachers and the poor learning outcomes of the students weakens the teachers' learning quality (Pakistan Economic Survey 2019). The low quality of teaching-learning produces educational and programmatic gaps and influences the students' performance.

2.2.3 Out-of-School Children

Out-of-school children include not only those who never attended school but also those who dropped out. According to the P&D Population Projection Report -This constitutes 57% (BEMIS 2015) of the total of 395,207 school-age children (6–15 years) (Shah Bukhari, S.K.U., Said, H., Gul, R. and Ibna Seraj, P.M. 2022). In elementary and high schools, this percentage further rises, where 70% and 75% children are out of school (EMIS 2018). Similarly, among this population, 69% of girls and 77% pf boys (6–15 years) are out of school (EMIS 2018).

2.2.4 Lack of Facilities and School Environment

The absence of highly necessary facilities such as functional toilets, boundary walls, drinkable water, and electricity are other major concerns in majority of the schools in Quetta, especially in rural areas. According to the BEMIS (2018) report, 21% of the girls in primary schools have no boundary wall, 87 % have no drinkable water, 43% have no toilets (if available in some schools, they are not functional), and 72% have no electric supply. This situation needs the immediate attention of higher authorities for them to provide these basic facilities in all public schools to ensure access to quality education in the region.

2.2.5 Poverty

Despite full fee waiver in school tuition and admission fees and the provision of free textbooks by the government of Balochistan, poverty continues to hamper providing education to all children. It has been reported that other expenses like transportation costs, uniforms, and stationery expenses also create a hindrance for parents to send their children to schools (Gul, Khan, Mazhar, & Tahir 2020).

2.3 The Development Partners Supporting the Education Sector in Quetta, Baluchistan

At present, a number of national and international donor agencies are working in Baluchistan to uplift the standards of education in this region. Among them the Canadian International Development Agency (CIDA), the United Nations agency (WB), the Japan Bank for International Cooperation (JBIC), the Royal Netherlands Embassy (RNE), UNESCO, the United States International Development Agency (USAID), UNICEF, the World Food Program (WFP), and UNHCR are the closest partners within the education sector of the province. These organizations have provided support in the areas of teacher preparation, community school development, preservice teacher education, the provision of needed facilities, preschool education, and Education for All, or EFA (Gul, Khan, & Akhtar 2020). These agencies may support the government in initiating an alternative/online system of education for the students.

2.4 Rationale of the Study

The quality of education and access to it in Quetta, Balochistan, is greatly influenced by the unavailability of basic facilities and resources in schools. Due to school closures in the COVID-19 pandemic, the future of 1.3 million students enrolled in 1,3729 schools (EMIS 2018) of Balochistan and 105,236 students enrolled in 529 schools in Quetta District is at risk (Quetta District Education Plan 2017–2020). The local and provincial governments have not proposed any framework to impart an alternate system of education for these enrolled students.

Besides restricted access to education, particularly in rural areas, educational supplies, demand-side issues, a huge gender gap (25% girls are allowed to attend school), lack of basic facilities in schools, and 75 % out-of-school children are the major challenges to the education system. In this situation, online education is a potential replacement for formal education (Baloch, Shah, Noor, & Lacheheb 2017). The existing literature (Bukhari, Gul, Bashir, Zakir, & Javed

2021; Cavus & Ibrahim 2007; Gul, Ayub, Mazhar, Uddin, & Khanum 2021; Gul, Talat, Mumtaz, & Shaheen 2021; Odell, Abbitt, Amos, & Davis 1999; Peterson & Bond 2004) also affirms that online courses yield student results more comparable to those generated by face-to-face courses (Ayub, Gul, Ali, & Rauf 2021). With this motive, the present study has investigated the readiness of the public schools in terms of the availability of different digital devices, the availability of technology-expert teachers, and curriculum responsiveness for online learning.

2.5 Conceptual Framework

The COVID-19 pandemic is a completely new phenomenon to health professionals, the general mass, and education researchers. Different studies identify major challenges and highlighted the gray areas where the education system must respond for the continued learning of children, which will otherwise be interrupted due to this menace (Ahmad & Gul 2021; Ali, Gul, Khan, & Karim 2021). The education systems should immediately equip teachers with technologies required for online learning in the time of emergency situations like COVID-19. These technologies may include FaceTime, Zoom, and Google Classroom; online assessment like reading assignments, quizzes, MCQs, etc.; video lectures/PowerPoint presentations; e-portfolios; students discussion forums; and so on (LaRose, Gregg, & Eastin 1998; Gul, Zakir, Ali, Karim, & Hussain 2021; Zayapragassarazan 2020).

Similarly, research (Gul, Tahir, Gul, & Batool 2022; Malkus, Christenson, & Schurz 2020) was carried out by American Enterprise Institute to analyze the response of the districts to the COVID-19 pandemic. Their analysis yielded that it is mandatory for the schools to provide the children with resources, including internet, technological devices, and instruction for remote learning. Furthermore, they identified huge gaps in curricular materials (Al-Oteawi 2002); Bukhari, Said, Gul, & Seraj 2021; Figlio, Rush, & Yin 2010; Fry 2001). The curriculum, according to them, should be supported by digital technologies. Zhang, Wang, Yang, and Wang (2020) conducted a study that identified possible difficulties in the pandemic situation in China, including: the weakness of the online teaching infrastructure, the inexperience of teachers (including unequal learning outcomes caused by teachers' varied experience), the information gap etc. They suggested that the government needs to further promote the construction of the educational information superhighway, consider equipping teachers and students with standardized home-based teaching/learning equipment, conduct online teacher training, include the development of massive online education in the national strategic plan, and support academic research into online education, especially education to help students with online learning difficulties (p. 1).

2.6 Research Objectives

The objectives of the study were the following:

1. To investigate the readiness of the schools, teachers, and the curriculum for initiating an online system of education at Quetta, Balochistan, amid the COVID-19 pandemic.
2. To explore the major challenges that hinder the launching of an effective online/alternate education at the public school level and suggest proposals to cope with these challenges.

2.6.1 Survey Questions

1. What digital devices are presently available in schools that can help teachers to provide interactive audio/video instruction to students?
2. To what extent do teachers have expertise in the use of different digital gadgets and technologies in instruction?
3. To what degree can the schools use all possible delivery methods to ensure students have accessible lesson plans, videos, tutorials, and other resources?
4. What are the major challenges that hinder the schools from initiating an online system of education amid COVID-19?

2.6.2 Interview Questions

5. To what extent do the current curriculum and textbooks support independent learning in an online system of education, and to what exent are they responsive to a sudden situation like COVID-19?
6. Suggest some proposals on how to cope with the challenges that hinders the schools from initiating an online system of education amid COVID-19?

2.7 Materials and Methods

2.7.1 Research Design

A mixed method was applied to understand the phenomenon under investigation. According to Fanghanel, Pritchard, Potter, and Wisker (2015) & Toquero (2020), mixed-method research involves both quantitative and qualitative approaches in conducting a research study. The design applied to this research was the explanatory methodology of sequential mixed methods (quantitative → qualitative = explanation), which initially involves a quantitative survey and a qualitative follow-up interview with priority given to quantitative intervention.

Accordingly, the explanatory design was best suited for this study because the researcher wanted to fully understand the survey findings through a follow-up interview. Following this approach, quantitative data were collected first through a questionnaire, and then focus group interviews were conducted and analyzed using thematic analysis.

2.7.2 Study Population

The target population for the study were school principals and teachers serving in different public high schools in the rural and urban areas of Quetta, Balochistan. According to the Balochistan Education Management Information System 2019 report, there are 59 urban and 18 rural high schools in Quetta District (Quetta District Education Plan 2017–2021). In urban areas, there are 33 boys' and 26 girls' schools, while in rural areas, there are 12 boys' and 6 girls' schools.

2.7.3 Sampling and Sample Size

For quantitative data collection, a proportionate sampling technique was used to select a sample of the study. This technique is considered good when the subgroups are vastly different in numbers, and the sample selected through this technique best represents the entire population being studied (Mumtaz, Saqulain, & Mumtaz 2021; Salkind 2010).

Using the criteria of sample size proposed by Gay, Mills, and Airasian (1996), 38 high schools (29 schools from urban areas and 9 schools from rural areas) were proportionally selected (50% of each subgroup population). From each high school, two teachers and one school principal were randomly selected. Thus, a total of 116 participants, including 38 principals and 76 teachers, responded from both rural and urban areas of the Quetta District.

For interviews, 10 principals, 10 SSTs, and 7 curriculum experts of the curriculum wing of Quetta were purposively selected from the same sample group and interviewed via phone.

2.7.4 Instrumentation

The research instruments used in the study were a survey questionnaire and interview questions. Details of both the instruments are given as follows.

2.7.4.1 Survey Questionnaire

For quantitative data collection, a survey questionnaire was applied. Using Google Forms, the researchers developed the questionnaire with the help of the available online surveys (Al-Oteawi 2002; Chen, Holton, & Bates 2005; Isleem 2003;

Gulbahar & Guven 2008). The survey questionnaire consisted of questions regarding the readiness of the schools, the readiness of the teachers, and the readiness of the curriculum for online education. Details of the questions are given in the results section.

2.7.4.2 Interview Questions

To get a more in-depth insight into the curriculum responsiveness for an online system of education, a panel of 27 participants (10 principals, 10 SSTs, and 7 curriculum experts) were interviewed using a focused group interview. The interview included questions on curriculum responsiveness to the COVID-19 situation, contextual responsiveness of the curriculum to local and global needs, textbook support for e-learning/distance learning, curriculum support for parents, and a curriculum allowing for independent learning. Additionally, during the interviews, suggestions were also taken from the interviewees on how to cope with the challenges that hinders the initiation of an online system of education.

2.7.5 Pilot Testing

To ensure the appropriateness of the questions and to detect any unexpected issue during data collection, the instruments were piloted. For validation, data was collected through survey questionnaires from five high school participants, including five principals, 10 SSTs, three curriculum experts. To determine their observations, the respondents were interviewed, and multiple questions were asked regarding clarity, adequacy, objectivity, relevance, etc. The respondents showed satisfaction with the questions, except for minor revisions in some questions that were incorporated in both the instruments. For reliability, the Cronbach's alpha for the survey questionnaire questions was found to be high ($\alpha = .87$).

2.7.6 Data Collection and Analysis

Due to the lockdown situation, the quantitative survey was administered electronically to all sample schools located in urban and rural areas of the district. Before the data collection, permission was granted by the district education department. The confidentiality of the respondents was maintained in the overall process of the study. The responses on the survey questionnaire were analyzed in SPSS version 23 using descriptive statistics (frequencies, mean, standard deviation).

After the analysis of the quantitative data, qualitative interviews were conducted on the phone for an in-depth understanding of the opinions, experiences, and beliefs of principals, teachers, and curriculum experts regarding curriculum responsiveness, the challenges to schools, and the suggested solutions to an online system of education during the COVID-19 pandemic. The interviews were recorded after taking verbal consent. The recorded interviews were later transcribed and analyzed using a thematic analysis (Braun & Clark 2006) model. According to Braun and Clark (2006), thematic analysis is "a tool for finding, analysing and reporting trends within data" (p. 79).

In this thematic analysis, the researchers' applied the six-stage method suggested by Braun and Clarke (2006). Data were evaluated using these six stages: 1. familiarity; 2. coding; 3. generation; 4. searching themes; 5. naming and defining themes; and 6. final reporting. The reason for using this structure is its consistency and practicality, and it is an effective and powerful approach to conduct social science research (Polit & Beck 2008) that helps the researcher to avoid obstacles during the study.

2.8 Results

Demographic Information of the Participants: The participants were asked to mark their gender, school location, designation, highest academic qualification, highest professional qualification, and experience in teaching. The responses were analyzed using descriptive statistics (see Table 2.1).

Table 2.1 indicates that among the respondents, school principals with a ratio of (F: 38), SSTs/SETs with (F: 65), SSs with (F: 6), and five respondents holding the designation of CT (certificate of teaching to elementary school level) participated in the study. The highest academic qualification of most of the respondents (F: 75) was MA/M.Sc. While the second largest bulk (F: 22) was observed with MS/M. Phil. degrees. Similarly, for professional qualification, the highest qualification of most of the respondents (F: 82) was M.Ed. Data also reveal that majority of study respondents (F: 56) have 5–10 years' experience, whereas the other largest group of respondents (F: 29) have experience of 11–15 years.

Research Question 1: What digital resources are presently available in your schools that can help teachers to provide interactive audio/video instruction to students?

School principals were asked to report all the digital devices presently available in their schools. Their responses are mentioned in terms of frequencies, mean, and standard deviation.

Table 2.2 indicates that among the available digital resources within the schools, 16 (41%) schools have an internet facility while 30 (77%) schools have computers. Additionally, 20 (51%) schools have projectors, and 13 (33%) schools have audio recorders. Besides, six (15%) schools have digital camera facilities while 14 (36%) schools have video recorder facilities.

Research Question 2: To what extent do teachers have expertise in the use of different digital gadgets and technologies in instruction?

Table 2.1 Descriptive Statistics of the Designation, Highest Academic Qualification, Highest Professional Qualification, and Experience in Teaching

Gender		School Location		Desig.	F	Highest Acad. Qual.	F	Highest Prof. Qual.	F	Experience in Years	F
M	F	Urban	Rural	Head	38	MS/MPhil	22	M.Ed.	82	5–10	56
57	57	30	08	SST	65	MA/MSC	75	B.Ed.	22	11–15	26
				CT	5	BA/BSC/BS	16	CT	3	16–20	14
				SS	6	FA/FSC	1	Other	0	21–25	9

Table 2.2 Available Digital Resources in Schools

	Internet Devices	Computers	Projector	Audio Recorder	Digital Camera	Video Recorders
Frequency	16	30	20	13	6	14
Mean	1.57	1.21	1.47	1.65	1.84	1.63
Std. Deviation	.500	.413	.506	.480	.369	.488
Minimum	1.00	1.00	1.00	1.00	1.00	1.00
Maximum	2.00	2.00	2.00	2.00	2.00	2.00

Table 2.3 Level of Skill in Using Different Digital Gadgets

Question Statement		Excellent %	Very Good %	Good %	Fair%	Not Capable%
I can use/ operate this tool/ equipment during teaching.	Digital camera	15	26	39	13	7
	Smartphone	26	48	13	10	3
	Projector	7	31	37	18	7
	Audio recorder	18	47	25	7	3
	Video recorder	23	43	21	8	5
	Computer/laptop	22	46	12	15	5

a) Teachers' Expertise in the Use of Different Digital Gadgets

To analyze the question regarding the skills of the teachers in using different digital gadgets, the teachers were asked to rate their skills for being excellent, very good, good, fair, and not capable of using different equipment during teaching. As school principals were also engaged in teaching practices, their responses were therefore taken as well. Table 2.3 presents the data in terms of percentages for each level.

Table 2.3 shows that most of the participants (39%) were good at using the digital camera while 26% were very good and 15 % were excellent in using this equipment. Similarly, 48% of the respondents were very good and 26% were excellent in using smartphones during teaching. Moreover, 37% of the respondents marked themselves good in using projectors while 31% possessed very good skills. Interestingly, most of the respondents (47%) rated themselves very good and 25% marked themselves good in using audio recorders, while 18% regarded themselves excellent in using this tool. For the skill on using video recorders during instruction, surprisingly, 43% rated themselves very good and 21% marked themselves good. Similarly, for the use of computer/laptop, 46 % of the respondents rated themselves very good and 12 % rated themselves good.

b) Teachers' Expertise in the Use of Most Popular Technologies

Data in Table 2.4 show that for the use of Google Classroom in teaching students, most of the respondents (36%) rated themselves less confident and 31 % rated themselves as confident. Similarly, for the use of Zoom and Microsoft Teams, majority of the respondents (34% and 75%, respectively) were not confident. Besides, respondents with a percentage of 42% and 40% rated themselves as not confident in the use

Table 2.4   Level of Skills in Using the Most Popular Technologies in Teaching

Question		Very Confident	Confident	Less Confident	Not Confident
What are the most popular technologies you can use to teach students online and guide parents about the topics of different subjects?	Use of Google Classroom	13%	31%	36%	20%
	Use of Zoom	20%	19%	27%	34%
	Use of Microsoft Teams	00%	8%	17%	75%
	Use of Skype	11%	18%	29%	42%
	Use of WhatsApp	26%	45%	23%	06%
	Use of Facebook	13%	36%	47%	04%
	Use of Emails	8%	16%	43%	33%
	Use of YouTube channels	02%	28%	30%	40%

Table 2.5   Different Modes of Delivery Schools Can Use to Ensure That Learning Resources Are Available for Students Online

	Social Media	Recorded Lessons	TV	Radio	Any Other
Frequency	30	10	2	7	7
Mean	1.21	1.73	1.94	1.81	
Std. Deviation	.41	.44	.22	.39	
Minimum	1.00	1.00	1.00	1.00	
Maximum	2.00	2.00	2.00	2.00	

of Skype and YouTube channels. On the contrary, majority of the respondents (47% and 43%) regarded themselves less confident in the use of Facebook and emails.

> Research Question 3: To what degree can the schools use all possible delivery methods to ensure students have accessible lesson plans, videos, tutorials, and other learning resources?

Data in Table 2.5 reveal that majority of the principals (F: 30 with M: 1.21) reported social media as a major mode to deliver lesson plans, videos, tutorials, and other resources to the students. Ten principals (with M: 1.73, SD: .44) reported that they can record the lessons and send them through CDs and other flash drives to students' homes. Two principals (with M: 1.94, SD: .22) stated that they can use TV as a mode of instruction by providing links and details of the programs offered for students. Seven principals (with M: 1.81, SD: .39) mentioned that they can use radio as a mode for delivering learning resources. Some of the principals (F: 7) stated that they cannot use any mode of delivery as they do not have any digital gadgets available in schools nor have the proper light system at school.

> Research Question 4: What are the major challenges that hinder the schools from initiating an online system of education? Suggest proposals on how to tackle these challenges.

Participants were asked to mark their opinions on all those challenges that hinder the schools from initiating an online system of education. The responses of the participants were analyzed using frequencies, mean, and standard deviation (See Table 2.6).

Table 2.6 indicates that the major challenge that hinder majority of the schools (F: 77 with M: 1.32, SD: .470) from initiating an online system of education is untrained teachers. Their teachers are not trained well enough to use different advanced technological tools in instruction. Similarly, 54 participants (with M: 1.52, SD: .501) reported that their schools do not have enough computers at schools for online education. Other participants with a ratio of F: 50 and F: 49 reported that their teachers and students have weak internet access and schools do not have enough funding to facilitate teachers and students in providing this facility. Fifty-four respondents with (M: 1.52, SD: .501) also reported that textbooks do not support online learning. In the same loop, some respondents (F: 42, with M: 1.63, SD: .484) stated that their teachers don't have smartphones to use for online teaching and due to the lockdown, they can't go and take online classes at school. Some respondents (F: 41, with M: 1.64, SD: .482) stated that the lack of digital devices for audio/video presentations is a big hurdle in running an online program. Similarly, 83 respondents with (M: 1.27, SD: .446) reported electric supply as a big challenge in an online system of education. The light mostly remains off for hours in schools.

Table 2.6 The Major Challenges That Hinder the Schools to Initiate Online Teaching

Major Challenges	F	M	SD
There is a lack of proper training on the use of technology in online instruction.	77	1.32	.470
Schools do not have enough computers.	54	1.52	.501
Teachers and students have no internet access at school or at home.	50	1.56	.498
Schools do not have enough funding to facilitate schools in online education.	49	1.57	.497
Textbooks do not support online learning.	54	1.52	.501
Internet connections are available but too slow to run an online program.	46	1.59	.492
Teachers do not have smartphones to use for online teaching.	42	1.63	.484
There is a lack of digital devices for audio/video presentations at schools or the teachers' home.	41	1.64	.482
There is an issue of electric supply.	83	1.27	.446

Research Question 5: To what extent do the current curriculum and textbooks support independent learning in an online system of education, and to what extent are they responsive to a sudden situation like COVID-19?

To get a more in-depth insight into curriculum responsiveness for an online system of education, 10 school principals, 10 SSTs from the survey participants, and 7 curriculum experts from the curriculum wing in Quetta were purposively selected and interviewed. Their responses were analyzed using thematic analysis (Braun & Clarke 2006). The following themes emerged upon the analysis of the data.

i. Responsiveness of the Curriculum to the Current Situation

The participants exclaimed that the curriculum has never been prepared for emergencies such as COVID-19, particularly in the elementary grades. However, alternative modalities could be used for the continuity of students' learning at the secondary level. One of the participants opined that apart from COVID-19, "we could be confronted with more natural disasters such as floods, earthquakes, and wars, which may cause the closure of schools."

The participants pointed out that there could be some covert guidelines relating to such incidents, but the curriculum is mostly silent on this matter. Such material is not particularized and explicit. The participants highlighted that COVID-19 is a test case for their schools to design the curricula, making it configured with digital sources of learning. One of the participants claimed that,

> Our curriculum is not prepared for such incidents because our curriculum is predetermined and outcome based. It is harshly controlled by the authorities. The curriculum would have been responsive had it been somewhat flexible. The curriculum should be redesigned so that it produces analytical and critical souls.

This respondent's opinions reflected that the participants are aware of the weaknesses of a predetermined and controlled curriculum. This predetermination snatches away teachers' autonomy and places her/him as a mere distributor of knowledge. The participants believe that there should be some percentage of autonomy for both teachers and students so that the curricula could be redirected as per the contextual realities.

ii. Contextual Responsiveness of the Curriculum to Local and Global Needs

The study participants believe that the current curriculum has manifold deficiencies in responding to both local and global needs at the same time. However, this situation could be handled through the local teachers who have been appointed to the village, tehsil, and district. At the local level, the local teachers are in contact with parents and community members. The teacher may prepare lessons and home-based assignments so that the disruption of studies could be remedied. A participant commented, "The role of a local teacher is very important. They can help students sequentially by teaching them the geography, history, culture, flora, and fauna of the vicinity. This would keep their learning context specific."

The participants reiterated that formal schooling necessitates organized curricula, trained teachers, and a conducive learning environment for the required growth of the children. They complained that teachers have given due support and space. Teachers' capacities have never been built for innovations in teaching. On the other hand, the curriculum is rigid and controlled. This situation has made the schooling nonresponsive to both the local context and global needs.

iii. Textbooks Support for E-Learning/Distance Learning

Most of the participants believe that online learning/e-learning and home-based learning could be some of the alternative modalities with which students can continue their learning. However, all the mentioned modalities have pressing challenges. For example, some of the participants expressed that they haven't had electricity in their districts for the last two months. Others mentioned that there is a limited electric supply in some districts. Therefore, there would be huge hurdles in the way of online/e-learning.

Apart from the access issues, some of the participants highlighted that online learning/e-learning is only feasible in higher grades, where students can independently respond to the online lecture, screen sharing, and assignments. Students in lower grades like primary wouldn't be able to be part of online learning with the teacher's mentorship.

The participants encouraged online learning/e-learning with the condition that the issues of access are resolved. The participants expressed,

> The online methods may help students for the continuity of their education during the COVID-19 situation, but there are heavy issues of access/support to online resources, especially in rural areas where the electricity supply is suspended for long hours.

The participants believe that online-e-learning would depend on two major factors—the education level of the parents and the support system and facilities available at home. This means that online e-learning needs prerequisites before it is taken to the implementation level. The participants highlighted huge issues of internet availability and connectivity.

iv. Parents' Support and Independent Learning

The participants highlight the need for parents' involvement in the learning of children. The participants argued that the government needs to prepare parents for this task before making them responsible for the learning of children at home as most of the parents are uneducated. However, one of the participants pointed out that,

> The situation has convinced us that the relationship of schools with parents must be redefined and revitalized.

The participants suggested that parents should be prepared to engage their children in learning at home. This may be easy through social media to teach parents to supervise their children in times of emergency such as COVID-19. In response to the question of whether the curriculum allows for independent learning, the participants said that there is no room in the curriculum for self-learning. The participants believe the curriculum is politically influenced; therefore, it does not allow for independent learning.

Research Question 6: Suggest some proposals on how to cope with the challenges that hinders the schools from initiating an online system of education amid COVID-19.

The participants extended the following proposals to tackle the situation.

1. "Must do" topics/themes should be identified from the curriculum. Special lessons could be prepared on the identified topics/themes so that they can be shared with students through various channels—social media, screen sharing, YouTube channels, or other methods. In this way, the students' learning progression would not be disrupted. Curriculum experts can identify these "must know" concepts and share them with education authorities. The authorities should prepare teachers to develop lessons to be shared with students. "Must know" topics should be identified both for instruction and assessment.
2. There should be a separate curriculum ready for times of emergency, which may be a specialized curriculum to be used when things transcend normalcy. Or portion in the curriculum must be designed as an emergency curriculum that guides them on how to face such situations and get along. If a course is designed, an assessment should also be designed for this emergency situation. Primary level classes don't need assessment.
3. The best way to respond to such a situation is to prepare students as critical and analytical thinkers. This way, students, as future citizens, would be able to find ways to deal with such challenges.
4. There should be a separate subject area related to health and hygiene—particularly, precautionary measures to avoid pandemics such as COVID-19.
5. Learning should not be limited to the written text only. There could be alternative ways of educating children through social learning concepts.
6. Let the schools open. The loss can be compensated for through the condensed curriculum or curriculum mapping of identifying and teaching the most significant themes/concepts, skills, and behaviors.
7. There should be learning material in the curriculum that is specially designed for self-directed learning, particularly at lower level and in the social sciences.
8. One suggestion is that a teacher guide on natural or man-made disasters should be prepared, which should be a core part of preservice teachers' training curriculum.
9. The condensed curriculum would not be as effective as the yearlong formal curriculum that allows for reinforcement and revisions that are necessary for understanding.
10. School heads could play a role in this situation by inviting teachers to schools by turns. Head teachers/principals could play their role by weekly directing a teacher to map course content to be taught, as per the requirement of the current situation.
11. The teacher can play a pivotal role in being aware of the realities of the local context. She/he can immerse herself/himself in creating opportunities for children so the children continue their learning. Currently, teachers are being posted on the village level. Therefore, they can arrange to facilitate students in their studies. However, this would need a staunch commitment

from the top-down education hierarchy. Directives could be issued to cluster heads to assign responsibilities to teachers of her/his cluster. Teachers also need to be incentivized through some additional amount to motivate them for this task.

12. The entire subject curriculum doesn't need to be taught. There could be a mapping of subjects as well. For example, subjects that could be learned as independent learning should be left out. Science, English, and mathematics could be focused on.

13. Another way could be telecasting prepared lessons through TV and radio channels.

14. It is hoped that arranging some possible ways for the continuity of students' learning would bring at least a 10% improvement. We believe something is better than nothing. We have to introduce this positive trend. We expect the multiplication effect of forming this healthy culture would challenge the multiplication effect of COVID-19.

2.9 Discussion

The current study encompassed the major research questions on readiness of the schools, teachers, and the curriculum for initiating an online system of education amid the COVID-19 outbreak. The study has investigated all the available essential digital infrastructure required for the execution of an online system of education, the hands-on practice of teachers on using different digital gadgets, and the flexibility of the curriculum to fulfill its suitability during the articulation of online classes amid the COVID-19 pandemic.

Analysis of the data collected through survey and interviews suggested that schools are prepared for online classes as they have enough devices and facilities that can help teachers to provide interactive audio/video instruction and can use all possible delivery modes, including TV, radio channels, and social media, to assure that lesson plans, videos, tutorials, and other resources are available for students. However, interrupted power supply, paucity of dedicated funds, and slow internet speed are some of the major challenges for them. The findings are consistent with previous reports (Gul, Kanwal, & Khan 2020; Ahmad, Gul, & Zeb 2022; Gul, Tahir, Ishfaq, & Batool 2021; Kaur & Bishnoi 2014; Kaur, Pragna, & Ankit 2019) that districts in Balochistan have always been under educational crises due to the nonavailability of very basic facilities in schools, including boundary walls, net facilities, potable water, lack of teacher training, and lack of electricity supply at schools and colleges. The literature shows that the availability of basic facilities, especially electric supply, directly affects students' learning (Miller & Salkind 2002; Mote, Bhoite, Bangar, & Mandakmale 2018).

Findings further suggested that teachers also have the skills to use all available digital devices and, to some extent, are familiar with the latest software, including YouTube channels, Google Classroom, Zoom, Skype, social media, etc., which can help them in teaching online. But they have never received any proper training on the use of technology for teaching and assessment purposes. Technical abilities bear a strong impact on the teachers online teaching. Research has revealed that if teachers become more acquainted with technology (computers, internet, and media tools), they are more ready to teach online (Rees, Gay, & McKinley 2016).

Additionally, in interviews show disappointment in terms of the responsiveness of the curriculum in that the predetermined and controlled curriculum is mostly silent in responding to the needs of the students and teachers in the online system of education; the textbook material is not particularized and explicit and has manifold deficiencies in responding to both local and global needs. Considering these deficiencies, proposals were suggested to cope with the existing situation.

2.10 Conclusion

The findings of the study, as discussed in the discussion section, reflect major challenges to schools to initiate an online system of education. In light of the discussion, this study concludes that many issues exist in implementing an online system of education, and these issues are not inescapable. If the government gets stuck in a vicious cycle where net connectivity and electric supply hinders the initiation of an online system of education, it will lead to widespread unemployment. Keeping pace with the rest of the world will be just a pipe dream, and there will be nothing more for the wondering youth of the Balochistan. As change is not optional, it is time for the academia to transform into an online system of education. The literature has affirmed that online teaching yields student results more comparable to those generated by face-to-face teaching (Caldwell 2006; Mentzer, Cryan, & Teclehaimanot 2007; Vaidya & Saini 2021). Therefore, our educational stakeholders and elected representatives need to work with their fingers crossed with national and international donor agencies (see detail in the introduction section), like the CIDA, UN agencies, World Bank, JBIC, UNESCO, USAID, UNICEF, UNHCR, technology benefactors, and telecommunication operators to start a coordinated effort in developing digital infrastructure, enhancing global cooperation, and building public-private relationships to provide all students with access to quality education and lifelong learning through various pathways. As in France, China, and the UAE, 60-plus educational institutions, publishers, media organizers, and industry experts are providing computers and tablets along with subsidizing mobile data packages, printed assignments, and other educational resources, including books, evaluations, assessment tools, and videos to students who do not have access to the internet (Sooknanan & Karen 2014). Additionally, training programs including technical skills, online methods of education and pedagogy, online educational content, etc. should also be carried out to support various aspects of online teaching (Eslaminejad, Masood, & Ngah 2010; Morris & Frey 1997; Ncube, Dube, & Ngulube 2014).

The crisis has changed the globe, and there are plenty of options—for development practitioners, planners, education experts, investors, policy makers, and electric companies—to provide light, connectedness, comfort, and above all, the capacity and learning opportunities to primary and secondary school students.

2.11 Study Implications

The results of this study are specific to online schooling in Balochistan, but the findings may be generalized to other provinces of Pakistan as public schools in Pakistan are confronting the same issues and an online system of education for students has not been initiated to date. The study implications are significant for higher-level studies and researchers of national and international levels as well. The study findings are also beneficial for developing countries whose demographic and economic conditions are the same as Pakistan—e.g., India, Sri Lanka, Bangladesh, etc.—where the education sector, specifically at the rural side, is confronting similar issues.

2.12 Study Limitations

There were some methodological limitations in this study. First, the study was limited to a single district because Quetta is a capital district of the province and is more developed compared to rest of the districts in Balochistan. Further study can be extended to the whole province by increasing the sample schools. Secondly, the study was limited to the technical skills of the teachers in using digital resources; further studies could examine teachers' competencies in online teaching methodologies and assessments as the shift from conventional teaching to online teaching requires good preparation for teachers to adapt to the new paradigm shift. Third, this study was limited to online education at the school level; further studies can be conducted at a higher education level. Fourth, only those demographic variables that had some relation with the research questions were tested. Finally, all data were self-reported due to the nature of the study. Some teachers may not be familiar with all the competencies for online teaching, and there might be a response bias.

1. Conflict of Interest and Funding: The authors declare that the research was conducted in the absence of any commercial or financial relationships that could be construed as a potential conflict of interest. Furthermore, no funding has been received for this research project.

2. Author Contributions: My co-author, Dr. Gulab, has contributed to data collection and qualitative data analysis.
3. Acknowledgments: The authors acknowledge the contribution of all study participants.
4. Participants' Consent: Before data collection, prior consent was taken from all study participants, and their confidentiality was maintained throughout the study.

References

Ahmad, I., Gul, R., and Zeb, M. "A Qualitative Inquiry of University Student's Experiences of Exam Stress and its Effect on Their Academic Performance." *Human Arenas* (2022): 1–16. https://doi.org/10.1007/s42087-022-00285-8.

Ahmad, Iqbal, and Rani Gul. "Impact of Online Service-learning on Civic and Social Justice Behavior of Undergraduate Laboratory-Based Graduates." *Human Arenas* (2021): 1–16.

Ali, Imran, Rani Gul, Syed Khan, Sulaiman, and Kamran Karim. "An Evaluative Study of English Contrastive Rhetoric in Pashtu Speaking Areas of Pakistan: A Case Study of District Swat." *Linguistica Antverpiensia* (2021): 2183–2203.

Al-Oteawi, Saleh Mohammed. *The perceptions of administrators and teachers in utilizing information technology in instruction, administrative work, technology planning and staff development in Saudi Arabia.* Ohio University; 2002.

Ayub, Alia, Rani Gul, A. Ali, and Bin Maroof Rauf. "Cultural and Educational Stress: A Case Study of Brahui Speaking ESL and EMI Periphery Students." *Asian EFL Journal* 28, no. 2.3 (2021).

Baloch, Amdadullah, Said Zamin Shah, Zaleha Mohd Noor, and Miloud Lacheheb. "The Economic Effect of Refugee Crises on Neighbouring Host Countries: Empirical Evidence from Pakistan." *International Migration* 55, no. 6 (2017): 90–106.

Balochistan education management information system planning and management unit, Directorate of Education, Quetta, Balochistan. BEMIS; 2018.

Balochistan education management information system planning and management unit, Directorate of Education, Quetta, Balochistan, Pakistan. BEMIS; 2015.

Braun, Virginia, and Victoria Clarke. "Using Thematic Analysis in Psychology." *Qualitative Research in Psychology* 3, no. 2 (2006): 77–101.

Bukhari, Syed Kaleem Ullah Shah, Rani Gul, Tayyaba Bashir, Sumaira Zakir, and Tariq Javed. "Exploring Managerial Skills of Pakistan Public Universities (PPUs)' Middle Managers for Campus Sustainability." *Journal of Sustainable Finance & Investment* (2021): 1–19.

Bukhari, Syed Kaleem Ullah Shah, Hamdan Said, Rani Gul, and Prodhan Mahbub Ibna Seraj. "Barriers to Sustainability at Pakistan Public Universities and the Way Forward." *International Journal of Sustainability in Higher Education* 23, no. 4 (2021): 865–886. https://doi.org/10.1108/IJSHE-09-2020-0352.

Caldwell, Elvira Rebecca. *A comparative study of three instructional modalities in a computer programming course: Traditional instruction, web-based instruction, and online instruction.* The University of North Carolina at Greensboro; 2006.

Cavus, Nadire, Huseyin Uzunboylu, and Dogan Ibrahim. "Assessing the Success Rate of Students Using a Learning Management System Together with a Collaborative Tool in Web-based Teaching of Programming Languages." *Journal of Educational Computing Research* 36, no. 3 (2007): 301–321.

Chen, Hsin-Chih, E. F. Holton III, and Reid Bates. "Development and Validation of the Learning Transfer System Inventory in Taiwan." *Human Resource Development Quarterly* 16, no. 1 (2005): 55–84.

Education Management Information System. *Directorate of elementary and secondary education*. Quetta, Balochistan, Pakistan. EMIS; 2018.

Eslaminejad, Tahereh, Mona Masood, and Nor Azilah Ngah. "Assessment of Instructors' Readiness for Implementing E-learning in Continuing Medical Education in Iran." *Medical Teacher* 32, no. 10 (2010): e407–e412.

Fanghanel, Joelle, Jane Pritchard, Jacqueline Potter, and Gina Wisker. *Defining and Supporting the Scholarship of Teaching and Learning (SoTL): A Sector-wide Study. Executive Summary: Preliminary Contribution*. Higher Education Academy York Science Park, Innovation Way, Heslington; 2015.

Figlio, David N., Mark Rush, and Lu Yin. "Is It Live or Is It Internet? Experimental Estimates of the Effects of Online Instruction on Student Learning." *NBER Working Paper No. 16089*. National Bureau of Economic Research; 2010.

Fry, Kate. "E-learning Markets and Providers: Some Issues and Prospects." *Education+ Training* 43, no. 4 (2001): 233. Retrieved July 22, 2021 from https://www.learntechlib.org/p/92498/.

Gay, L. R., Mills, G. E., and Airasian, P. *Educational research: Competencies for analysis and applications*. Merrill, Upper Saddle River, NJ; 1996.

Gul, N., Tahir, T., Gul, R., and Batool, S. "Investigating Teachers' Knowledge About Dyslexia: A Study at Primary School Level." *International Journal of Early Childhood Special Education* 14, no. 3 (2022).

Gul, R., Tahir, T., and Ishfaq, U. "Teaching as a Profession, Exploring the Motivational Factors, and the Motives to Stay in the Field of Teaching." *Ilkogretim Online – Elementary Education Online* 19, no. 4 (2020): 4560–4565. https://doi.org/10.17051/ilkonline.2020.04.764861.

Gul, Rani, Alia Ayub, Shumaila Mazhar, Syed Shahab Uddin, and Muhammad Khanum. "Teachers' Perceptions on Students' Cultural and Linguistic Diversity and its Impact on their Approaches towards Culturally Teaching Practices." *TESOL International Journal* 16, no. 3.2 (2021).

Gul, Rani, Shazia Kanwal, and Sadia Suleman Khan. "Preferences of the Teachers in Employing Revised Blooms Taxonomy in Their Instructions." *SJESR* 3, no. 2 (2020): 258–266.

Gul, Rani, Sadia Suleman Khan, Shumaila Mazhar, and Tehseen Tahir. "Influence of Logical and Spatial Intelligence on Teaching Pedagogies of Secondary School Teachers." *Humanities & Social Sciences Reviews* 8, no. 6 (2020): 1–9.

Gul, Rani, Sulaiman Syed Khan, and Syed Akhtar. "Organizational Politics as Antecedent of Stress in Public Sector Universities of Khyber Pakhtunkhwa." *International Review of Management and Business Research* 9, no. 2 (2020): 150–161.

Gul, Rani, and Gulab Khilji. "Exploring the Need for a Responsive School Curriculum to Cope with the Covid-19 Pandemic in Pakistan." *Prospects* 51, no. 1 (2021): 503–522.

Gul, Rani, Tehseen Tahir, Umbreen Ishfaq, and Tayyaba Batool. "Impact of Teachers' Workload on Their Time Management Skills at University Level." *Indian Journal of Economics and Business* 20, no. 3 (2021).

Gul, Rani, Muhammad Talat, Majid Mumtaz, and Lubna Shaheen. "Does Intelligence Matters in Teaching? Exploring the Impact of Teachers Intelligence on Teaching Pedagogies of Secondary School Science Teachers." *Multicultural Education* 7, no. 3 (2021).

Gul, Rani, Sumaira Zakir, Imran Ali, Hafsa Karim, and Rashid Hussain. "The Impact of Education on Business Opportunities for Women Entrepreneurs in Public & Private Television Advertisements in Pakistan." *Industrial Engineering & Management Systems* 20, no. 2 (2021): 140–147.

Gulbahar, Yasemin, and Ismail Guven. "A Survey on ICT Usage and the Perceptions of Social Studies Teachers in Turkey." *Journal of Educational Technology & Society* 11, no. 3 (2008): 37–51.

Humaira, Akhter, and Munazza Mahmood. "Study of the Impact of Online Education on Students' Learning at University Level in Pakistan." *Online Submission* 3, no. 2 (2018).

Isleem, Mohammed I. *Relationships of selected factors and the level of computer use for instructional purposes by technology education teachers in Ohio public schools: A statewide survey.* The Ohio State University; 2003.

Kaur, Jasleen, and Bishnoi Anjali. "Investigating the Ways Through Evaluation Practice in Higher Education: The Value of Learner's Need." *International Journal of Engineering and Computer Science* 3, no. 12 (2014): 9560–9563.

Kaur, Jasleen, Bishnoi Anjali, Mistry Pragna, and Mishra Ankit. "Educational Institutes: Creators of Socially Responsible citizens." *9th International Conference in Engineering and Business Education (ICEBE)*, Gujarat Technological University Gandhinagar, Gujarat; 2019: 302–305. ISBN 978-3-942100-43-4.

LaRose, Robert, Jennifer Gregg, and Matt Eastin. "Audiographic Telecourses for the Web: An Experiment." *Journal of Computer-Mediated Communication* 4, no. 2 (1998): JCMC423.

Malkus, Nat, Cody Christensen, and Jessica Schurz. "School District Responses to the COVID-19 Pandemic: Round 6, Ending the Year of School Closures." *American Enterprise Institute* (2020). Washington, D.C.; April 7, 2020. https://www.aei.org/research-products/report/school-district-responses-to-the-covid-19-pandemic-round-1-districts-initial-responses/.

Mentzer, Gale, JohnRobert Cryan, and Berhane Teclehaimanot. "Two Peas in a Pod? A Comparison of Face-to-face and Web Based Classrooms." *Journal of Technology and Teacher Education* 15, no. 2 (2007): 233–246.

Miller, D. C., and N. J. Salkind. "Introduction: Understanding Basic, Applied, and Evaluation Research." In D. C. Miller and N. J. Salkind (eds.), *Handbook of Research Design & Social Measurement*, pp. 1–2. SAGE Publications, Inc; 2002.

Morris, R. G., and B. B. S. Frey. "Hippocampal Synaptic Plasticity: Role in Spatial Learning or the Automatic Recording of Attended Experience?" *Philosophical Transactions of the Royal Society B Biological Sciences* 352, no. 1360 (1997): 1489–1503.

Mote, M. G., S. U. Bhoite, Y. C. Bangar, and S. Mandakmale. "Genetic Divergence Studies on Reproduction and Production Traits Among Gir Crosses." *Tropical Animal Health and Production* 50 (2018): 1881–1885. https://doi.org/10.1007/s11250-018-1639-y.

Mumtaz, N., G. Saqulain, and N. Mumtaz. "Online Academics in Pakistan: COVID-19 and Beyond." *Pakistan Journal of Medical Sciences* 37, no. 1 (2021): 283–287.

National Education Statistics. Retrieved from Performance Management Cell (PMC), Policy, Planning and Implementation Unit (2018–2019). www.emis.gob.pk/.

Ncube, Siphamandla, Luyanda Dube, and Patrick Ngulube. "E-learning Readiness among Academic Staff in the Department of Information Science at the University of South Africa." *Mediterranean Journal of Social Sciences* 5, no. 16 (2014): 357–357.

Odell, Mike, Jason Abbitt, Doug Amos, and John Davis. "Developing Online Courses: A Comparison of Web-based Instruction with Traditional Instruction." In *Society for Information Technology & Teacher Education International Conference*, pp. 126–130. Association for the Advancement of Computing in Education (AACE); 1999.

Pakistan Economic Survey. Department of Planning and Development, Islamabad, Pakistan (2018–2019).

Pakistan Social and Living Standards Measurement. Performance Management Cell (PMC), Policy, Planning and Implementation Unit, PPIU, Quetta, Balochistan, Pakistan (PSLM, 2019–2020).

Peterson, Cynthia L., and Nathan Bond. "Online Compared to Face-to-face Teacher Preparation for Learning Standards-based Planning Skills." *Journal of Research on Technology in Education* 36, no. 4 (2004): 345–360.

Polit, Denise F., and Cheryl Tatano Beck. *Nursing research: Generating and assessing evidence for nursing practice*. Lippincott Williams & Wilkins; 2008.

Quetta District Education Plan Directorate of E&S Education, Quetta, Balochistan, Pakistan (2017–2020).

Rees, Eliot L., Simon P. Gay, and Robert K. McKinley. "The Epidemiology of Teaching and Training General Practices in England." *Education for Primary Care* 27, no. 6 (2016): 462–470.

Salkind, Neil J., ed. *Encyclopedia of Research Design*. Vol. 1. Sage; 2010.

Shah Bukhari, S.K.U., Said, H., Gul, R. and Ibna Seraj, P.M. "Barriers to sustainability at Pakistan public universities and the way forward." *International Journal of Sustainability in Higher Education* 23, no. 4, (2022): 865–886. https://doi.org/10.1108/IJSHE-09-2020-0352.

Sooknanan, Prahalad, and Karen Crichlow. "The Role of Technology in the Marketing Communications Industry: An Exploratory Study of the Impact of North American Influence on Business in Trinidad and Tobago." *Advances in Journalism and Communication* 2, no. 3 (2014). https://doi.org/10.4236/ajc.2014.23009.

Toquero, C. M. "Challenges and Opportunities for Higher Education amid the COVID-19 Pandemic: The Philippine Context." *Pedagogical Research* 5, no. 4 (2020): 1–5.

Vaidya, A., and J. R. Saini. "A Framework for Implementation of Learning Analytics and Educational Data Mining in Traditional Learning Environment." In S. Fong, N. Dey, and A. Joshi (eds.), *ICT Analysis and Applications*. Lecture Notes in Networks and Systems, vol. 154. Springer; 2021. https://doi.org/10.1007/978-981-15-8354-_11

Zayapragassarazan, Zayabalaradjane. "COVID-19: Strategies for Online Engagement of Remote Learners." *F1000Research* 9, no. 246 (2020): 246.

Zhang, Wunong, Yuxin Wang, Lili Yang, and Chuanyi Wang. "Suspending Classes without Stopping Learning: China's Education Emergency Management Policy in the COVID-19 Outbreak." *Journal of Risk and financial management* 13, no. 3 (2020): 55.

Chapter 3

Opinion and Perception of Mentors and Interns in the Academic Domain for E-Internships during COVID-19

Vikas S. Chomal, Jatinderkumar R. Saini, and Ketan Kotecha

Contents

DOI: 10.1201/9781003328438-3

3.1 Introduction

This century belongs to digital transformation thanks to the internet, which made it possible and provided a platform for businesses and the academic domain to continue their operations distantly. To stay engaged with business partners, clients, colleagues, and students, varieties of online collaboration platforms and videoconferencing are effectively utilized. Universally, there has been a conditional transformation to remote working and learning due to COVID-19. During these last two years, many studies and research have been conducted to explore the students', faculty's, as well parents' perceptions of the adoption, use, and acceptance of online education. On the contrary, modest information is known about the quality of academic software projects developed by computer science students during their internships [1].

There was a global societal change due to the novel coronavirus. Governing authorities around the world issued an overnight restriction on mass gatherings as well as shut down business and academic functioning and encouraged and introduced a new concept of work from home [2]. Further, much of the prevailing literature on internships is conducted largely considering the perception of the students only. This chapter describes the impact of COVID-19 on academic software project development internships and evaluates interns' and mentors' perception on their experience in the internships before and during the pandemic. Moreover, much of the available literature on internships is focused largely on perceptions by students and less on supervisors. The mentors included in the survey also played the role of examiners in evaluating these academic software projects developed.

An internship can be defined as a supervised, controlled, practical oriented and structured knowledge-learning experience that provides students a prospect for career exploration and expansion and to learn new or interesting skills [3]. Due to use of online platforms, traditional internship termed as "e-internship" refer to computer-oriented, domain-driven projects assigned to interns by academic authorities, where interns work online and/or remotely. Internships in courses of computer science and engineering as well as information technology encompass software project development. Moreover, the duration of this internship is basically six months. Particularly, for our research work, we considered the internship of only final-year students of the master's level of computer science and information technology.

The aims of this research are as follows:

- To learn and analyze the perception of students and mentors about e-internships
- To explore student and mentor perceptions on internships before and during COVID-19
- To explore the engagement of IT students in e-internships
- To investigate the effort and performance of students in each phase of the software project development
- To examine the overall quality of software project development during e-internships

The organization of the chapter is as follows: A comparative literature review is discussed in section 2. The research methodology is presented in section 3. The experiment and result of the research are presented in section 4. Lastly, conclusions and future enhancements drawn from this research are highlighted in section 5.

3.2 Related Literature Review

E-internships are defined as digital oriented and materialized with the advent of information and communication technology and provides benefits to those who face challenges and obstacles in traditional on-site internships [4][5][6]. Adedoyin and Soykan [1] stated that online teaching and learning is still in the emerging period, and long-lasting research, benefits, implications, and effects are still unidentified and will persist in imminent years.

Ahmad et al. [2] in their study categorized and characterized factors that described the experience of e-learning for secondary schoolteachers and undergraduate students. In research work, parameters considered were namely experience, ease of use, attitude, self-efficiency, outcome expectation, and technical support. The study of Zaman et al. [3] focused on investigating the obstacles faced by students in their final-year internship. They also summarized the challenges and opportunities that were tackled the internship during the pandemic period. The preference of students for remote internships, the problems faced during internships, and the collaboration and coordination of virtual teams were research criteria considered in exploring the research area. Teng et al. [7] explored and explained the impact of COVID-19 on internships carried out by public health workers. Further, quality of work, problem-solving, and critical thinking and overall performance were main decision parameters taken into account while exploring the impact of e-internship. Bilsland et al. [8] presented an in-depth discussion about existing studies on virtual internship and training executed during the pandemic in view of hospitality and tourism as their domain area. Elsalem et al. [9] and Hassan et al. [10] in their research described the perceptions, experiences, and opinions of students about their online internship, learning, teaching, and examination. They contributed that examinations taken online added stress and anxiety among medical students. Jeske and Axtell [11] presented an exclusive comparison about on-site internship and e-internship as well as expressed various criteria that are needed to make e-internships successful. In continuation, with the previous work, Jeske and Linehan [12] also executed their work on identifying how mentoring and skill can be developed during e-internships.

Through their research work, Nguyen et al. [13] shared and highlighted medical professionals and practitioners using virtual platforms to impart medical knowledge. Wilson and Major [15] published a detailed study and report that focused on various innovative practices carried out in career and technical education. The report also describes various innovative tools as well as challenges that were faced by services provided by career counseling hubs. Mishra et al. [16] stated the importance and adaptation of online teaching-learning processes applied in education during the pandemic. In their work, they focused on various forms of online teaching-learning modes and perceptions and obstacles experienced by undergraduate and postgraduate faculty and students. Hora et al. [17] in their work analyzed, examined, and stated the role, importance, and success of the new dimension of e-internships provided by a large number of technical training institutes. The research emphasis was on factors such as the prevalence of e-internships, the quality of internship provided, commitment, and accessibility. The proposed work of Blankstein et al. [18] highlighted the challenges faced by academic institutions in implementing online education and the strengths and gaps of opportunities in online education. Institutional policies, significant challenges, physical as well as mental health, and perceptions were significant parameters of their study. Koopman and Emmett [14] in their work inprogress articulated a review of literature on virtual internships. The major finding of their research work was on opportunities and limitations in virtual internships. Mishra et al. [19] stated that many Indian institutes were successful in imparting basic course curriculum knowledge as well as training to students through the use of digital tools during the pandemic.

Hermida [20] studied and explored the opinions of students on the adoption and use of online learning. Attitude, motivation, self-efficacy, use of technology, perceptions, and improvements are predominantly constraints considered for opinion mining. Khalil et al. [21] revealed the usefulness of synchronized online learning platforms in medical education.

The study of Anjum [22] showcased and evaluated the dimensional impact that internships have on the personal and skills development of students. Jayadeva [23] focused on the plans of students regarding studying for a postgraduate degree abroad during the pandemic. Seladorai and Mohamed [24] described an evaluation-based theoretical work on digital-oriented learning among postgraduate students for the duration of COVID-19. Asgari et al. [25] identified and listed various negative considerations, rumors, and concerns that influenced online education. Chaturvedi et al. [26] reviewed and presented effective valuable practices and procedures that can be followed to make online teaching a success story. Thandevaraj [27] et al. conducted research work to study the psychological impact of COVID-19 on students in Malaysia. The research was review based, and the authors were interested to uncover the obstacles such as (a) various difficulties students faced in getting internships during the pandemic and how they can overcome it; (b) the role played by institutes as well as universities in helping out students to be absorbed by industries for internships; and (c) the success ratio of remote internship. Vaidya and Saini [28] proposed a model for executing learning analytics and education data-mining practices in a face-to-face teaching environment. Virani et al. [29] examined and validated the acceptance ratio of teachers toward the use of MOOCs. Wall [30] highlighted the impact of COVID-19 on internships as well the placement of postgraduate students. Zimmerman [31] articulated that all over the globe, students as well as faculty, despite obstacles, had a great experience as well as were successful in imparting online education as well as training students. Further, a comparative analysis of the proposed work of Teng et al. [5] is presented in Table 3.1.

3.3 Research Methodology

For the said research, we followed an evidence-based systematic methodology, which is graphically represented in Figure 3.1.

The prime goal of an evidence-based systematic methodology is to methodically study and explore the criteria's (a) engagement; (b) the performance of the IT students in their e-internship; and (c) the quality of the software developed by the IT students during their e-internship. Further, we called our research "evidence-based systematic phase" since the examination of the stated criteria is systematically synthesized based on the primary data collected through an online survey of final-year IT students who carried out e-internships and supervisor/mentors who guided as well as evaluated the software projects of these students in their e-internship. This study will provide with the synopsis of e-internship pros and cons for the IT students.

Table 3.1 Comparative Analysis of Proposed Work

Sr. No.	Point of Comparison	Proposed Work	Teng et al. [5]
1.	Research domain	Academic	Public health
2.	Internship Duration	4 to 6 months	3 months
3.	Questionnaire	Divided into 3 parts, which consist of (a) organizational environment and support where e-internships were executed; (b) professional development; and (c) involvement of mentors	Generalized questionnaire regarding experience and perceptions. Further, information from learning management system (LMS) is also utilized.
4.	Sample Size	92 Mentors + 211 Students = 303	Not mentioned
5.	Assessment Attribute	Software developed and development activities carried out during e-internship	Public health services
6.	Examination of Opinion, Perception, Experience of Internship	During COVID-19	Before and during COVID-19

Hypotheses

The hypotheses of the study are as follows:

1. H1:E-internship has an impact on the involvement of the IT students.
2. H2:E-internship has an impact on the technical support and understanding of the IT students.
3. H3:E-internship has an impact on the performance of the IT students.
4. H4:E-internship has an impact on the project scheduling and completion of the IT students.
5. H5:E-internship has an impact on project tracking and reporting to the mentors.

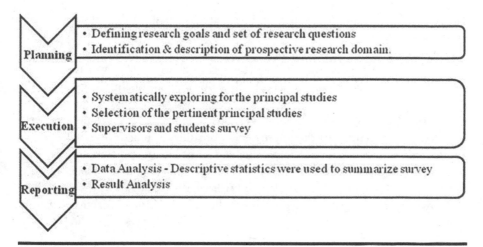

Figure 3.1   Evidence-based systematic phase.

6. H6:E-internship has an impact on the project evaluation done by the mentors.
7. H7:E-internship has an impact on the overall quality of the software developed by the IT students.

3.3.1 *Methods*

This segment of the study describes the methods of data collection, population and sampling procedures, the investigation of data, and the study design. For a comprehensive study, we assembled primary data from the final year IT students of a two-years postgraduate course who did e-internships for six months in eight prestigious educational institutes of the South Gujarat region as well faculty members of the same institutes who acted as mentors and examiners for the said e-internships' duration. The data for exploration were collected in May and June for the academic year 2021. Further, 350 questionnaires were circulated overall. The questionnaire survey for the students comprised 18 questions and a five-point Likert scale where the higher values indicated immense fulfillment and "good" as the middle point. Part A consisted of eight questions related to the IT industries where the students needed to carry out their e-internships. These questions consisted of (1) appropriate support; (2) a suitable atmosphere for learning and training provided by the IT industries for the e-internship; (3) ample resource provision; (4) the project schedule and reporting procedures and the policies followed; (5) the level of technical support provided; (6) the level of involvement; (7) the prospect of employment; and (8) the e-internship experience.

Part B consists of five professional developments during the e-internship and questions on (1) the focus on the achievement of career goals; (2) skill identification; (3) field of interest; (4) the level of achievement in technical work knowledge in the concerned domain and technology platform; and (5) enhancement in problem-solving and critical thinking skills. Part C consists of five questions related to the involvement of supervisor(s) or mentors. These questions are on (1) availability; (2) the involvement of the supervisor with the interns during the e-internships; (3) periodic and productive feedback on technical work; (4) evaluation during e-internships; (5) the level of guidance. The online questionnaire for mentors consists of 11 questions, namely on (1) the punctuality of students; (2) the fulfillment of intern-supervisor communication; (3) satisfaction regarding the periodic tasks fulfilled by the interns; (4) the improvement of students' practical knowledge during the e-internship; (5) timely reporting and involvement; (6) stated instructions and guidelines being followed properly; (7) the completion level of each phase of the project development; (8) the adaptability level; (9) the quality of the work done; (10) overall performance during the e-internship; and (11) the satisfaction regarding the expected outcome.

3.3.2 *Population and Sampling*

The final-year IT students and faculty members were considered as the population for the said research work. A sample of the study included 211 IT students who were part of the e-internship and 92 faculty who guided these interns as well as served as examiners for evaluating and assessing these curriculum software project developments. These interns and faculty represent the esteemed institutes of the South Gujarat region.

3.3.3 *Methodology*

This assessment is also termed a quantitative research, to better figure out the potency and flaws of e-internships in the curriculum of IT courses. A few of the qualitative study criteria were also taken into consideration. This study is a quantitative research, but in order to better comprehend the potency and weakness of the e-internship programs, some qualitative research elements were also utilized. The study makes use of both descriptive as well as statistical investigation to evaluate the impact of the e-internship prospect for employment and the experience and skill identification of the IT students. It also evaluates the perception of the mentors on e-internships and the quality of the work done, overall performance, and satisfaction regarding the expected outcome. This descriptive method of the study includes a percentage and frequency analysis of the participants' responses. Further, the statistical technique consists of scale analysis comprising normality and reliability tests.

The consistency and trustworthiness of the survey was examined and tested using Cronbach's alpha. A well-prepared and well-structured questionnaire technique was used for both students' and mentors' survey. Part A consists of nine questions related to the IT industries where students need to carry out their e-internships, part B consists of five professional developments during the e-internship, and part C consists of five questions related to the involvement of supervisors or mentors during the e-internship. The mentor online survey questionnaire consists of 11 questions. Each criterion of the questionnaire was assessed using a 5-point Likert scale, where 1 is below average, 2 is average, 3 is disagree, 2 is disagree, 3 is good, 4 is very good, and 5 is excellent.

3.4 Results

This section deals with experimental findings and their inferences. The first part of the section consists of descriptive analysis and second part consists of scale analysis.

3.4.1 Descriptive Analysis

In total 250 online questionnaire(s) were given to students, out of which 211 students participated; therefore, the survey rate for the students' responses was 84.4%, whereas 100 online questionnaires were submitted to faculty/supervisors/mentors, and the response rate was 92%.

3.4.2 Scale Measurement

3.4.2.1 Reliability Test

Cronbach's coefficient alpha was used to check the reliability of the research questionnaire. Cronbach's alpha test is one of the most popular measures that is used to evaluate and assess the reliability of a survey, which consists of multiple Likert scales and attributes. Anjum [13] stated that if Cronbach's coefficient alpha ranges from 0.6 to 0.9, then the questionnaire of the study is reliable. The Cronbach's coefficient alpha is 0.9641 for the faculty survey and 0.6841 for the students' survey. As the decisive values fall in the acceptable range, the questionnaire of the study is reliable and acceptable. In Table 3.2 and Table 3.3, the implementation of Cronbach's alpha test for the mentors' and students' surveys is presented. The Google Form links to the mentors' and students' questionnaires are mentioned as follows:

(a) https://forms.gle/sUUftmjd74wYyW667
(b) https://forms.gle/Cu6ZX3GGEHU3ZsSF7

3.4.2.2 Students' Evaluation Survey

In Table 3.4 we represent the distribution of responses in the percentage of students' experience related to the IT organization where they executed e-internships for their final-year semester. Figure 3.2 (a), (b), (c), and (d) graphically represent

Table 3.2 Implementation of Cronbach's Alpha Test for Mentors' Survey

ANOVA: Two-Factor without Replication						
Summary	*Count*	*Sum*	*Average*	*Variance*		
1.086956522	4	98.91304	24.72826	194.844833		
5.434782609	4	94.56522	23.6413	152.3117517		
3.260869565	4	96.73913	24.18478	229.5014178		
1.086956522	4	98.91304	24.72826	222.4125709		
1.086956522	4	98.91304	24.72826	283.0615942		
3.260869565	4	96.73913	24.18478	179.8794896		
2.173913043	4	97.82609	24.45652	209.9086326		
2.173913043	4	97.82609	24.45652	240.6269691		
3.260869565	4	96.73913	24.18478	220.8372716		
2.173913043	4	97.82609	24.45652	212.2715816		
3.260869565	10	35.86957	3.586957	1.588426801		
29.34782609	10	275	27.5	16.8163201		
33.69565217	10	355.4348	35.54348	4.47647553		
31.52173913	10	308.6957	30.86957	16.33060281		
ANOVA						
Source of Variation	SS	df	MS	F	P-value	F crit
Rows	4.164697543	9	0.462744	0.035826205	0.999993	2.250131
Columns	6088.226607	3	2029.409	157.1192513	3.35E-17	2.960351
Error	348.7417297	27	12.91636			
Total	6441.133034	39				
Cronbach's Alpha	0.964173795					

Table 3.3   Implementation of Cronbach's Alpha Test for Students' Survey

ANOVA: Two-Factor without Replication						
Summary	*Count*	*Sum*	*Average*	*Variance*		
3.791469194	4	93.09901	23.27475	145.9479		
2.714932127	4	92.76018	23.19005	159.0706		
1.809954751	4	93.66516	23.41629	159.8896		
3.167420814	4	92.30769	23.07692	186.0459		
2.714932127	4	92.76018	23.19005	113.7535		
4.07239819	4	91.40271	22.85068	163.8651		
2.262443439	4	93.21267	23.30317	220.648		
36.65158371	4	58.82353	14.70588	281.2528		
2.714932127	4	92.76018	23.19005	186.2336		
3.167420814	4	92.30769	23.07692	163.7968		
3.619909502	4	91.8552	22.9638	172.4473		
4.07239819	4	91.40271	22.85068	210.4107		
2.262443439	4	93.21267	23.30317	223.9239		
1.357466063	4	94.11765	23.52941	175.1261		
2.262443439	4	93.21267	23.30317	160.0431		
1.357466063	4	94.11765	23.52941	158.7464		
1.809954751	4	93.66516	23.41629	146.5128		
0.904977376	4	94.57014	23.64253	159.0706		
9.954751131	18	137.5115	7.639529	66.47221		
14.47963801	18	371.4246	20.6347	23.04836		
30.76923077	18	548.4163	30.46757	39.64846		
35.29411765	18	581.9005	32.3278	42.90566		
ANOVA						
Source of Variation	SS	df	MS	F	P-value	F crit
Rows	278.6234	17	16.38961	0.315822	0.994264	1.827147
Columns	6913.707	3	2304.569	44.40828	2.96E-14	2.786229
Error	2646.646	51	51.89503			
Total	9838.977	71				
Cronbach's Alpha		0.684178				

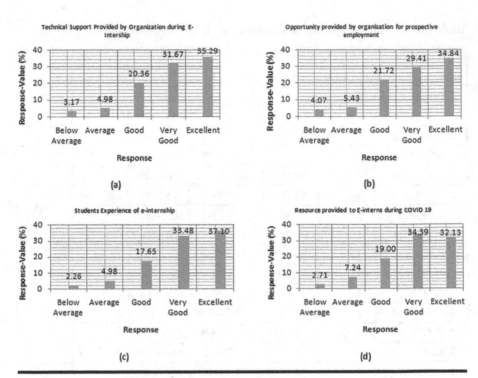

Figure 3.2   Distribution of responses from e-interns on (a) technical support provided by the organization during e-internship; (b) opportunities for prospective employment during COVID-19; (c) e-internship experience during COVID-19; and (d) resources provided to e-interns during COVID-19.

the students' e-internship experience, which was executed at various individual organizations.

3.4.2.3 Students' Perception of Technical Support during E-Internship and COVID-19

The survey response indicates that a greater number of students were satisfied with the universal and technical support (35.29% response rate) as well as the resources provided by the organization during the e-internship (34.39% response rate), as highlighted in Figure 3.2 (a).

3.4.2.4 Students' Perception of Prospective Employment during E-Internship and COVID-19

A significantly large number of students were in favor that the organization provided a good opportunity for their prospective career and employment. It can be

Table 3.4 Distribution of Responses (as Percentages) in Student Evaluation Surveys for Part A

Sr. No.	Criteria	1 Below Average	2	3	4	5 Excellent
1	Organization provided appropriate support during e-internship.	4.98	9.95	14.48	30.77	35.29
2	Organization provided suitable environment for learning and training for e-internships.	3.79	9.00	18.48	28.96	36.65
3	Organization provided ample resources to execute e-internships.	2.71	7.24	19.00	34.39	32.13
4	Procedures and policies were followed by the organization for project schedule and reporting.	1.81	7.69	19.00	31.22	35.75
5	Level of technical support provided by organization	3.17	4.98	20.36	31.67	35.29
6	Level of involvement by the organization during e-internships	2.71	8.14	23.08	30.77	30.77

(Continued)

Table 3.4 (Continued) Distribution of Responses (as Percentages) in Student Evaluation Surveys for Part A

Sr. No.	Criteria	1 Below Average	2	3	4	5 Excellent
7	Opportunity provided by the organization for prospective employment	4.07	5.43	21.72	29.41	34.84
8	Individual experience of e-internships carried out at the organization	2.26	4.98	17.65	33.48	37.10

observed from Table 3.4 and Figure 3.2 (b) (34.84%, response rate) that students thought that excellent career and employment prospects were provided by the organization (29.41% and 21.72% response rate), whereas student experience was rated as very good and good related to the prospective employment.

3.4.2.5 Students' Individual E-Internship Experience during COVID-19

E-interns were more satisfied with the e-internship carried out at the respective organization. From the distribution of responses presented in Table 3.4 and the graphical representation in Figure 3.2 (c), it can be examined that 37.10% and 33.48% of students had an excellent and very good experience during their e-internship, whereas 2.26% and 4.98% had a below average and average experience.

Further, the distribution of responses in percentage regarding the students' perception on professional development during COVID-19 is summarized in Table 3.5.

3.4.2.6 Students' Perception of Professional and Skill Development during E-internship and COVID-19

Most of the e-interns had an outstanding experience and were satisfied with the professional and skills development throughout their e-internship. In Table 3.5, the response rate shows a higher percentage for the achievement of Achievement of career goals during e-internships, attainment of domain and technology knowledge, as well as the enhancement of problem-solving and critical thinking skills, with a response rate of 34.38%, 36.6,5% and 36.65%, respectively.

Table 3.5   Distribution of Responses (as Percentages) in Student Evaluation Surveys for Part B

Sr. No.	Criteria	1 Below Average	2	3	4	5 Excellent
1	Achievement of career goals during e-internships	2.71	4.07	23.08	30.77	34.84
2	Satisfaction level in identifying skills during e-internships	3.17	4.98	23.08	32.13	32.13
3	E-internships were executed and help to work with your field of interest.	3.62	5.43	20.36	32.58	33.48
4	Achievement of technical work knowledge in concerned domain and technology platform	4.07	5.88	15.84	33.03	36.65
5	Enhancement in problem-solving and critical thinking skills during e-internships	2.26	3.62	19.91	33.03	36.65

The research study also focuses on the significant aspect of students' perceptions toward the involvement of mentors during the e-internship. The distribution of responses in percentages are highlighted in Table 3.6 and graphically represented in Figure 3.3 (a), (b), (c), and (d).

3.4.2.7 Students' Perceptions of Mentor Involvement

Most of the students found that the involvement of mentors during the e-internship was pleasant. The mentors guided them appropriately during the software project development. It can be observed from Figure 3.3 (a) that the highest response rate

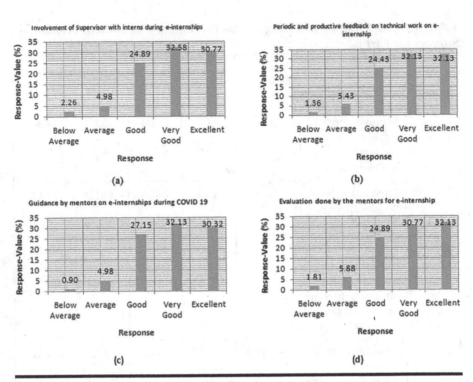

Figure 3.3 **Distribution of responses from e-interns on (a) involvement of supervisors/mentors with e-interns during e-internship; (b) periodic and productive feedback from supervisors/mentors; (c) guidance by supervisors/mentors; and (d) evaluation done by supervisors/mentors.**

was rated very good, with a 32.58% response rate, followed by 30.77% for excellent and 24.89% for good.

3.4.2.8 Students' Opinion of Mentor Feedback

In the analysis in Figure 3.3 (b), it is significant to note that students got exceptional as well as timely and periodic feedback from supervisors/mentors for their technical queries and difficulties and had a response rate percentage of 32.14% for scale very good and excellent and 24.43% for good.

3.4.2.9 Students' Perception of Guidance and Evaluation

Figure 3.3 (c) and (d) depict that students' response rate for mentors guidance during COVID-19 for the academic software project handled through an online platform was very good (32.13% response rate) since students found the guidance very good. A 30.32% and 27.15% response rate, respectively, was given for the ratings excellent and good. Similarly, a greater number of the students were satisfied

Table 3.6 Distribution of Responses (as Percentages) in Student Evaluation Surveys for Part C

Sr. No.	Criteria	1 Below Average	2	3	4	5 Excellent
1	Supervisor was dependable and available to assist when needed.	1.36	4.98	23.08	33.48	32.58
2	Involvement of supervisor with interns during e-internships	2.26	4.98	24.89	32.58	30.77
3	Periodic and productive feedback on technical work	1.36	5.43	24.43	32.13	32.13
4	Evaluation done during e-internships	1.81	5.88	24.89	30.77	32.13
5	Level of guidance	0.90	4.98	27.15	32.13	30.32

with the evaluation by their supervisors/mentors on their software project development. The response rate for their evaluation was 32.13% for excellent, followed by 30.77% and 24.89% for very good and good.

The software project development is considered as the most significant phase for the completion of final year of computer science curriculum. During this phase, students learn and explore practical as well as industrial knowledge. Students' involvement in software project development during their e-internships was appraised by mentors on the basis of the criteria intern punctuality, communication and feedback, reporting of various phases, overall performance, and quality of the software project developed by the students. Table 3.7 and Figure 3.4 (a), (b), (c), and (d) summarize and provide the evaluation survey of mentors involved in the e-internships during COVID-19.

Table 3.7   Distribution of Responses (as Percentages) in Mentor Evaluation Surveys

Sr. No.	Criteria	1 Below Average	2	3	4	5 Excellent
1	Punctuality of students during e-internships	2.17	3.26	29.35	33.70	31.52
2	Fulfillment of intern-mentor communication	1.09	4.35	30.43	35.87	28.26
3	Satisfaction of periodic tasks contributed by interns	5.43	6.52	22.83	31.52	33.70
4	E-internship improved student's practical knowledge.	3.26	3.26	22.83	35.87	34.78
5	Timely reporting and involvement	1.09	3.26	26.09	35.87	33.70
6	Follow-up taken in consideration with stated instructions and guidelines	1.09	2.17	21.74	39.13	35.87
7	Phase completion during project development	3.26	4.35	28.26	33.70	30.43
8	Adaptability level	2.17	3.26	27.17	34.78	32.61
9	Quality of software developed during e-internship	2.17	3.26	33.70	38.04	22.83

(Continued)

Table 3.7 (Continued) Distribution of Responses (as Percentages) in Mentor Evaluation Surveys

Sr. No.	Criteria	1 Below Average	2	3	4	5 Excellent
10	Overall performance of interns during e-internship	3.26	2.17	30.43	34.78	29.35
11	Satisfaction regarding expected outcome	2.17	3.26	31.52	33.70	29.35

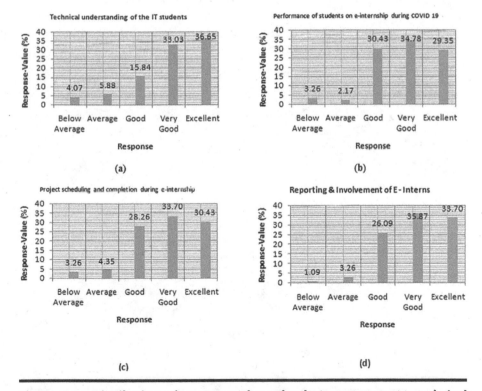

Figure 3.4 Distribution of responses from faculty/mentors on (a) technical understanding of e-interns; (b) performance of e-interns; (c) project scheduling and completion during e-internship; and (d) reporting and involvement of e-interns.

3.4.2.10 Mentors' Perception of Student Performance

From Table 3.7 and Figure 3.4 (b), it can be observed that the mentors were satisfied by the performance of the students during e-internship. The response rate was high for very good and good, with 34.78% and 30.43% response rate, respectively, whereas a 29.35% response rate was for excellent. Similarly, Table 3.7 and Figure 3.4 (c) and (d) state that activities such as scheduling, reporting, and completing project tasks were done remarkably by students on the e-internship for their academic software project development during COVID-19. The response rate was 33.70% and 35.87% for very good for scheduling and completion and reporting, followed by 30.43% and 33.70% for excellent, respectively.

3.4.2.11 Mentors' Perception of the Improvement of E-Interns' Practical Knowledge

From Table 3.7 and Figure 3.5 (a), it can be observed that mentors strongly believe and are in favor that the e-internship improved the practical knowledge of students

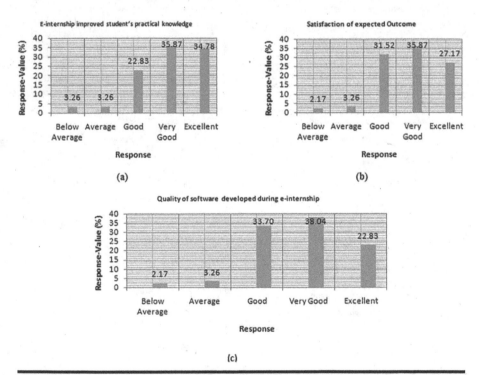

Figure 3.5 Distribution of responses from faculty/mentors on (a) e-internship improving the technical knowledge of students; (b) supervisor/mentor satisfaction regarding the expected outcome; and (c) quality of software developed during the e-internship.

undergoing the software project development. The response rate for the same shows a higher scale for very good with a 35.87% response rate, followed by a 34.78% response rate for excellent and a 22.83% response rate for good.

3.4.2.12 Mentors' Perception of E-Internship's Expected Outcome and Quality of Academic Software Project

Mentors' perception on the expected outcome of the e-internship and the quality of the software developed during the e-internship was acceptable but not exceptional or outstanding. In Table 3.7 and Figure 3.5 (b) and (c), it can be examined that mentors agree that e-internships were successful in achieving the expected outcome of industrial training. In total, a 35.87% response rate came out for very good, followed a by 31.52% response rate for good followed by 27.17% for excellent. A similar pattern was found for the quality of the academic software project developed by the students during the e-internship. A response rate of 38.04% from faculty claimed that the quality of the software project developed was very good, whereas 33.70%, stated that the quality was good and only 22.83% rated the quality is excellent. Regarding supervisors'/mentors' survey evaluation, it can be recognized that there is a need for closer supervision and direction to compensate and improve the performance of students and the expected outcome and quality of the software project in the e-internship. Further, we would like to emphasize the benefits and challenges of e-internship. These benefits and challenges are identified and listed on the basis of the response rate of students/e-interns and faculty/supervisors/mentors in the evaluation survey, presented in Table 3.8.

Table 3.8 Benefits and Challenges of E-Internship

Sr. No.	Description	Values
1.	Benefits	Handiness, flexibility, self-sufficiency, supportive and encouraging environment, enhancement and improvement in practical knowledge, effective use of communication techniques
2.	Challenges	Scope of improvement for performance of e-interns, to deliver good quality of academic software project, sense of isolation, project scheduling, and task completion

3.4.3 Study Limitations

In total, 303 out of 350 respondents' surveys were analyzed and evaluated, which consist of mainly 211 students and 92 faculty. The results and perceptions may yield variations in response rate if a greater number of responses were received, analyzed, and evaluated. Further, only students and faculty of institutes located in the South Gujarat region were considered.

3.5 Discussion

The research study intended to evaluate the impact of e-internships on professional, personal, and skill development as well as to evaluate criteria related to the IT industries where these interns executed their e-internship. The study also intended to evaluate the involvement of the mentors in the e-internships during COVID-19. Mentors involved in the e-internships who provided guidance and mentoring to students were also included in the study, and their survey responses were evaluated and presented. The data of the study comprised of 211 final-year IT students as well as 92 computer science faculty from South Gujarat region universities and colleges. A structured-questionnaire technique was used for collecting responses. Each criterion of the questionnaire was assessed using a 5-point Likert scale. The study employed various statistical analyses, such as descriptive analysis and scale measurement. Further, for test reliability, Cronbach's coefficient was used for the students' survey evaluation as well as faculty's survey evaluation. The Cronbach's coefficient alpha is 0.9641 for the faculty survey and 0.6841 for the students' survey. As critical values fall in a satisfactory range, the questionnaire of the study is trustworthy and acceptable. In general, the results depict that e-the internships carried out during COVID-19 by IT students were found favorable and have a good impact on (a) learning and understanding technical aspects; (b) prospective employment; (c) the involvement of mentors; (d) the guidance and evaluation provided by faculty; (e) periodic feedback provided by mentors; and (f) the enhancement of problem-solving and critical thinking skills.

Similarly, the faculty and mentors involved in the e-internships strongly and positively supported the following aspects, namely (a) punctuality of students during e-internship; (b) scheduling and reporting throughout the e-internship; (c) involvement, learning, and understanding regarding the concerned technology and IT domains; (d) follow-up on stated instructions for the academic software project development; and (e) improvement in practical knowledge.

3.6 Conclusion and Future Enhancement

On the basis of the survey evaluations, we conclude that the e-internships gave favorable outcomes to e-interns and mentors as well as resulted in knowledge gains. We also claim that e-internships materialize a new dimension of training and show a positive approach in the IT academic domain. Considering the research results, we must also state that due concern is needed to improve the performance of the students, the expected outcomes, and the quality of the software project developed during the e-internships. Further, the proposed research provides a platform for other academic domains such as management, law, and social science to study and explore the opportunities, challenges, and impact of e-internships in their respective fields.

References

[1] O. B. Adedoyin, and E. Soykan (2020) "Covid-19 Pandemic and Online Learning: The Challenges and Opportunities." *Interactive Learning Environments*, 1–13. http://doi.org/10.1080/10494820.2020.1813180.

[2] Ahmad Hamza Obidat, Mahmoud Alquraan, and Malak Hamza Obeidat (2020) "Data on Factors Characterizing the Elearning Experience of Secondary School Teachers and University Undergraduate Students in Jordan." *Data in Brief*, 33, 106402. Contents lists available at Science Direct, https://doi.org/10.1016/j.dib.2020.106402.

[3] Asif Zaman, Hasanul Banna, Mohammad Arshadul Alam Rakib, Shakil Ahmed, and Mohammad Monirujjaman Khan (2021, August) "Impact of Covid-19 on University Final Year Internship Students." *Journal of Software Engineering and Applications*, 14, 363–388. www.scirp.org/journal/jsea. ISSN Online: 1945–3124, ISSN Print: 1945–3116.

[4] E. T. Baloran (2020) "Knowledge, Attitudes, Anxiety, and Coping Strategies of Students during COVID-19 Pandemic." *Journal of Loss and Trauma*, 25(8), 635–642. http://doi.org/10.1080/15325024.2020.1769300.

[5] R. Dani, R. Kukreti, A. Negi, and D. Kholiya (2020) "Impact of COVID-19 on Education and Internships of Hospitality Students." *International Journal of Current Research and Review*, 12(21), 86.

[6] H. Dent, and B. J. White (2020) "Virtual Internships: Interdisciplinary Remote Work for Undergraduates During a Pandemic." *Issues in Information Systems*, 21(3), 11–19. http://doi.org/10.48009/3_iis_ 2020_11-19.

[7] Cecilia Woon Chien Teng, Raymond Boon Tar Lim, Dana Wai Shin Chow, Suganthi Narayanasamy, Chee Hsiang Liow, and Jeannette Jen-Mai Lee (2021, August) "Internships Before and During COVID-19: Experiences and Perceptions of Undergraduate Interns and Mentors." Higher Education, Skills and Work-Based Learning Emerald Publishing Limited 2042–3896. http://doi.org/10.1108/HESWBL-05-2021-0104.

[8] Christine Bilsland, Helga Nagy, and Phil Smith (2020) "Virtual Internships and Work-Integrated Learning in Hospitality and Tourism in a Post-COVID-19 World." Special Issue. Responding to COVID-19: Understanding and conceptualizing challenges for work-integrated learning, *International Journal of Work-Integrated Learning*, Special Issue, 21(4), 425–437.

[9] L. Elsalem, N. Al-Azzam, A. A. Jum'ah, N. Obeidat, A. M. Sindiani, et al. (2020) "Stress and Behavioral Changes with Remote E-exams During the Covid-19 Pandemic: A Cross-sectional Study Among Undergraduates of Medical Sciences." *Annals of Medicine and Surgery*, 60, 271–279. https://doi.org/10.1016/j.Amsu.2020.10.058. PMID: 33163179.

[10] B. Hassan, A. A. Shati, A. Alamri, A. Patel, A. A. Asseri, et al. (2020) "Online Assessment for the Final Year Medical Students During COVID-19 Pandemics; the Exam Quality and Students' Performance." *Onkologia i Radioterapia*, 14, 1–6.

[11] D. Jeske, and C. M. Axtell (2019) "Virtuality in E-internships: A Descriptive Account." Lazazzara, A., Nacamulli, R., Rossignoli, C. and Za, S. (Eds), *Organizing for Digital Innovation*. Lecture Notes in Information Systems and Organisation. Springer, Cham, pp. 219–233. http://doi.org/10.1007/978-3-319-90500-6_17.

[12] D. Jeske, and C. Linehan (2020) "Mentoring and Skill Development in E-internships." *Journal of Work Applied Management*, 12(2), 245–258. http://doi.org/10.1108/JWAM-09-2019-0028.

[13] Khang D. Nguyen, Tyler Travis Vandergriff, Rebecca Vasquez, Ponciano D. Cruz, Heidi T. Jacobe, and Melissa M. Mauskar (2020) "Opportunities for Education During the COVID-19 Pandemic." 2020 by the American Academy of Dermatology, Inc. Published by Elsevier Inc. https://doi.org/10.1016/j.jdin.2020.04.003.

[14] Kristen Koopman, and Robert S. Emmett (2020) "Work in Progress: Examining the Literature on Virtual Internships for Insights Applicable to Engineers." *American Society for Engineering Education, 2021 ASEE Annual Conference, Virtual Meeting*, July 2021, American Society for Engineering Education. https://peer.asee.org/38156.

[15] LeAnn Wilson, and Doug Major (2021) "High-quality CTE During COVID-19: Challenges and Innovations." *Association for Career and Technical Education*. www.acteonline.org.

[16] Lokanath Mishra, Tushar Gupta, and Abha Shree (2020) "Online Teaching-learning in Higher Education during Lockdown Period of COVID-19 Pandemic." *International Journal of Educational Research Open*, 1(2020), 2666–3740. https://doi.org/10.1016/j.ijedro.2020.100012; Available online 10 September 2020.

[17] Matthew T. Hora, Changhee Lee, Zi Chen, and Anthony Hernandez (2021, June) "Exploring Online Internships Amidst the COVID-19 Pandemic in 2020–2021: Results From a Multi-Site Case Study." *WCER Working Paper No. 2021-5*. https://wcer.wisc.edu/publications/working-papers.

[18] Melissa Blankstein, Jennifer K. Frederick, and Christine Wolff-Eisenberg "Student Experiences during the Pandemic Pivot." *ITHAKA*. https://creativecommons.org/licenses/by/4.0/.

[19] L. Mishra, T. Gupta, and A. Shree (2020) "Online Teaching-Learning in Higher Education during Lockdown Period of Covid-19 Pandemic." *International Journal of Educational Research Open*, 1, 100012. http://doi.org/10.1016/j.ijedro.2020.100012.

[20] Patricia Aguilera-Hermida (2020, September) "College Students' Use and Acceptance of Emergency Online Learning Due to COVID-19." *International Journal of Educational Research Open*. https://doi.org/10.1016/j.ijedro.2020.100011.

[21] Rehana Khalil, Ali E. Mansour, Walaa A. Fadda, Khaled Almisnid, Mohammed Aldamegh, Abdullah Al-Nafeesah, Azzam Alkhalifah, and Osama Al-Wutayd (2020) "The Sudden Transition to Synchronized Online Learning During the COVID-19 Pandemic in Saudi Arabia: A Qualitative Study Exploring Medical Students' Perspectives." *BMC Medical Education*, 20, 285. https://doi.org/10.1186/s12909-020-02208-z.

[22] Sadia Anjum (2020) "Impact of Internship Programs on Professional and Personal Development of Business Students: A Case Study from Pakistan." *Future Business Journal*, 6(1), 2. https://doi.org/10.1186/s43093-019-0007-3

[23] Sazana Jayadeva (2020) "The Impact of Covid-19 on Postgraduate-level Student Migration from India to Germany." https://education-services.britishcouncil.org/node/40584?no_cache=1594843497, www.timeshighereducation.com/news/pandemic-redistribute-international-student-flows-report.

[24] D. Seladorai and M. Mohamed (2021) "Digital Learning among Postgraduate Students in the Times of Covid-19: A Literature Review." *Creative Education*, 12, 1494–1502. https://doi.org/10.4236/ce.2021.127114.

[25] Shadnaz Asgari, Jelena Trajkovic, Mehran Rahmani, Wenlu Zhang, Roger C. Lo, and Antonella Sciortino (2021, April) "An Observational Study of Engineering Online Education During the COVID-19 Pandemic." https://doi.org/10.1371/journal.pone.0250041.

[26] Shakti Chaturvedi, Sonal Purohit, and Meenakshi Verma (2021, June) "Effective Teaching Practices for Success during COVID-19 Pandemic: Towards Physical Learning." *Educational Psychology*, 6, Article 646557, a section of the journal Frontiers in Education. www.frontiersin.org.

[27] E. Thandevaraj, N. Gani, and M. Nasir (2021) "A Review of Psychological Impact on Students Online Learning during Covid-19 in Malaysia." *Creative Education*, 12, 1296–1306.

[28] Vaidya Anagha, and Jatinderkumar R. Saini (2020, Springer) "A Framework for Implementationof Learning Analytics and Education Data Miningin Traditional Learning Environment." *Proceedings of ICT4SD-2020*, Springer, and vol: 154, pp. 105–114. https://doi.org/10.1007/978-981-15-8354-4_11.

[29] Shreya R. Virani, Jatinderkumar R. Saini, and Sharma Sarika (2020) "Adoption of Massive Open Online Courses (MOOCs) for Blended Learning: The Indian Educators' Perspective." *Interactive Learning Environments*. Taylor and Francis, pp. 1–17, https://doi.org/10.1080/10494820.2020.1817760, London, UK.

[30] K. Wall (2020) "COVID-19 Pandemic: Impacts on the Work Placements of Post Secondary Students in Canada." https://files.eric.ed.gov/fulltext/ED605407.pdf (accessed 2 November 2020).

[31] J. Zimmerman (2020) "Coronavirus and the Great Online-Learning Experiment. The Chronicle of Higher Education." www.chronicle.com/article/Coronavirusthe-Great/248216 (accessed 10 March 2020; 29 April 2020).

Chapter 4

The Role of Smartphones in E-Learning: A Case Study of Tribal Students in Jharkhand State

Amiya Kumar Sarkar, Alamgir Biswas, and Dr. Saheli Guha Neogi Ghatak

Content

4.1 Introduction

Education is one of the essential means to achieve the destiny of human life. Education inculcates social values, ethics, and responsibilities. The primary principle of education is to learn. Learning is a method of obtaining knowledge, information, and skills through study, understanding, and experience. All the disasters of the world always leave an impression on education. The COVID-19 pandemic also has its footprints on education. The outbreak of the COVID-19 virus across the world has enforced educational foundations to shut down to resist the spread of the virus. E-learning has become the only alternative way to teach students during the shutdown of educational institutes. In the present scenario, learning has transformed, where teachers and students are digitally connected.

India is diverse in terms of multiple religions, ethnic groups, and languages, but it has diversified learner groups in more than 1.6 million schools with more than 265 million enrollments (Wikham, 2019). E-learning includes learning using mobile devices like smartphones, tablets, laptops, etc. Besides smartphones being compact and easy to carry, features like blogs, chat rooms, electronic resource sharing, content development, and access have made mobile use more popular and effective.

According to Technopedia (2019), "A smartphone is a mobile phone with highly advanced features. A typical smartphone has a high-resolution touch screen display, WiFi connectivity, Web browsing capabilities, and the ability to accept sophisticated applications." The smartphone is a device that allows students to complete the information-seeking process faster than any other device.

Vidyasaarthi, a scholarship management portal promoted by NSDL e-Governance to assist students in their financial process, surveyed India Lockdown Learning and reported that 79% of students in India use smartphones for online learning. In contrast, only 17% have laptops, and 4% have tablets. The same study shows that 59% of students attended their online classes on WhatsApp and Zoom. Sixty percent of the students have spent 1–4 hours/day on online learning whereas 31% have reported spending around 4–8 hours, and 8% said to have used 8–12 hours.

Smartphones have become an essential part of people's lives because of their mobility, entertaining, and communication features like camera, GPRS, email, and social media (WhatsApp, Facebook, etc.) During the pandemic, smartphones became the most crucial too for communication, necessary payments, and education. Students use smartphones to maintain daily schedules, save study materials, watch educational videos, have videoconferences, share presentations, etc.

Again, the usage of smartphones is not limited to just online class delivery but also curricular, cocurricular and extracurricular. Assignments, project submissions, parent-teacher meetings, arts and crafts, music, etc. are other areas in which the students have been guided through online education. With Jharkhand being one of the poorest states, its education departments have made the remarkable journey of offering online classes to the students, especially classes IX, X, XI, and XII during the COVID-19 pandemic lockdown period.

4.1.1 Scope

This study intends to know the education system of four significant districts of Jharkhand State—i.e., Pakur, Ranchi, Dumka, and Dhanbad. During the pandemic, all schools were forced to shut down, and online education became the trend in teaching the students. Since online education was a new technology for the students at government schools, it could have been a more significant challenge to adopt it. This study looks into situations where smartphones played a vital role to continue online education.

4.2 Objectives of the Study

The study was conducted based on the following objectives:

1. To find out teachers' and students' perceived ease of use of a smartphone in online teaching-learning
2. To know the affordability of smartphones to the students with Jharkhand being a poor state
3. To investigate the engagement and learning effect through online learning
4. To investigate the factors that inhibit challenges in smartphone use as an online learning tool

4.3 Literature Review

A study (Eden & Jacqueline, 2014) was conducted for over three years at the University of Central Florida among 1,181 students on mobile technologies in education. The study showed that 95% of the students own at least one smartphone and 57% a tablet. It was also found that there are more smartphone users among undergraduate students than there are among graduate students. When asked about the medium they prefer for learning, the younger students prefer the smartphone to other devices.

The online education market generates over US$100 billion each year and is expected to grow to US$446.85 billion by 2020 (CB Insights, 2016). It includes traditional MOOCs and various MOOC-ish pedagogical, technological, and business models. Instead of being massive and open, these platforms may limit enrollment to a smaller subset of students. Rather than entire courses, many offer modular options oriented around a narrow skill set. Learners' educational experience online may be supplemented by in-person instruction or meetings. Some students earn credits or degrees online from traditional accredited higher education institutions (Shah, 2016a).

Radha et al. (2020), in their study among 175 national and international students, found e-learning as the most popular form of study among national and international students during the COVID-19 pandemic. They have mentioned e-learning as the forthcoming trend as it is best suited to everyone per the convenience, comfort, and availability. The students get access to updated content based on their convenience. The study also found the positive effects of e-learning among the students.

The smartphone has become an indispensable device when it comes to online learning. According to the study conducted by Fordjour et al. (2015), a "smartphone is a mobile phone with more advanced computing capability and connectivity than a feature phone which has limited functionality." Ifeanyi and Chukwuere (2018) postulated in their study that the use of smartphones by students has both a negative and positive effect depending upon the users and on how they are used. Further, the researchers emphasized the darker side of the coin where the smartphone has become an excellent distraction for the students. To check mobile notifications almost every minute has been an addiction, and this creates a disturbance in their regular study; focus on serious study is hampered. Being in the class makes us think of notifications as soon as the mobile vibrates or rings. It is not rare for a serious class to get distracted by a ringing phone. This is a serious concern and should be controlled strictly for students to excel academically.

4.4 Method

A survey method was adopted for this study as it tends to study a large number of populations across five different districts of Jharkhand State. The population for this study comprises 200 school students who were engaged in online learning through their smartphones. To validate the idea and obtain accurate information, the matured standard like IX, X, XI, and XII students were chosen for data collection. The questionnaire was framed in a simple and legible format to maximize their interest. The questions consisted of both open-ended and closed-ended categories.

4.4.1 Data Collection and Analysis

The study was conducted Jharkhand, India. Four districts were under this study: Pakur, Ranchi, Dumka, and Dhanbad. Four higher secondary schools were chosen from each district. They were assumed to be the fittest for understanding the aim of the research and validity of answers. Students of class 9, 10, 11, and 12 standards were considered the respondents of the questionnaire. A questionnaire having 12 closed-ended questions was framed to collect the data. Two hundred copies of the questionnaire were equally distributed, and among them, 175 were collected.

To conduct the survey, the researcher physically visited the schools in July 2021. After a long detachment with regular physical classes due to the COVID-19 pandemic, it was assumed that an interactive physical survey might give better survey results. It was assumed that the students might behave like strangers, so the researchers contacted the class teachers first to brief them on the aim of the study. The teachers circulated the questionnaires among the students for them to answer the questions in the researcher's presence. Their extended support made this study successful. Data were analyzed using a simple percentage analysis.

4.5 Result and Analysis

Table 4.1 shows the sociodemographic background of the respondents. The data reveal that 60% of the student respondents are boys and 40% are girls; the percentage of students representing four districts of Jharkhand are 26.2% from Pakur,

Table 4.1   Distribution of Respondents Based on Sociodemographic Background

Item		No.	Percentage
Gender	Boys	105	60%
	Girls	70	40%
Area	Pakur	46	26.2%
	Dumka	60	34.2%
	Dhanbad	36	20.5%
	Rachi	33	18.8%
Educational Status	Class IX	74	42.2%
	Class X	36	20.5%
	Class XI	40	22.8%
	Class XII	25	14.2%
Age	15	18	10.2%
	16	50	28.5%
	17	42	24%
	18	28	16%
	19	23	13.14%

34% from Dumka, 20.5% from Dhanbad, and 19% from Rachi; the educational status of the respondents are 42% from class IX, 21% from class X, 23% from class XII, and 14% from class XII; and the age group of the students are 10% 15 years old, 29% 16 years, 24% 17 years, 16% 18 years, and 13% 19 years old.

Table 4.2 shows that most of the students (63%) do not have personal smartphones; students have engaged in classes by borrowing (61%) a smartphone from their parents, brothers, uncles, or relatives. Sixty-seven percent of the students have discontinued online classes due to the unavailability of smartphones. Fifty-eight percent of the students have also informed that tariff unavailability is another reason for discontinuing their classes. Figure 4.1 shows the distribution of respondents on the basis of access of smart phone.

Smartphones have taken over many other devices that are helpful in our day-to-day lives. Now without smartphones, it is tough to think of what our lives would be like. Smartphones in e-commerce have made them among the most necessary items. Smartphones are much cheaper now, but when we consider the case of Jharkhand, it is still a matter of struggle to afford a smartphone for many families. The cost of a smartphone becomes higher when the government imposes higher taxes as customs duties when imported from abroad. Indian mobile manufacturers are still to get world recognition as far as the global market is concerned. The table shows the ground facts and the challenges that school-going students still face. To show a way to afford mobile uses, Aker and Mbiti (2010) have shown in their study that prepaid mobile phones require extensive credit support schemes from the mobile network providers in developing and underdeveloped countries. This idea is also applicable in the poorest states like Bihar, Jharkhand, etc.

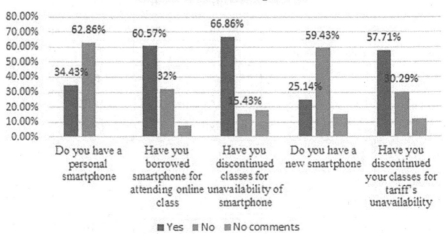

Figure 4.1   Access of smartphone.

Table 4.2   Distribution of Respondents Based on Smartphone Access

No.	Items	Yes	No	No Comments
1	Do you have a personal smartphone?	62 (34.43%)	110 (62.86%	3 (0.17%)
2	Have you borrowed a smartphone to attend an online class?	106 (60.57%)	56 (32%)	13 (7.43%)
3	Have you discontinued classes because of the unavailability of a smartphone?	117 (66.86%)	27 (15.43%)	31 (17.71%)
4	Do you have a new smartphone?	44 (25.14%)	104 (59.43%)	27 (15.43%)
5	Have you discontinued your classes because of tariff unavailability?	101 (57.71%)	53 (30.29%)	21 (12%)

The complexity theory suggests that the living organism acclimatizes to the changing situation. To survive in the changing situation, the living organism modifies the external situation, and during that process, new composite and stable systems emerge (Veletsianos, 2010). As per the complexity theory, e-learning becomes the new education system during social change caused by pandemics, which provides learning growth. However, this learning platform is still out of reach for many unprivileged. Wheeler et al. (2001) and Wesolowski et al. (2012) reported that members shared a single phone in a low-income family. This definition of poor excludes this section from this technological benefit. They have also found that solid econometric factors play a significant role in showing cross-country diffusion patterns.

Table 4.3 shows the opinions of the respondents about online learning. Most of the students (77.71%) attended regular online classes; data also reveals that students face different negative aspects of online studies, such as 13.14% facing power interruption; 58.86% lacking sufficient data for online classes; and 51.43% facing negative aspects and different types of other technical glitches during online classes. The respondents also inform about some positive aspects of online classes—73. 71% of the respondents have informed that the online classes are beneficial for ease of individual doubt clearance, and 48.47% also think online classes are more interactive than physical classes. Figure 4.2 shows opinion about online learning as effective learning environment.

Constructivism emphasizes that learning is possible when the completed tasks embrace meaning for the learners and remain contextual (Veletsianos, 2010).

Table 4.3 Distribution of Respondents Based on Opinion about Online Learning as an Effective Learning Environment

No.	Items	No	Rarely	Occasionally	Yes
1	Attended regular online class	3 (0.17%)	27 (15.43%)	9 (5.14%)	136 (77.71%)
2	Power interrupted online learning	72 (41.14%)	41 (23.43%)	39 (22.29%)	23 (13.14%)
3	Insufficient data	27 (15.43%)	12 (6.86%)	33 (18.86%)	103 (58.86%)
4	Technical glitch	45 (25.71%)	19 (10.86%)	21 (12%)	90 (51.43%)
5	Ease of individual doubt clearance	17 (9.71%)	11 (6.29%)	18 (10.29%)	129 (73.71%)
6	More interactive than physical class	71 (40.57%)	02 (1.14%)	17 (9.71%)	85 (48.57%)

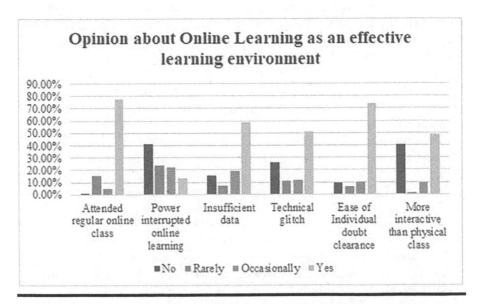

Figure 4.2 Opinion about online learning as an effective learning environment.

E-learning provides meaning for learners and becomes more convenient for students.

Learning has been extended from traditional classroom learning to virtual classrooms. Visual and audio learning has become routine, and the students are finding it to be very effective. The e-learning industry is witnessing a growth of 25% each year. *India Today* in 2020 reported that the e-learning industry will see a growth of US$1.96 billion (India Today, 2021). Apart from these fascinating facts, it is surprising that when the whole world has adopted the e-learning platforms as their regular classroom, few unfortunates still lack the services (Agarwal, 2021).

The responses in Table 4.4 shows that the students face different challenges in using smartphones for online classes: 43.43% of respondents strongly agreed about the problems of poor internet connectivity; 9.14% agreed that the smartphone is an uncomfortable device to handle;19.43% agreed that not all file format are supported in their smartphone; 13.71% agreed that the smartphone hangs during operation; 34.86% agreed that their online education was interrupted because of unwanted calls during online learning; and 52% also agreed that the challenges involve expensive tariff also. Figure 4.3 shows distribution of respondents based on challenges of using smartphone. Table 4.5 is a small table showing the tariff for prepaid mobile services in different countries.

Table 4.4   Distribution of Respondents Based on Challenges of Using Smartphone

No.	Items	Strongly Disagree	Disagree	Neutral	Agree	Strongly Agree
1	Poor internet connectivity	12 (6.86%)	17 (9.71%)	13 (7.43%)	57 (32.57%	76 (43.43%)
2	Smartphone is uncomfortable device to handle	32 (18.29%)	53 (30.29%)	59 (33.71%)	16 (9.14%)	15 (8.57%)
3	Not all file formats supported	16 (9.14%)	27 (15.43%)	66 (37.71%)	32 (18.29%)	34 (19.43%)
4	Smartphone hangs during operation	29 (16.57%)	43 (24.57%)	57 (32.57%)	24 (13.71%)	22 (12.57%)
5	Unwanted calls during online learning	14 (8%)	31 (17.71%)	57 (32.57%)	61 (34.86%)	12 (6.86%)
6	Expensive tariff	09 (5.14%)	13 (7.43%)	44 (25.14%)	91 (52%)	18 (10.29%)

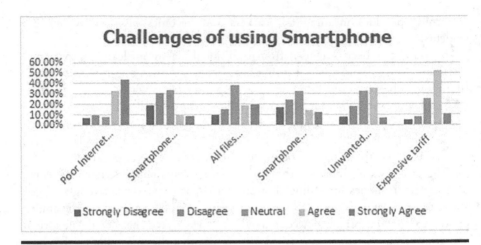

Figure 4.3   Distribution of respondents based on challenges of using smartphone.

Table 4.5   Selected Asian Countries and Tariff Rate in US$

Country Name	Rate
Bangladesh	1.41
Pakistan	3.65
India	2.91
Sri Lanka	0.95
Philippines	10.15
Thailand	5.36

Source: ITU (2014)

It is self-explanatory that the tariff is not significantly higher than other Asian countries. However, as these tariffs do not facilitate all people, a standard resolution is expected from government initiatives that allow for affordable mobile phones even for marginalized families. Again, a shocking study was conducted by Murphy and Carmody (2015) where they found that the people of Uganda reduced their grocery expenses to afford a mobile phone and its tariff. A study by Rashid and Elder (2009) also brings out the struggle for the poor to get a mobile phone. They mentioned, "Affordability is a key barrier for the rural poor's adoption of essential mobile services."

Smartphones are becoming an effective learning tool used in teaching and learning. Modern smartphones have the potential of computers and even function faster than computers. In an article on using cell phones as learning tools, Becton Loveless pointed to the massive growth of smartphones. The number of smartphones used globally increased to 3.2 billion in 2019 and was expected to reach 4.5 billion in 2022 (Data Reportal, 2021). Regarding tariffs, a report by ITU, 2014 explains that the cheapest prepaid mobile cellular tariff is available in Asia, where Sri Lanka and Bangladesh are among the cheapest in the world. The following statistics give an idea that smartphones are yet to design a device for the masses that all can afford and use smoothly.

In this study, the following other challenges were also reported by the respondents:

1. The student community mentioned technical reasons to be the biggest reason for their reluctance to use mobile technology. Teachers mentioned lack of training, technical support, and connectivity issues among the challenges in mobile learning.
2. Students reported that they had faced sudden calls, notification rings, unwanted chaos, unwanted calls, and disturbance during an online class.
3. Students have reported that they had audiovisual issues during their online classes. Voice break is among the most common issues.
4. Most of the students have also reported that the class link sent by the teachers did not work many times, which led them to being absent.

While the world considers smartphones as a potential learning tool for online resources, communication, and multimedia creativity, there is a segmented population that sees them as a nuisance. Trilling and Fadel (2009) said mobile phones are a learning tool for better education. However, many social and educational leaders find it a hindrance to meaningful learning considering the distraction from ring tones, emails, texting, tweeting, and cheating in the classrooms. Instant messaging services are the most common distraction. Hinduja and Patchin (2011) said an instant message can be a form of cyberbullying as "willful and repeated harm inflicted through the use of computers, cell phones, and other electronic devices." Numerous incidents of cyberbullying were reported in the United Stated in the year 2020. This act has been proven to be very dangerous as this happens outside the schools.

Durrani (2009) expressed equally disturbing facts when most school-going students share nude photos to known or unknown people, also known as sexting. This has created massive distractions among the youth. Parents and schools need to play a better role to curb this evil. Again, cheating through mobile is also a trend where fraudsters send a link or encrypted message, and as soon as the links are visited, the device gets hacked and sometimes bank frauds take place. The bank account is linked with the mobile number to notify a transaction to receive bank updates. However, cybercriminals have been taken this as an opportunity by fooling civilians.

4.6 Major Findings

1. Sixty-three percent of the respondents do not have personal smartphones.
2. Students have engaged in the classes by borrowing (61%) a smartphone from their parents, brothers, uncles, or relatives.
3. Thirty-two percent of the respondents use a smartphone pricing under 8–10 thousand rupees, and 48% use a smartphone ranging from 5–8 thousand.
4. Sixty-seven percent of respondents confirmed that they use used or refurbished smartphones. Only 18% use new smartphones.
5. Eighty-five percent of students used their parents' or relatives' phones, and the other 15% were the owners of their phones.
6. Students face different negative aspects of online studies: 13.14% face power interruption; 58.86% lack sufficient data for online classes; 51.43% face different types of other technical glitches during online classes; 43.43% face poor internet connectivity; 13.71% face the problem of the smartphone hanging; 34.86% face unwanted calls during online learning; and 52% face challenges from expensive tariffs.
7. Among the online class attendants, 98% of the population use smartphones, 1% tablets, and 1% laptops.
8. According to Niti Aayog's report in 2021, Jharkhand is the second poorest state of India after Bihar. As per the Multidimensional Poverty Index (MPI), 42.16% of the population of Jharkhand is poor. Ninety-two percent of the respondents reported that they face severe problems regarding recharging the internet tariff.
9. Gyan Vigyan Samiti (GVS) NGO has surveyed primary education in Jharkhand. They revealed that majority of students have not been able to access online classes during the pandemic (Sanjay Sahay, 2021).

4.6.1 Future of Education in Jharkhand

The present government of Hemant Soren has announced that Jharkhand is on its way to achieving the "schools of excellence" goal (India Times, 2021). The government wishes to convert 80 schools into schools of excellence. The aim is to facilitate 5,000 government-run schools with modern educational facilities. Labs, libraries, and STEM labs will be established to ensure quality education.

As per the "Adarsh Vidyalaya scheme," the government is trying to develop at least one model school in each panchayat. The targeted students under "school of excellence" schemes are preprimary to standard XII. It is expected that almost 15 lakh students will benefit from this scheme. As per the report of ASER (2014), one of the most important reasons for school dropout is the lack of sanitation and lavatory facilities. To tackle this issue, the state government has ordered school premises to have separate lavatory facilities for girls and boys.

4.7 Conclusion and Recommendation

Since the devastating effects of the COVID-19 pandemic started, the world has seen a rapid change in the education sector. Online education has become the new normal; though after April 2021, the cases of COVID-19 came down, which relaxed the regulating authority's mandates and allow education institutions to open slowly and start physical classes. Then in December 2021, the world was introduced to the Omicron variant, and again, the world came under the dark shadow of different uncertainties.

Jharkhand was declared the second poorest state by the recently published Multidimensional Poverty Index in 2021 by NITI Aayog in terms of poverty: 42.16% of the population are poor, and 47.99% of people are malnourished. The figures are a matter of great concern and quite alarming. The challenges have crumpled the education scenario as well. Amita Kumari (2020) has revealed in her study that basic facilities are not provided in the schools. The achievements of the schools are just ignorable. With these challenges aside, education must be continued to bring about personal and career growth for the individuals of Jharkhand and for them to prove the region's existence.

Composite schools (which will provide complete education from class 1 to postgraduation in one campus) are a great initiative by the Ministry of Education that promise to start opening schools in Ranchi, Palamau, Dumka, Chaibasa, and Hazaribagh. This will surely increase the number of students since now, SC, ST, and OBC students can get free education in IIT Dhanbad, but free education for every community shall increase the registration. Even a pilot project may be conducted where for 10 or 15 years, the students from less literate districts may be allowed to study free of cost at any institute, which can bring a positive change in education.

Since we fear that online education will continue for quite some time, the government should distribute smartphones to the students belonging to low-income-group families. Though Jharkhand police have formed a "gadget bank," requesting people to donate their old smartphones and computers that can be used by poor students for their online classes (Indian Mastermind, 2021), still, more such policy-level initiatives are required. Further, as this study reveals, the students face a significant hurdle in recharging the monthly tariff; the telecom industry may be requested to initiate a pocket-friendly recharge plan, especially for the student community. This will bring a positive change to bring the deprived under the online-education umbrella.

The Indian government takes unprecedented steps to promote tribal education: Ashram schools, Ekalavya Model Residential Schools, Kasturba Gandhi Balika Vidyalaya, prematric scholarships, and vocational training centers.

- ▪ The government, policy makers, and international development institutions should come forward to collaborate and address the root issues with tribal education. A special task force may be created to look into a specific challenge to resolve within a limited period.

■ The firm policy should have an adequate budget focusing on a long-term strategy to eradicate different challenges associated with tribal education.

■ Equal access and opportunity should be created as many tribal children feel detached from the mainstream children from an upper-caste society. This ease will help them to feel common rather than detached.

■ Economic and educational upliftment is necessary to promote the socioeconomic integration of tribal people.

■ It is high time for the government to think of a better job guarantee for the parents apart from their direct beneficiaries. Once the parents are economically efficient, they will encourage their ward to go to school.

Acknowledgment

The researchers are sincerely grateful to the headmasters and the class teachers of the schools of Jharkhand State, where the study was carried out. Their extended help in conveying the aim of the study to the students made it easier to get positive feedback. This work could not have been completed without their support and cooperation.

References

Agarwal, N. "The future of e-learning in India." *The Future of E-learning in India—Digital Learning Magazine*, 2021. https.eletsonline.com.

Aker, J. and Mbiti, I. "Mobile phones and economic development in Africa." *Journal of Economic Perspective*, 2010:24(3):207–232.

Annual Status of Education Report. *Pratham NGO*, 2014. https://img.asercentre.org/docs/Publications/ASER%20Reports/ASER%202014/National%20PPTs/aser2014indiaenglish.pdf.

Becton Loveless. "Using cell phones as learning tools (complete guide)," 2019. https://ducationcorner.com.

CB Insights. "Mega-rounds boost global Ed-tech funding to new record. CB Insights," 19 January 2016. www.cbinsights.com/blog/2015-global-ed-tech-funding/.

Data Reportal. 2021. https://datareportal.com/global-digital-overview.

Durrani, A. "'Sexting' growing trend among teens." *Getlegal.com*, 29 April 2009. http://public.getlegal.com/articles/sexting.

Eden, D., and Jacqueline. "ECAR study of undergraduate students and information technology." *EDUCAUSE Centre for Analysis and Research*, 2014. https://net.educause.edu/ir/library/pdf.

Fordjour, K. Andrews, Zakaria, Ismail Mahamud and Rockson, Afriyie. "Use of mobile phones to support coursework: Evidence from Wa Polytechnic, Ghana". *Ghana Journal of Development Studies*, 2015:12(1–2):195.

Hinduja, S. and Patchin, J. W. "Bullying, cyberbullying, and suicide." *Archives of Suicide Research*, 2011(14):206–221.

Ifeanyi, I. P. and Chukwuere, J. E. "The impact of using smartphones on the academic performance of undergraduate students." *Knowledge Management & E-Learning*, 2018:10(3):290–308.

India Times. "Explained: How Jharkhand is improving quality of education through schools of excellence." 2021. www.indiatimes.com/explainers/news/how-jharkhand-is-improving-quality-of-education-through-schools-of-excellence-547284.html.

Indian Mastermind. "Jharkhand cops come forward to help poor students." 2021. https://indianmasterminds.com/features/be-inspired/jharkhand-cops-come-forward-to-help-poor-students/.

IndiaToday. 2021. www.indiatoday.in/education-today/featurephilia/story/how-e-learning-is-transforming-the-education-sector-1759690-2021-01-16.

ITU. "Measuring the information society report." Geneva. www.itu.int/en/ITU-D/Statistics/Documents/publications/mis2014/MIS2014_without_Annex_4.pdf.

Kumari, A. "A study of the status of primary education in village area of Jharkhand: With special reference to chatra district." *Quest Journals of Research in Humanities and Social Science*, 2020:08(12):51–54.

Murphy, J. and Carmody, P. *Africa's information revolution.* Wiley-Blackwell, Hoboken, 2015.

Radha, R., Mahalakshmi, K., Sathish Kumar, V., and Saravanakumar, A. "E-learning during lockdown of COVID-19 pandemic: A global perspective." *International Journal of Control and Automation*, 2020:13(4):1088–1099. www.researchgate.net/publication/342378341

Rashid, A., and Elder, L. "Mobile phones and development: An analysis of IDRC-supported projects." *EJISDC*, 2009:36(2):1–16.

Sahay, S. "Most students in rural areas of Jharkhand lack access to online education: Survey." 2021. https://timesofindia.indiatimes.com/city/ranchi/most-students-in-rural-areas-lack-access-to-online-education-survey/articleshow/85607938.cms.

Shah, D. "MOOC trends in 2016: College credit, credentials, and degrees." 2016a. www.class-central.com/report/mooc-trends-credit-credentials-degrees/.

Technopedia. "What does Smartphone mean?" 2019. www.techopedia.com/definition/2977/smartphone.

Trilling, B., and Fadel, C. *21st Century Skills: Learning for Life in Our Times.* Jossey Bass, San Francisco, CA, 2009:3.137–159.

Veletsianos, G. *Emerging Technologies in Distance Education.* Athabasca University, Canada, 2010. http://tojde.anadolu.edu.tr/upload/files/tojde_16_1_2015.pdf.

Wesolowski, A., Eagle, N., Noor, A., Snow, R., and Buckee, C. "Heterogeneous mobile phone ownership and usage patterns in Kenya." *PLoS ONE*, 2012:7(4):e35319. http://doi.org/10.1371/journal.pone.0035319.

Wheeler, D., Dasgupta, S., and Lall, S. "Policy reform, economic growth, and the digital divide: An econometric analysis." *World Bank Policy Research Working Paper.* Washington, DC, 2001. http://doi.org/10.1596/1813-9450-2567

Wikham, B. "The school education system in India: An overview." *British Council,* 2019:187–193.

Chapter 5

Employing Google Classroom as a Tool for Teaching and Learning during the COVID-19 Pandemic among English as a Second Language Teachers in Selected Malaysian Secondary Schools

Charanjit Kaur Swaran Singh, Eng Tek Ong,
Revathi Gopal, Mahendran Maniam,
Mazura Mastura Muhammad,
Tarsame Singh Masa Singh,
Muhammad Fadzllah Zaini,
Nadiah Yan Abdullah, and Sasigaran Moneyam

DOI: 10.1201/9781003328438-5

Contents

5.1 Introduction

The COVID-19 pandemic has interrupted and affected the education system globally. Most of the teaching institutions, including universities and schools, were closed to curb the spread of the virus. The decision to enforce the lockdown and closure of schools has had a deep effect on teaching. Correspondingly, the decision to close schools has had a profound impact on educators, students, and parents. Thus, online distance learning and remote learning are the alternatives to ensure continuity in teaching and learning. Subsequently, educators from the tertiary, secondary, and primary levels had to modify and redesign different and unacquainted methods of teaching during the pandemic. In Malaysia, the federal government has announced and declared a movement control order (MCO) since March 18, 2020, as a precautionary measure to curb the spread of the COVID-19 pandemic. In Malaysia, home-based teaching and learning (PdPR) were one of the initiatives taken to ensure students' education would not be neglected and their morale was restored during the COVID-19 pandemic. Other initiatives announced by the Ministry of Education were the television-based learning sessions or programs that offered a range of practice activities for students having national examinations and also for those students who have difficulty accessing the internet or who have no internet access. The purpose of this study is to investigate how ESL teachers employ Google Classroom as a tool for teaching and learning during the COVID-19 pandemic, assess their experiences teaching remotely on digital platforms, identify their perceived impediments and the challenges of conducting online learning activities during the COVID-19 pandemic, and examine the factors affecting the practice and acceptance of online learning as a tool for teaching and learning within secondary schools. This article attempts to address this gap by focusing on two key research questions:

1. How did the ESL teachers carry out the teaching and learning activities during the COVID-19 pandemic?
2. What were the problems and challenges faced by the ESL teachers in conducting online learning activities during the COVID-19 pandemic?

5.2 Asynchronous Learning

Asynchronous learning refers to an approach that is based on student-centered teaching techniques extensively employed in an online learning platform. The teacher generally prepares the learning platform that will allow the student to take part and engage in learning conveniently at their own pace. In other words, the student will be engaged in learning independently without the presence of the teacher. Asynchronous learning can take place at any time and places specific toward individual learners' preference compared to synchronous learning, whereby the learning can take place at the same place and time as the instructor and learners.

5.3 Synchronous Learning

Synchronous learning occurs when teachers and students are positioned at the same time and in the same place (Rigo & Mikus, 2021). The learning occurs in real time.

This implies that both the teachers and the students are in class together, undergoing live online lessons. Both the teachers and students will go through the lesson and learning platform together. Teachers will be online to accompany the students to monitor and facilitate learning by giving them some support so that the students can accomplish the assignments or tasks given online. Synchronous learning is also beneficial for live classes online or interactions implemented to encourage a strong community among students.

5.4 Google Classroom as a Tool for Teaching and Learning

One of the reliable technology alternatives teachers have employed and explored within education was Google Classroom as it opened up solutions and impacted instruction. Google Classroom allows teachers to form and create an online classroom zone that allows teachers to store and manage all the teaching and learning documents they want students to access. All the teaching and learning documents saved and stored by the teachers on Google Drive can be edited by teachers and students with permission in Sheets, Google Docs, and others.

5.5 Past Studies on the Use of Google Classroom

5.5.1 Employing Online Educational Technology Tools

Iftakhar (2016) reported teachers and students' views on the use of Google Classroom and found that Google Classroom has the potential to be used and explored by teachers from different disciplines to make teaching more meaningful. Crawford et al. (2020) concur the need for teachers to master and internalize proper skills and knowledge in employing online educational technology tools and applications that they can use to effectuate teaching and learning. Teachers must equip themselves and keep abreast with the current technological hardware because online teaching and learning demands teachers' mastery of the use of current technology so that they can teach anytime and anywhere. Teachers must create a learning space similar to learning at school despite knowing the fact that students are still learning from home.

5.5.2 Use of Various Apps for Online Teaching and Learning

Singh et al. (2020) carried out a study to check how teachers implement online teaching during the COVID-19 pandemic in selected schools in Malaysia. The findings showed that the ESL teachers used social media such as Telegram and WhatsApp to engage students in the teaching and learning process. Teachers made use of other various apps, including Kahoot, Padlet, and Quizziz, to assess students' mastery of the content taught. Their findings showed that teachers must have a good mastery of the online technological tool to implement successful online teaching. Despite the challenges faced by the teachers, they expressed their concerns and the problems encountered while implementing online teaching with students, namely students' negative attitudes toward cooperating and submitting works assigned on the online platform. Irfan Fauzi and Iman Hermawan Sastra Khusuma (2020), Nambiar (2020), and Rasmitadila et al. (2020) have different views with regard to the online learning platform as they reported teaching online became more meaningful during the COVID-19 pandemic. The researchers reported that an online learning platform was the only alternative for them to implement and share teaching and learning resources. Teachers have to be selective in delivering online teaching and learning resources due to limitations such as access to the internet and computers, students living in rural areas, and lack of infrastructure. Chen (2021) compiled the effects of cooperative learning (CL) that can be advantageous to both teachers and students as CL allows for progress in learning and also increases their motivation. The students' attitude is an important variable to ensure growth in learning and academic performance (Okafor, 2021; Kiong et al., 2022).

5.5.3 Factors Affecting the Use of Google Classroom

Tahir et al. (2021) conducted a study to examine the factors affecting the use of Google Classroom in four selected states in Malaysia. The main aim of the study was to seek out the factors that had led teachers to employ GC in the classroom during the COVID-19 pandemic. Data were collected from a self-administered survey comprising 103 respondents. The findings showed that teachers still lack knowledge on the technical skills required to implement GC and other learning-management systems. Their study reported that teachers are not confident to master and learn about current technical technologies that can facilitate them in the instruction. Other interesting findings include internet-connectivity inaccessibility, which caused English teachers to take into account the implementation of GC or other learning-management systems and insufficient equipment to use and depend on to teach using GC.

5.6 Methodology

This study employed multiple case studies comprising the experiences of different teachers across different settings: nine ESL teachers from five different selected states in Malaysia.

5.6.1 Participants

Fourteen ESL teachers participated in this study, and they were selected based on the purposive sampling method. These teachers work in different states, namely Perak, Kuala Lumpur, Selangor, Melaka, Kedah, and Terengganu. These teachers have obtained their first degree in teaching English as a second language (TESL), and out of the 14 teachers, six teachers have obtained their master's degree in education (TESL). All these teachers have taught English for at least four years and more. These teachers have vast teaching experience in the English language as shown in Table 5.1. All these teachers were assigned to teach English for both the lower and upper secondary levels. The students' language proficiency was determined by the summative assessment scores shared by the teachers. Table 5.1 displays their demographic data.

Table 5.1 shows the demographic of a total of 10 English as second language teachers. Most of the teachers are from Kuala Lumpur.

Table 5.2 provides information on the ethnic background of 14 teachers, comprising Malay, Chinese, India, Punjabi, and others. "Most of the teachers are from the Indian ethnic background (Mertens, 2014)." Table 5.2 shows the ethnic background of the teachers. Five Malay teachers, one Chinese teacher, six Indian teachers, and two Punjabi teachers participated in the study to share their views in terms of how they employed Google Classroom as a tool for teaching and learning during the COVID-19 pandemic, assess their experiences teaching remotely on digital platforms, identify their perceived impediment and challenges in conducting online learning activities during the COVID-19 pandemic, and examine factors affecting the practice and acceptance of online learning as a tool for teaching and learning within secondary schools.

Table 5.3 shows information on the age group of the teachers. The most obvious age group of the teachers ranges from 41–50. There are seven teachers whose age range is from 41–50. Table 5.3 shows the age group of the teachers who have participated in this study based on the purposive sampling method. The purposive sampling method was used by the researchers in this study. Best et al. (2017) opined that the selection of samples in purposive sampling are based on participants who can offer the richest information or those who possess certain characteristics that the researcher is interested in. As for this study, the researchers selected 14 ESL teachers who have experience and expertise in teaching English as a second language.

The teachers' working experience reflect their pedagogical and technological knowledge that will benefit students in terms of mastery of knowledge, skills, and values that they can apply in the context of real-life situations. The teachers' good mastery in information communication technology (ICT) will provide them with more opportunities to develop and facilitate lessons more effectively using digital technologies.

All the fourteen teachers mentioned that they had taught students with varying language proficiencies. These varying language proficiencies are classified as

Table 5.1 ESL Teacher's Demographic Background

Teacher's Name	Gender	State	Teaching Experience	Qualifications	Students' Proficiency Level
Teacher A	Female	Perak (Kanmani)	18	Master of Education in TESL	Low
Teacher B	Female	Selangor (Kalai)	15	Bachelor of Education in TESL	High
Teacher C	Female	Selangor (Manimala)	4	Master of Education in TESL	High
Teacher D	Female	Selangor (Rohaya)	23	Master of Education in TESL	Low
Teacher E	Female	Kuala Lumpur (Nik)	22	Bachelor of Education in TESL	High
Teacher F	Female	Kuala Lumpur (Megha)	10	Bachelor of Education in TESL	High
Teacher G	Female	Kuala Lumpur (Ifa)	8	Bachelor of Education in TESL	High
Teacher H	Female	Melaka (tana)	14	Bachelor of Education in TESL	High
Teacher I	Female	Kedah (Manisha)	11	Master of Education in TESL	Low
Teacher J	Female	Kuala Lumpur (Kaya)	12	Master of Education in TESL	High
Teacher K	Female	Selangor (Teena)	10	Master of Education in TESL	Intermediate

(Continued)

Table 5.1 (Continued) ESL Teacher's Demographic Background

Teacher's Name	Gender	State	Teaching Experience	Qualifications	Students' Proficiency Level
Teacher L	Female	Terengganu (Tasha)	4	Bachelor of Education in TESL	Low
Teacher M	Female	Perak (Umi)	6	Bachelor of Education in TESL	Low
Teacher N	Female	Perak (Lim)	7	Bachelor of Education in TESL	Intermediate

Table 5.2 Ethnic Background

Ethnic Background	Malay	Chinese	Indian	Punjabi	Others	Total
Frequency (f)	5	1	6	2	-	14

Table 5.3 Age Group

Age Group (x)	25–30	31–40	41–50	Above 50
Frequency (f)	2	4	7	1

high, intermediate, and low. The teachers mentioned that they divided students' proficiency levels based on their summative test scores. Teachers B, C, E, F, G, H, and J taught students with a high level of English proficiency. Teachers K and N taught students with an intermediate level of English proficiency, and Teachers A, I, L, and M taught students with a low level of English proficiency.

5.6.2 Data Collection

All 14 teachers were contacted by the researchers via WhatsApp and email. The interview questions were shared using WhatsApp. The researchers contacted the participants via WhatsApp to get their consent to participate in the study. Upon getting the participants' consent, the researchers shared the interview questions using email. The researchers did not reveal the names of the participants to protect confidentiality and anonymity. The interview questions shared via email focused mainly on seeking out the tools the participants used for teaching and learning the English language during the COVID-19 pandemic, the implementation of the teaching and learning activities based on the tool mentioned, the challenges and problems faced while conducting online teaching, and how the participants would overcome the problems, challenges, and factors affecting the practice and acceptance of online learning as a tool for teaching and learning English within secondary schools during the COVID-19 pandemic.

5.6.2.1 Interview Questions

The researchers created seven questions for the interview with the teachers. All these seven questions were shared through WhatsApp and email.

1. Please state your working experience as a teacher.
2. Please write your current state of work: for example, Perak.
3. What tool did you use for teaching and learning the English language during the COVID-19 pandemic?
4. How did you carry out the teaching and learning activities for the English language during the COVID-19 pandemic based on the tool mentioned in question 2? Please explain step-by-step.
5. What are the challenges and problems you faced while conducting online teaching of the English language during the COVID-19 pandemic?
6. How do you overcome the challenges of teaching English online during the COVID-19 pandemic?
7. What factors would affect the practice and acceptance of online learning as a tool for teaching and learning the English language within secondary schools during the COVID-19 pandemic?

5.6.3 Data Analysis Technique

Bowen (2009) states that qualitative data analysis involves the reflexive and reiterative process in nature that starts from the time the data are assembled rather than after data collection has ended. The qualitative research approach is primarily designed to discover and project elements or ideas that can be interpreted and used in hypothesis testing in the quantitative method (Corbin & Strauss, 2015). This is further supported by Grbich (2007), stating that qualitative data analysis does not comprise hypotheses and variables; data analysis begins with the demystification of the text rather than numbers once the data analysis takes place. Hypothesis testing is not designed in qualitative research (Bowen, 2009). The interviews with 14 teachers in this study were carried out to obtain views concerning the implementation of Google classroom for teaching and learning purposes during the COVID-19 pandemic. The teachers recorded their feedback in written form. The researchers collected the feedback in written form to collect word-for-word transcripts from the interviewees (Corbin & Strauss, 2015). The researchers then collected the transcripts and analyzed them by recognizing and classifying themes that are meaningful and mutual by an "open coding" technique (Schmidt, 2004). The findings were analyzed solely based on the teachers' responses. This technique permits the researchers to narrate and relate categories in both multifaceted manners to ensure the thickness of interpretation and accuracy of the developed theory. Thus, the interview method is deemed important to collect the qualitative data in this study. The data obtained from the interviews were analyzed using thematic analysis. Fundamentally, the researchers carried out the analysis reflexively by encompassing the following steps, namely categorizing, analyzing, and reporting themes extracted within the data gained. Six main themes were taken inductively from the emails analyzed.

5.7 Findings

1. How did the ESL teachers carry out the teaching and learning activities during the COVID-19 pandemic?

5.7.1 Using Google Classroom as a Teaching and Learning Tool during the COVID-19 Pandemic

5.7.1.1. Special Features of Google Classroom

All the 14 teachers shared that they have used Google Classrooms as a teaching tool for teaching and learning purposes during the COVID-19 pandemic. For instance, Teachers G and J shared that during this pandemic, Google Classroom has played an important role in both teachers' and students' lives. As teachers, both Teachers G and J have to branch out in different ways to use Google Classroom. Google classroom is set up as a "stream."

Teachers G, L, M, and N shared that Google Classroom has special features, such as "Announcements" and "Assignments," which are posts that allow students to comment on both types of posts. Teachers A, B, C, E, and L mentioned that the purpose of an announcement on Google Classroom is to add something to the stream so that the class can view it and leave a comment on it. For example, Teachers A and D shared that they posted videos on how to use certain types of vocabulary to improve the students' speaking skills and fluency. Teacher J shared that the availability of the effective apps provided in Google Classrooms can engage and gauge students' learning in class. Teacher J expressed that Google Docs is user-friendly and deemed suitable as one of the tools employed for teaching. Teacher J further explained that the school had instructed all the teachers to teach through online and hybrid versions. Teacher L and J shared that Google Docs permits teachers to share links easily with students. Teachers, on the other hand, can monitor students' participation and contribution in the classroom. Teacher J also shared that by providing the link through Google Docs, teachers can request students to highlight and answer questions, and this is a good tool for teaching writing.

The teachers shared that DocHub is an extremely trouble-free platform that allows you to take down notes and type your work out freely. It allows you to make text boxes in the size and shape of your choice. After making your text box, you can type out the work that you were assigned. You will have to save this document

Figure 5.1 Announcement on Google Classroom shared by Teacher B.

into your devices' files. At the top bar, you can also see the icon labelled as "People." When you click this icon, you will be able to see the students' and teachers' names, including the number of how many students and teachers there are. There is also a platform called Google Drive. This platform is usually used when teachers or students need to save their work so they can review it later. It is easier for students to save their work here so they can send it to their teachers afterward. Figure 5.1 shows an example of announcement on Google Classroom shared by teacher B.

Teacher C, who is teaching in a boarding school, has used the following tools to teach during the COVID-19 pandemic. The tools Teacher C has used include Google Classroom, Google Meet, Zoom, Telegram, Google breakout rooms, Quizizz, Kahoot, Google Forms, YouTube, Canva, Jamboard, Padlet, and DELIMA. During the COVID-19 pandemic, Teacher C has conducted online classes using either Google Meet or Zoom since all the teachers are provided with a DELIMA account by the Ministry of Education. It was easier to conduct lessons using Google Meet because teachers do not have to admit the students to the meet one by one, so it saves time. For this, all the students in Teacher C's school are encouraged to also use their DELIMA email ID. Teacher C shared that the students would submit the task/work assigned via Google Classroom. Hence, it was very easy for Teacher C to keep track of the lesson because Google Classroom acts like a virtual book. Besides, Teacher C had used Telegram to notify the students especially about sharing a link or any important information. On the other hand, Teacher C has conducted the midterm assessment via Google classroom and Google Forms. Next, during the lesson, Teacher C used YouTube, Canva, Quizizz, Kahoot, Padlet, Jamboard, Google breakout rooms, and PowerPoint slides to engage the students better. Figures 5.2 and 5.3 show examples of Jamboard activities prepared by the students (Teacher H).

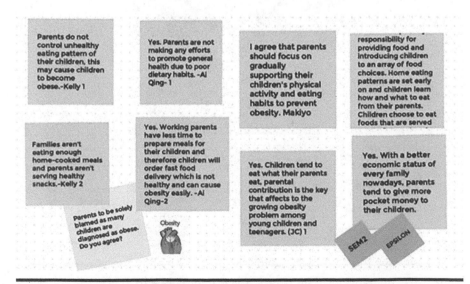

Figure 5.2   Jamboard activities prepared by the students (Teacher H).

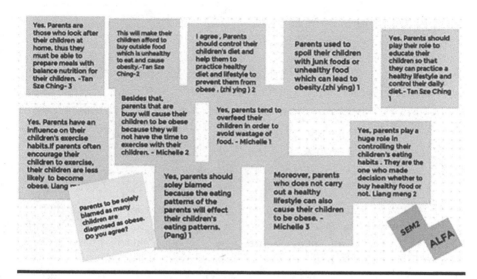

Figure 5.3   Jamboard activities prepared by the students (Teacher H).

Teacher D shared that both online and offline approaches were used for teaching and learning purposes during the pandemic. When Teacher D conducts the lessons online, Teacher D will share the Google Meet link with students, and for offline classes, Teacher D usually instructs students to watch YouTube or listen to the recorded lessons together with live worksheets or Google Forms exercises. The Google Meet link is created and shared by Teacher D. Next the Google Meet link is shared with the students earlier, 30 minutes or 10 minutes before class. Then, Teacher D will state the learning objectives so that they know what they are supposed to achieve by the end of the lessons. Teacher D will let them know which book, workbook, or module they should refer to. Normally, Teacher D will ask the students to use their textbook or workbook. Sometimes Teacher D uses the English module for teaching purposes. Teacher D gives the module before class so that they can print it out. The exercises were taken from their textbook or live worksheets. The links were given to them before classes. On the other hand, for the offline classes, Teacher D always made use of the YouTube and her recorded lessons based on the lesson of that day. Then, Teacher D ensures that the students are given quizzes or live worksheets based on the topic that they had learned. All the links were given in the class info for that day's lesson.

Teacher L claimed that the reason to embrace the new online learning mode was to assist the students so that they can benefit from learning during the pandemic. Teacher L used Google Classroom as it assisted Teacher L to be more creative in producing enjoyable English lessons; it offers various interesting templates such as quizzes, word searches, puzzles, and interactive slides for the students' learning progress in the classroom. Furthermore, Google Classroom is a flexible tool as the activities conducted in this tool can be accessed anywhere and everywhere, which is convenient for both the students and teachers.

Teacher E, who has been teaching English in a rural school, shared that the use of ClassDojo, online quiz websites (Quizziz, Wordwall), Padlet, Classkick, ClassPoint, flipped learning, YouTube, and Delima during the COVID-19 pandemic were very beneficial. Teacher E employed Google Meet sessions (virtual classroom), WhatsApp, and Telegram and shared learning materials offline with the students.

5.7.1.2 Uploading Files and Materials for Discussion

All the teachers claim that they can add files, drives, and web links for their students to refer to on Google Classroom. They shared that they upload files on the stream so that their students can go through the notes that had been discussed during the class. This can help the students in many ways. Students may log out of their classes, and this is when Google Classroom comes into action; the files that are uploaded daily usually contain all the main points that had been discussed during class. Therefore, this will give the students a chance to revise the notes well. Google Drive can be extremely useful as well. Google Drive allows you to save your files and access them anywhere.

5.7.1.3 Allowing Students to Comment on Assignments

All the 14 teachers mentioned that Google Classroom allows students to comment on assignments as well if they need help with anything specific, and they can even create discussions among themselves about a post. There is a download icon as well; if you click on it, you can download all of the assignments. The teachers mentioned that assignments are usually given out in different ways. Under the label "Classwork," teachers can simply divide the assignments into videos, reading lists, worksheets, etc. Google Docs is a very good platform for assignments. It is easy to adapt when using. It also saves your work immediately so the students don't have to stress out about whether they have saved their work or not.

5.7.1.4 Grading Students' Work

Teachers E, F, G, H, and I claimed that they can click on their students' work to view their assignments and add grades and leave a comment on them. The teachers explained they can give the students a grade by just clicking under "grade" and start typing. Once they are ready to send the grade to your students, teachers have to check the boxes next to all of the students they want to notify. They can click the blue "return" button at the top of the page. The students would then receive a link with the assignment that is returned. Figures 5.4 and 5.5 show the task graded by Teacher D.

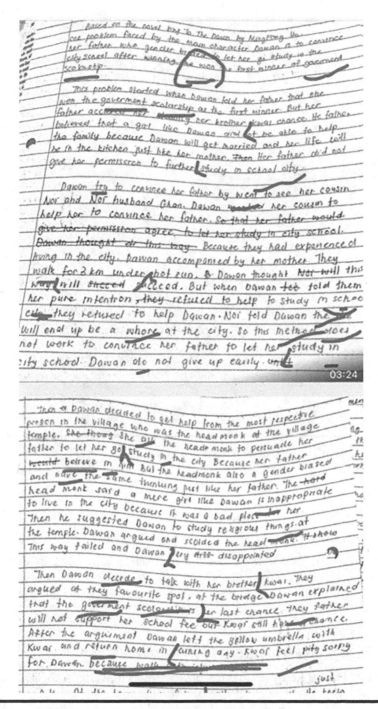

Figure 5.4 **Student's essay marked by Teacher D (an essay submitted via Google Docs).**

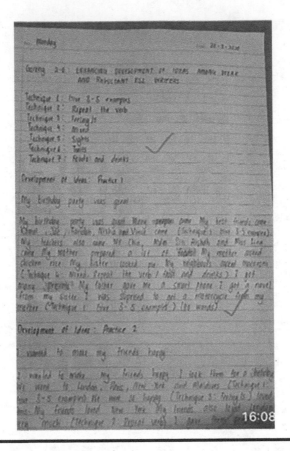

Figure 5.5   Graded work of a student.

5.7.1.5 Interactive Learning

All the teachers claim that they can also share a Jamboard link in Google Classroom so that the students can view the board, which acts as a whiteboard, as shown in Figure 5.6. If the teacher is writing anything on Jamboard, the students can view the writing actions immediately. This helps the students become more cooperative during lessons.

5.7.1.6 Engaging Students in the Learning Process

Teachers A, D, and J claimed that the primary tools or platform they had utilized was Google Meet and Google Classroom in order to engage with the students as well as to provide them with essential exercises for them to practice on. The use of Google Classroom as a teaching tool allowed the teachers to monitor the students'

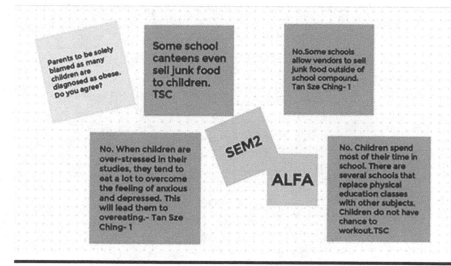

Figure 5.6   Jamboard activities posted by the students.

participation and contribution in class. Students are also allowed to post their written work through Google Classroom, as shown in Figure 5.7.

5.7.1.7 *Proper Planning and Announcement before Class*

Teachers A, B, C, D, H, and J believed that proper planning and announcements should be made clear before class so that the students are prepared for the lesson. Figure 5.8 is an example of an announcement made through Google Meet by Teacher D. The links for Google Meet should also be provided one day before the lesson. All the teachers shared that on the day of the class, the students are ordered to enter Google Meet punctually before they start the session. All the classes are to be conducted according to the duration allocated in the schedule. Once the teaching session is over, the teachers would then upload the exercises and homework on Google Classroom, which will later downloaded by the students for them to practice regularly.

Teacher F shared that the preparation of PowerPoint presentations beforehand should be planned earlier so that it is easier for the students to understand the specific topic that is being revised or taught. Teacher F explains certain subtopics in each slide of her liking. Teacher F also posts this presentation onto the Google Classrooms stream so that the students that were absent or had internet issues during the lesson can refer to it. Google Slides is also a great platform that is similar to PowerPoint. Google Slides is where anyone can create creative presentations smoothly. It saves your work automatically after you have completed typing as well. Teacher K agreed that the Google Classroom platform has been beneficial in terms

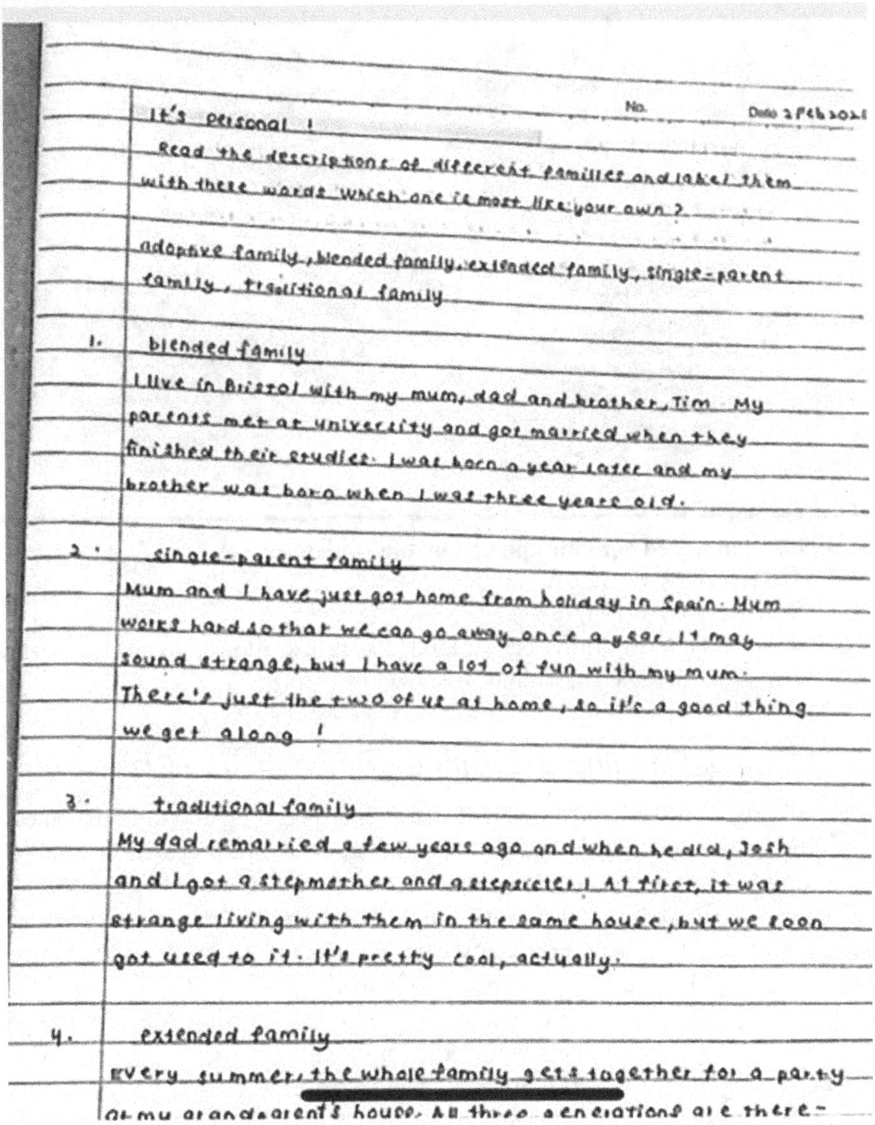
No. Date 2 Feb 2021

It's personal !

Read the descriptions of different families and label them with these words which one is most like your own ?

adoptive family, blended family, extended family, single-parent family, traditional family

1. blended family

I live in Bristol with my mum, dad and brother, Tim. My parents met at university and got married when they finished their studies. I was born a year later and my brother was born when I was three years old.

2. single-parent family

Mum and I have just got home from holiday in Spain. Mum works hard so that we can go away once a year. It may sound strange, but I have a lot of fun with my mum. There's just the two of us at home, so it's a good thing we get along !

3. traditional family

My dad remarried a few years ago and when he did, Josh and I got a stepmother and a stepsister ! At first, it was strange living with them in the same house, but we soon got used to it. It's pretty cool, actually.

4. extended family

Every summer, the whole family gets together for a party at my grandparent's house. All three generations are there -

Figure 5.7 Students' written work posted on Google classroom.

of approaching students during the pandemic. Teacher F also added that students are usually assigned with activities through Google Classroom. Google classroom has unique features that allow teachers to select options such as materials or assignments that they could assign to students for any form of activity. Table 5.4 shows the teaching and learning tools used by the ESL teachers during the COVID-19 pandemic to ensure continuity in instruction.

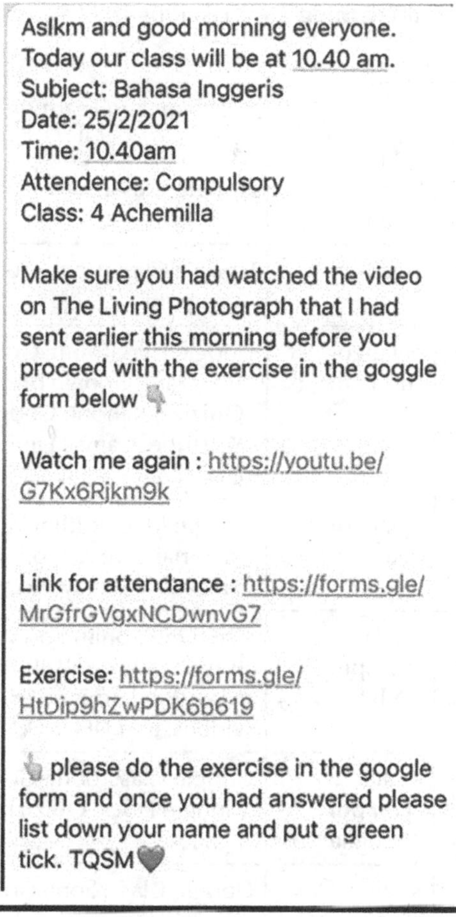

Aslkm and good morning everyone.
Today our class will be at 10.40 am.
Subject: Bahasa Inggeris
Date: 25/2/2021
Time: 10.40am
Attendence: Compulsory
Class: 4 Achemilla

Make sure you had watched the video
on The Living Photograph that I had
sent earlier this morning before you
proceed with the exercise in the goggle
form below 🖐

Watch me again : https://youtu.be/
G7Kx6Rjkm9k

Link for attendance : https://forms.gle/
MrGfrGVgxNCDwnvG7

Exercise: https://forms.gle/
HtDip9hZwPDK6b619

👆 please do the exercise in the google
form and once you had answered please
list down your name and put a green
tick. TQSM 💚

Figure 5.8 Announcement made through Google Meet by Teacher D.

Table 5.4 shows the teaching and learning tools used by the ESL teachers during the COVID-19 pandemic. The most apparent teaching and learning tool employed was Google Classroom. What are the problems and challenges faced by the ESL teachers in conducting the online learning activities during the COVID-19 pandemic?

5.7.1.8 Access to the Internet

Teachers A, D, E, J, M, and N revealed that the primary issue they had while using Google Classroom to conduct online lessons was that the internet connection was not always steady, causing interruptions throughout the class. Teacher C shared that all the students had good internet access, and for this reason, the challenges

Table 5.4 Teaching and Learning Tool Used by the ESL Teachers during the COVID-19 Pandemic

Teacher's Name	Gender	State	Teaching and Learning Tool Used during the COVID-19 Pandemic
Teacher A	Female	Perak (Kanmani)	Google Classroom, Google Meet
Teacher B	Female	Selangor (Kalai)	Google Classroom, Google Meet, Zoom, Telegram
Teacher C	Female	Selangor (Manimala)	Google Classroom, Google Meet, Zoom, Telegram, Google breakout room, Quizizz, Kahoot, Google Forms, YouTube, Canva, Jamboard, Padlet, and DELIMA
Teacher D	Female	Selangor (Rohaya)	Google Meet, offline and online materials, workbook, English module, quizzes or live worksheets
Teacher E	Female	Kuala Lumpur (Nik)	ClassDojo, online quiz websites (Quizizz, Wordwall), Padlet, Classkick, ClassPoint, flipped learning, YouTube videos, and DELIMA
Teacher F	Female	Kuala Lumpur (Megha)	Google Classroom, Google Meet, Google Docs, Quiziziz, DocHub
Teacher G	Female	Kuala Lumpur (Ifa)	Google Classroom, Google Meet, Google Docs, Quiziziz, DocHub
Teacher H	Female	Melaka (Tana)	Google Classroom, Google Meet, Zoom, Telegram
Teacher I	Female	Kedah (Manisha)	Google Classroom, Google Meet, Zoom, Telegram
Teacher J	Female	Kuala Lumpur (Kaya)	Google Classroom, Google Docs
Teacher K	Female	Selangor (Teena)	Google Classroom, Webex, Zoom
Teacher L	Female	Terengganu (Tasha)	Google Classroom, Google Docs
Teacher M	Female	Perak (Umi)	Google Classroom, Google Docs
Teacher N	Male	Perak (Lim)	Google Classroom, Google Docs

and problems in conducting online lessons were fewer while teaching her upper-form students. This is because most of the time, there will be a full attendance and the students will submit the work assigned to them. Besides, the students were also very cooperative as they would participate actively during the lesson most of the time. However, when it comes to the lower secondary student (Form 1), some of them do not have the motivation to participate in the lesson. Next, a few of Teacher C's students who were in Form 1 were facing internet-connectivity issues; hence, they would miss the online session often. Teacher E faced a similar problem as mentioned and shared that most of the students who fall under the category of B40 (parents with low income) do not have proper devices/gadgets. Teacher L explained some technical problems encountered when using the online learning tools, and preparing online materials can be time-consuming and overwhelming.

Teachers K, M, and N shared that it was quite difficult to keep students engaged when teaching them via the online platform. They also shared that the activities must be creative to attract students to the lesson so that they do not get distracted easily. These teachers mentioned that students preferred activities that embed YouTube during the online learning session. She also reminds her students to switch on their videos throughout the lesson so that she could monitor interaction online. Teachers K, M, and N also admit that when it comes to face-to-face lessons, interaction is limited between the teacher and students online. Therefore, as a teacher, it is crucial to find ways to establish a positive relationship between the teacher and students. To ensure the continuity of teaching and learning online, teachers must establish two-way communication. For this to take place, both teachers and students must be committed to fostering a conducive and interactive environment by progressing toward their social presence.

Teachers D, E, and K shared that those students were reluctant to join the online classes as they lack the motivation to learn. All these three teachers (Teacher D, E, and K) had to constantly remind them to join their classes. Students who failed to join online classes are instructed to view the recorded videos of the respective lesson. Teacher E mentioned that the same group of students were the ones who always skipped the online classes. These students were very passive in the class and seldom participated. Teacher E expressed her concern about some students who do not have proper devices/gadgets to commit to online classes as they had to share internet data with other siblings. Some of her students have a poor internet connection at home. Most of her students depend on the prepaid mobile data and when they are unable to reload the data, the students are unable to attend the online classes planned by Teacher E. Teacher J mentioned that some of her students do not answer despite calling their names for many times. Teacher J had to wait for the students to respond first before she could proceed to the next stage of the lesson, and this would then interrupt the flow of the online teaching session. Teacher J opines that students' cooperation is important to ensure that the learning standards set for the particular lesson are achievable. Teacher J also feels that students who refused to cooperate during the online learning session always tend to interrupt the flow of the lesson as she had to ensure the students demonstrated good mastery of the content being taught.

Teachers D, K, M, and N all stated that they continue to encourage and persuade their students to participate in online classes. Teachers D and K attempt to personally phone and occasionally video call their pupils to learn about their condition and problems. Students answer positively at times, while at other times, they may not reply at all. Regarding the internet coverage, Teacher D experienced a similar problem accessing the internet for teaching purposes. Teacher D suggested her students go to a place where they can get good internet coverage.

5.7.2 Overcoming Problems and Challenges Faced While Teaching English Online during the COVID-19 Pandemic

This section reports findings by teachers in terms of overcoming problems and challenges while teaching English online during the COVID-19 pandemic, namely, providing prerecorded lessons, assigning offline work to students, students' negative attitudes, integration of interesting and creative lessons, and also stability of internet connection.

5.7.2.1 Providing Prerecorded Lessons

Teachers A and D shared some of the strategies they had used to overcome the challenges of teaching English online during the COVID-19 pandemic. Teacher A usually provides prerecorded classes, and daily quizzes and challenges will make the students more alert and engaged with the subject. Teachers A, D, and E claimed that they overcome the challenges of teaching English online during the COVID-19 pandemic by sharing the link of the Google Meet recording for the students to view during their free time. Teacher E has used Hyperdoc with her students. Teacher E shared that teaching and learning materials were posted through Google Classroom.

5.7.2.2 Assigning Offline Work to Students

Teachers C and D shared that teachers need to constantly check on the students who miss the online lesson. This is to ensure they are not left out when they come back to school. Teacher C also assigns some offline work to her students who constantly have issues with internet connectivity. Since Teacher C is also a class teacher, she always checks on her students on how they are feeling at home and if they can cope with online learning.

5.7.2.3 Students' Negative Attitude

Teachers C, D, E, K, L, M, and N shared some of the factors that would affect the practice and acceptance of online learning as a tool for teaching and learning the English language within secondary schools during the COVID-19 pandemic. Teachers C, E, K, M, and N shared that students' negative attitudes could affect the good practice and acceptance of online learning. This is because students must be active participants to ensure effective learning takes place. If students lack motivation and confidence, this would impede and obstruct the teaching process. Therefore, students' positive attitude and participation during online learning are crucial toward language learning. Students' motivation factor would drive their learning and grasping language better. Teacher E shared that her students are lazy and always wake up late although they know they have to attend the online classes.

5.7.2.4 Integration of Interesting and Creative Lessons

Second, teachers' efforts in conducting an interesting lesson to engage the students would also determine the students' excitement toward language learning. Teachers have to be creative in their pedagogical approach to make learning more meaningful, such as gamifying language learning to increase students' excitement and focus to learn English. Positive communication between students and teachers is another factor that would affect the good practice and acceptance of online learning. Teacher L mentioned the importance of equipping oneself with good technological knowledge that will assist with the preparation and creation of good online materials for her students.

5.7.2.5 Stability of Internet Connection

All 14 teachers have agreed that the stability of internet connection plays an important role to ensure the smoothness and continuity of online teaching and learning. Stakeholders, including parents, must find ways to ensure their children have reliable internet access and technology that will permit them to take part and contribute to e-learning. Teachers mentioned that students who have sufficient access to the internet and technology can learn more effectively. Teachers mentioned that students tend to learn faster when they are online as the tasks posted would require their immediate response. Students are also allowed to learn at their own pace, reread materials posted, flip through learning materials, or hasten through ideas and concepts as they select them.

5.8 Discussion

Teaching strategies, especially incorporating technology into pedagogical practices in virtual learning, ensures continuity in the teaching and learning process. Traditional face-to-face teaching and the integration of technology into instruction cannot be ignored as teachers must use either blended or Web 2.0 to adapt to the needs of the current situation due to the COVID-19 pandemic. Good technological knowledge and skills will be an advantage for the teachers to embrace the challenges and shortcomings of traditional face-to-face teaching. Teachers cannot ignore the importance and integration of technology into instruction and must always keep abreast with the latest innovations in education so that students can benefit and sustain lifelong learning despite the pandemic. Dhawan (2020) divulged that online learning will benefit both the teachers and students as teachers can develop teaching and learning materials via the online platform for the learners to access and make learning more meaningful. However, to ensure smooth teaching and learning via the online platform, students must be equipped with the necessary infrastructure, technological tools, accessibility to the internet, and good technology support for the teachers to implement virtual learning. Mahyoob (2020) mentioned that more initiatives are needed to assist the students to attend e-learning, create awareness among students to participate actively during virtual learning and submit tasks or assignments given, spend time completing the tasks given for certain projects, and attend classes to ensure knowledge is transferred. Students must understand the synchronous and asynchronous learning approaches that they can choose to ensure learning takes place. There is also an urgent need to accept and validate the usage of technology in instruction and its major role in the learning and e-learning process. Suggate et al. (2013) assert that for the ensured success online learning, students must be equipped with ample opportunities to be the creator or participant in an online learning session. Teachers must take the initiative to guide students and apply their pedagogical and technological content knowledge so that students are given equal opportunities to participate and learn actively in an online learning platform. Collaboration and cooperation between teachers and students are crucial to show the importance of learning in line with the current development and modernization in the education landscape.

5.9 Conclusion

Based on the findings, it is apparent that participants display their commitment to flexible learning through the use of different technological tools to ensure continuity in instruction. Teaching and learning are possible with the incorporation of technology whether through online asynchronous or synchronous learning. The findings also highlight the problems faced by the students in terms of accessing the internet that limited their engagement and interaction with teachers for teaching and learning purposes. Teachers, on the other hand, had issues managing students' negative and passive attitudes toward gearing their interest to learn online so that they can sustain their academic development and performance. These results showed that both teachers and students have roles to play to ensure continuity and a successful online learning experience. Both students' positive attitudes and mindset needed to achieve effective online learning goals. Thus, it is the students' responsibility to ensure they set up a conducive and reliable learning environment to promote learning. Students' readiness and acceptance to learn in online learning will demand their ability to equip themselves with proper online tools and identify individual student learning styles, self-discipline, attentiveness, and respect shown to teachers and peers. When students can practice these online learning strategies, it would then assist the teachers in focusing on their instruction and creating an effective online learning community. The challenges and struggles shared and experienced by both the teachers and students are real, but the mutual understanding between teachers and students can decrease challenges in an online learning setting. Teachers can always motivate and get the students to take part in an online learning environment. Teachers should state the goals of the instructions clearly and inform students on the expectations of the tasks given with proper guidelines. With proper planning and guidance from the teachers, students will be more prepared to participate in the activities given, and this will become a habit to practice with a positive mind geared for learning. Teachers must rethink and reconsider ways or strategies that they can implement for those students who are unable to join the online learning sessions as some of them do not have proper devices/gadgets to commit to online classes. Teachers in this study have provided prerecorded videos for students to view at their own pace independently and have prepared an English-language module to assist students who cannot access the internet. This study is beneficial in enhancing the mastery of pedagogical and technological content knowledge due to the challenges faced by the education landscape. Teachers, stakeholders and scholars throughout the world must adopt and implement different measures and alternatives in dealing with the transformational changes in the learning system.

References

Best, M., MacGregor, D., & Price, D. (2017). Designing for Diverse Learning: Case Study of Place-Based Learning in Design and Technologies Pre-Service Teacher Education. *Australian Journal of Teacher Education, 42*(3), 91–106. http://doi.org/10.14221/ajte.2017v42n3.6

Bowen, G. A. (2009). Document Analysis as a Qualitative Research Method. *Qualitative Research Journal, 9*, 27–40. http://doi.org/10.3316/QRJ0902027

Chen, R. (2021). A Review of Cooperative Learning in EFL Classroom. *Asian Pendidikan, 1*(1), 1–9. https://doi.org/10.53797/aspen.v1i1.1.2021

Corbin, J., & Strauss, A. (2015). *Basics of Qualitative Research.* Thousand Oaks, CA: Sage.

Crawford, J., Butler-Henderson, K., Rudolph, J., et al. (2020). COVID-19: 20 Countries' Higher Education Intra-Period Digital Pedagogy Responses. *Journal of Applied Teaching and Learning, 3*, 1–21. https://doi.org/10.37074/jalt.2020.3.1.7

Dhawan, S. (2020). Online Learning: A Panacea in the Time of COVID-19 Crisis. *Journal of Educational Technology. Systems, 49*(1), 5–22.

Fauzi, I., & Khusuma, I. (2020). Teachers' Elementary School in Online Learning of COVID-19 Pandemic Condition. *Jurnal Iqra': Kajian Ilmu Pendidikan, 5*(1), 58–70. https://doi.org/10.25217/ji.v5i1.914

Grbich, C. (2007). *Qualitative Data Analysis: An Introduction*. London: SAGE Publications Ltd.

Iftakhar, S. (2016). Google Classroom: What Works and How? *Journal of Education and Social Sciences*, *3*, 12–18. ISSN 2289–9855

Kiong, T. T., Ramla, A., Azman, M. N. A., Bagus, N. R. P., Sukardi, R., & Abdul, H. R. I. (2022). Mastery Issues and Teaching Approaches for the Electrical Technology Certificate Programme at Community Colleges on the Topic of Measuring Instruments. *Asian Pendidikan*, 2(1), 1–7. https://doi.org/10.53797/aspen.v2i2.2.2021

Mahyoob, M. (2020). Challenges of e-Learning during the COVID-19 Pandemic Experienced by EFL Learners. *Arab World English Journal*, *11*(4), 351–362. https://doi.org/10.24093/awej/vol11no4.23

Malaysia Education Blueprint (2013–2025). https://www.moe.gov.my/en/dasarmenu/pelan-pembangunan-pendidikan-2013-2025

Mertens, D. M. (2014). *Research and Evaluation in Education and Psychology: Integrating Diversity with Quantitative, Qualitative, and Mixed Methods*. Sage, Gallaudet University, USA.

Nambiar, D. (2020). The Impact of Online Learning During COVID-19: Students' and Teachers' Perspective. *International Journal of Indian Psychology*, *8*(2), 783–793. DIP: 18.01.094/20200802. http://doi.org/10.25215/0802.094

Okafor, P. I. (2021). Influence of School Variables on Students' Attitude Towards Schooling in Upper Basic Schools in Ilorin South LGA, Kwara State. *Asian Pendidikan*, *1*(2), 73–81. https://doi.org/10.53797/aspen.v1i2.12.2021

Rasmitadila, R., Aliyyah, R. R., Rachmadtullah, R., Samsudin, A., Syaodih, E., Nurtanto, M., & Tambunan, A. R. S. (2020). The Perceptions of Primary School Teachers of Online Learning During the COVID-19 Pandemic Period: A Case Study in Indonesia. *Journal of Ethnic and Cultural Studies*, *7*(2), 90–109. https://doi.org/10.29333/ejecs/388

Rigo, F., & Mikus, J. (2021). Asynchronous and Synchronous Distance Learning of English as a Foreign Language. *Media Literacy and Academic Research*, *4*(1), 89–106.

Schmidt, C. (2004). The Analysis of Semi-Structured Interviews. In: Flick, U., von Kardoff, E. and Steinke, I. (Eds.), *A Companion to Qualitative Research*, Reinbek bei Hamburg: Rowohlt Taschenbuch Verlag GmbH, 253–259.

Singh, C. K. S., Singh, T. S. M., Tek, O. E., Moneyam, S., Abdullah, N. A., Singh, J. K. S., Chenderan, K., Singh, M. K. R., & Karupayah, T. (2020). Rethinking English Language Teaching Through Telegram, Whatsapp, Google Classroom and Zoom. *Systematic Review Pharmacy*, *11*(11), 45–54.

Suggate, S., Schaughency, E., & Reese, E. (2013). Children Learning to Read Later Catch up to Children Reading Earlier. *Early Childhood Research Quarterly*, *28*, 33–48. https://doi.org/10.1016/j.ecresq.2012.04.004

Tahir, M. H. M., Adnan, A. H. M., Piaralal, S. D., Shah, D. S. M., & Shak, M. S. Y. (2021). *Factors Influencing the Use of Google Classroom for Lessons During Covid-19 Pandemic Among Secondary ESL Instructors*. e-Proceedings of International Conference on Language, Education, Humanities &Social Sciences (i-LEdHS2021).

Chapter 6

Perception of Undergraduate Students on Online Education during COVID-19 Pandemic in Purulia District of West Bengal

Santosh Kumar Behera, Mazhar Shamsi Ansary, and Sodip Roy

Content

DOI: 10.1201/9781003328438-6

6.1 Introduction

Education is that dream tool that makes human beings more liberal, efficient, and honest. Our ancestors realized the importance of education well; that is why the process of imparting knowledge is continuing to date everywhere. New pedagogies, methods, and techniques have made education much more effective for us. Experts and scientists are continuously investing much effort to make education more feasible for all. The rapid development of technology attracted education researchers as well. They are highly interested to utilize technology in the field of education (Raja & Nagasubramani, 2018). However, the concept of online education was invented a long time ago; it became very popular for learners at large. Moreover, with their complex and busy schedule, people are fascinated by online education, and through this mode of education, anyone can learn anytime and anywhere at their own pace. It offers an amazing scope to learn many topics and issues without investing much time and resources that make learners' journey convenient and effective (Ghavifekr & Rosdy, 2015). Nowadays, developed and developing countries are encompassing online platforms and resources inevitably for their educational development.

People in 2020 witnessed a menane of a pandemic that broke down their lives. Everything was tremendously affected due to COVID-19, which originated in Wuhan, China (Jena, 2020). Although the origin of this virus was China, many countries suffered from this pandemic. India also suffered shabbily during this pandemic. It is a highly densely populated country with more than 1.30 billion people. The density of the population has become a big headache for the government because the virus infects fast in crowded environment. A large number of people in India have been infected so far by this virus. The world scenario is more horrible. The entire country was in lockdown like many other countries. This pandemic affects all sectors of human life, such as business, communication, daily life, economy, education, and so on, but the education system is affected shabbily. The daily class system, internal-external examination system, etc. are broken down. The in-person classroom is collapsed (Koul & Bapat, 2020). Therefore, teachers, administrators, and academicians thought about the alternative to formal education. To overcome this situation, various online modes of education are brought forth to continue education services.

Most of the areas in Purulia District in the Indian state of West Bengal are remote rural areas. Majority of the people in this district live in rural areas (Manna & Mondal, 2017). But their inclusion in higher education is eye-catching. As a result of the unimaginable advancement of technology in the world today, the education system has also turned to technology-based and online education (Budhwar, 2017). Students in remote areas like Purulia also kept pace with the new normal and have become interested in online education. This online education did not spread overnight. The National Center for Educational Statistics (NCES) published a research in 2008 that concluded many positive aspects of online learning (Sun & Chen, 2016). Since then, people have gradually become interested in this teaching. Students in Purulia district oftentimes have to work in the field during their study period. And now almost everywhere, there is internet and the student can study and work conveniently. Although the online education system is reaching out to people fast, many students have not been able to adapt properly to the system as the whole process has suddenly gone online. The only reason for the sudden transformation is COVID-19 (Pokhrel & Chhetri, 2021). Compared to urban pupils who are a little more proficient with mobiles, laptops, and computers, students in rural areas in Purulia could not connect to the online education system easily. However, as time goes by, this class of students will also be capable of integrating themselves into the online system.

During that terrifying time, educators and researchers were highly worried about the education system. It can be realized that if the lockdown system will be going on for the next few months, then it will be a great loss for learners, especially at the undergraduate college level. This is the first step of higher education in the Indian educational system. Put differently, the undergraduate level is the base of Indian higher education. Educators know that they cannot take classes in normal ways, and also the government declared the slogan "Stay Home, Stay Safe" for public safety. So keeping in mind the safety of the learners and educators, there needs to be some alternative option. That is why educators resorted to an online mode of education to continue the teaching-learning activities till the unlock process is commenced. Online education is flexible because, through this method, learners can learn flexibly at their own pace. The diversified topics make the learner more interested. This mode of education provides joyful learning that keeps learner away from monotony.

Purulia District is situated in the western part of West Bengal, India. This district is mainly known as the poorest district of West Bengal. The locality consists of economic and social classes. Some are living with high status, some are below poverty line, and sometimes they are categorized according to their caste such as general, other backward caste (OBC), scheduled caste (SC), and scheduled tribes (ST). Online education was an essential alternative during COVID-19 for undergraduate students who were from various socioeconomic backgrounds. Since every student went through the experience of online education, it is high time after the pandemic to investigate their perception about this medium of education for better application of the platform in future.

The chapter proceeds in five sections. While the introductory section has delineated the study background on students' perception to online education and its rationality, the second section reviews the relevant literature to figure out research gaps to fill in through proper study methods. The third section underpins the applied materials and methods of the study that to ascertain such perception of the students, survey-based quantitative methods can effectively achieve the objectives of the study. The fourth, result and discussion, illustrates the findings and analysis of the study. Briefly the result indicates to a mixed perception about online education of the said student group, but most of the students have perceived the online modes positively irrespective of their gender, location, and caste. And the final section, the conclusion, sheds light on the result of the study with an emphasis on government and other stakeholders' effective actions to continue this spirit about online education.

6.2 Literature Review

Online education is not the counter product of COVID-19, but it boosted the growth of its application mandatorily. First world countries have been exercising this mode of teaching-learning, even India, for decades before the pandemic. Indian open universities are specialized for the application of the online platform. Thus, there are some studies on the perception of teachers and learners about this tool. Tellingly, COVID-19 incorporated all sorts of academics and students under online education, particularly students from conventional institutions in India. Astani et al. (2010) students have significantly different perceptions of online education, with experienced students having a satisfied perspective. Many aspects of online education were unfamiliar to students who have no prior experience with it. Ghandforoush (2013) demonstrated that some professionals have a negative perception of online education; that is why the author developed a research approach for measuring various backgrounds of professionals. Kaur and Bishnoi (2014) indicated that pupils are more likely to prefer innovative teaching approaches such as Computer Aided Method (CAM) or Team Based Methods (TBM). For example, 70% of students in chemical engineering and environmental science and technology rated the industrial visit as good. We can argue that they desired to learn more through practice or by experiencing the actual world. Bhagat et al. (2016) found that their developed tool (POSTOL) is very much a reliable tool, and it will be helpful for educators and instructional designers. Bali and CLiu (2018) argued that there is no discernible difference between online and face-to-face learning. It is also observed that some students have positive perceptions of online education, which led them to use innovative computer technology. Pasha and Gorya (2019) revealed that through online education, learners can easily receive educational services via this mode. They can search their desired topics and materials in the hundreds of online platforms. Dhawan (2020), in a study on this time of crisis, underlines the relevance of online education and application of e-learning modes using the

SWOC (strengths, weaknesses, opportunities, and challenges) method. The rise of educational technology start-ups in the face of pandemics and natural disasters was also explored in this study, as well as advice for academic institutions on how to manage the difficulties of online learning. Another similar survey was conducted by Muthuprasad et al. (2020) in order to better understand agricultural students' perceptions and preferences for online education. They are also keen to know about preferences of students for various features of online classes. According to the findings of the study, majority of the respondents (70%) are willing to employ online classes to handle the curriculum throughout the epidemic. For online education, the majority of students choose to utilize their smartphone. On the basis of content analysis, students prefer recorded classes with some questions at the end of each session. Menon et al. (2021) investigated how undergraduate medical students manifested their satisfaction in joining online classes. According to the findings, 53.6% of students rated their satisfaction as moderate, 31% as high, and 15.4% as low. Attending classes from home dissatisfied 49.8% of the students, while 15.7% students thought it was beneficial. Furthermore, 57.1% of the students opined online learning to be fairly useful, 31.4% found it to be little effective, and 11.5% students found it to be extremely valuable. Bast (2021) carried out a similar study to compare students' perceptions of online education to conventional teaching methods in this new setting. The findings highlighted a number of fascinating aspects of pupils' views. Those from metropolitan areas were considerably more receptive to online education than students from rural areas. Naik et al. (2021) attempted to compare the effectiveness of online teaching and learning methods to traditional teaching methods. The absence of facilities, infrastructure, technology infrastructure, and internet connection (weak) are the key drawbacks for conducting online sessions as per this investigation. During the COVID-19 outbreak in Bangladesh, Sarkar et al. (2021) attempted to unfold public university students' perceptions toward online classes. Majority of the students failed to participate in virtual classes and were unable to communicate effectively with their classmates, according to the survey. As a result, they struggled with online education; majority of the students preferred traditional learning techniques to virtual classrooms and found it difficult to comprehend virtual class materials. They further maintain that majority of the students in online classes were uncomfortable and unattentive. Shrestha et al. (2022) conducted another similar type of study in the context of Bangladesh and Nepal, in which they attempted to analyze the experiences of teachers and students in Bangladesh and Nepal on online education in higher education during the pandemic. According to the findings, students and teachers adapt the action potential of digital art effects to local circumstances and use them in the best possible ways to increase communication and promote student learning in challenging situations. Poor network, a lack of digital skills, and a lack of institutional technological support are the main problems and limitations they faced when switched to online education. During the COVID-19 epidemic, Thanavisuth (2021) sought to understand more about students' perceptions regarding online learning. The study's findings revealed that students enjoy both online and onsite learning. The most significant benefit of online learning is that it allows participants to stay at home (72.15%), while the most significant disadvantages are technological difficulties (73.33%percent) and a lack of social connection (71.37%). Participants thought online learning was successful in increasing knowledge (35.29%), active classroom activities (33.33%), and enjoyment (30.2%).

The previously mentioned studies have investigated the issue of online education from diversified angles and geographies as well as the perception of academic stakeholders toward that mode of education. The contributions of the studies can also be realized to make the education more accessible, particularly for the students from low socioeconomic background. Other noticeable important issues of those studies are that perceptions vary from place to place, class to class, or in other categories. Taking up the previous issues, the present study also strives and hopes it will contribute to enrich this scholarship of online education at least a bit. It is a study on a remote and backward group of students of Purulia District of India. Moreover, it focuses on the largest group of higher education in India, the college level. There are not many studies on the perceptions of college-level students on teaching and learning in online mode. Therefore, this study, after an extensive literature review, fixes the following objectives to add value to online education.

6.3 Objectives of the Study

1. To ascertain the perception of undergraduate students in Purulia District on online education
2. To identify the distinction between the perception of undergraduate students on online education with regard to their gender (male and female), locality (rural and urban), and semester of study (fourth and sixth)
3. To seek out the differences among the perception of undergraduate students on online education with relation to their stream (arts, science, and commerce) and caste (General, OBC, SC and ST).

6.4 Hypotheses of the Study

The following are the null hypotheses:

H_{01}: There'll be a low perception of undergraduate students in Purulia District on online education.

H_{02}: The perception of the undergraduate students on online education does not differ significantly based on their gender (male and female), locality (rural and urban), and semester (fourth and sixth) of study.

H_{03}: There are no significant differences among the perception of undergraduate students on online education with relation to their stream (arts, science, and commerce) and caste (General, OBC, SC and ST).

6.5 Delimitations of the Study

The study maintained the following delimitations:

(A) Geographical Region

The inquiry was carried out only in Purulia District of West Bengal.

(B) Education Level

(i) The research focused on the undergraduate college students under Sidho-Kanho-Birsha University of Purulia District.

(ii) Of the undergraduate students, arts, science and commerce streams (fourth and sixth semesters) of Purulia District were considered the subjects of this study.

(C) Type of Study

This study was conducted only at the surface level. It had been not an "in-depth" study. It plans to determine the students' perception by administering a perception scale developed by the investigators. There was no interstate/college comparison. Only intra district/college comparisons were drawn between the male and female; rural and urban; fourth semester and sixth semester; arts, science, and commerce; and General, SC, ST and OBC students.

6.6 Materials and Methods

A descriptive Survey method was followed for this study. The population of this study consisted of all undergraduate level students affiliated to Sidho-Kanho-Birsha University in Purulia District of West Bengal, India. A total number of 100 undergraduate students of Purulia District (50 male and 50 female), those who are studying in the fourth and sixth semesters under Sidho-Kanho-Birsha University, Purulia, constituted a representative sample of the entire population. The sample was chosen using a simple random sampling procedure. During the COVID-19 lockdown, an online perception scale was utilized to determine how undergraduate students at Sidho-Kanho-Birsha University perceived online education. The scale was developed by the researchers; the link is: https://forms.gle/h7djDCaYKGDrnBry5. It consists of 20 parameters. Out of these, there were 13 positive and 7 negative statements. For positive items, the scoring procedure was 5, 4, 3, 2, and 1, and for negative items, reverse scoring was followed. The value of the reliability of the tool is 0.89. In measuring the validity of the tool, the judgment or opinion of experts was taken by the researchers. The acquired data was analyzed and verified using the mean, SD, percentage, t-test, and ANOVA. The formulas for t-test and F-test are given as follows:

$$t = \frac{D}{S_{\in_D}}$$

$$S_{\in_D} = \sqrt{\left(\frac{\sum x_1^2 + \sum x_2^2}{N_1 + N_2 - 2}\right)\left(\frac{1}{N_1} + \frac{1}{N_2}\right)}$$

$$F = \frac{Between\ Group\ Mean\ Square}{Within\ Group\ Mean\ Square}$$

6.7 Results and Discussion

This section analyzes the collected data and discusses the results. Each hypothesis was verified one by one and interpreted in the appropriate manner. T-test and F-test were computed to find out the significance of difference between two or more means. The descriptive statistics of the study is reported in Table 6.1.

Table 6.1 and Figure 6.1 show that among the five-point scale, the minimum score is 43 and the maximum is 86. The range for this group is 43. For the total sample, the mean, median, and mode are 61.49, 61.00, and 58, respectively. The kurtosis is 0.475, which indicates that the distribution is quite a flat and thin tail. It is a leptokurtic distribution. The data in the present study are positively skewed. Against zero, the value of skewness in the present study is 0.257, which indicates the symmetrical nature of the data.

6.7.1 Testing of H_{01}

There is a low perception of undergraduate students in Purulia District toward online education during COVID-19.

Category	N	Mean	SD
Undergraduate Students	100	61.49	8.89

Table 6.1 Descriptive Statistics

Statistics		Score
N	Valid	100
	Missing	0
Mean		61.49
Std. Error of Mean		.889
Median		61.00
Mode		58
Std. Deviation		8.887
Variance		78.980
Skewness		.257
Std. Error of Skewness		.241
Kurtosis		.475
Std. Error of Kurtosis		.478
Range		43
Minimum		43
Maximum		86
Sum		6149

The cutoff point is used for analyzing the data. The investigators verified the H_{01}. M ± 1σ is the formula for the cutoff point in this case. The mean is 61.49, N is 100, and the standard deviation is 8.89. As a result, M +1 σ equals 61.49 + 1 × 8.89 = 70.38, while M −1 σ equals 61.49 − 1× 8.89 = 52.6. The majority of undergraduate students (71 in number), i.e., 71% of undergraduate students, have scored ranging from 52.6 to 70.38 (Table 6.2 and Figure 6.2). Thus, it can be said that the perceptions of undergraduate students toward online education in Purulia District during COVID-19 are neither high nor low, which manifests a moderate or average degree of perception about online education. So H_{01} is rejected.

From Table 6.3 and Figure 6.3, it is found that for item 1, 61% (61 students) of undergraduate students agreed that the online education is continuous learning, and 21% disagree. In a response to item 2, 60% of undergraduate students' opined that in online education, there is a lack of discipline, and 19% students disagreed. In the next item, 72% of UG students responded that through online education,

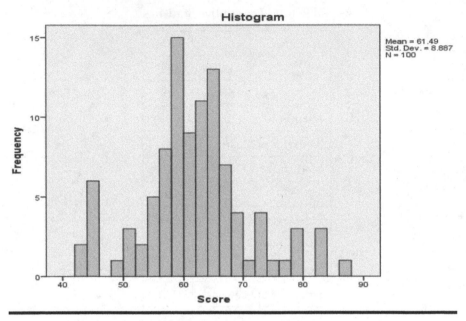

Figure 6.1 Histogram of Descriptive Statistics.

Source: (Authors' depicted)

Table 6.2 Undergraduate Students' Overall Perception on Online Education throughout COVID-19 Pandemic

Scores	Frequency	Percentage	Levels of Perception
Above 70.38	15	15%	High
Between 52.60–70.38	71	71%	Moderate/Average
Below 52.60	14	14%	Low
TOTAL	100	100	

students can learn flexibly, whereas 16% students disagree. For item 4, 40% of undergraduate students' agreed that online education squeezes learners' creative thinking, and 31% students disagree. In response to item 5, 56% of UG students think that online education is a flexible learning process, and 24% students disagree. For item 6, 80% of undergraduate students agreed that an online education system is an expensive method, and 10% disagree. In reply to item 7, 82% of UG students agreed that through online education learners can learn at their own pace and 12% disagree. In reaction to the item 8, 61% of UG students agreed that

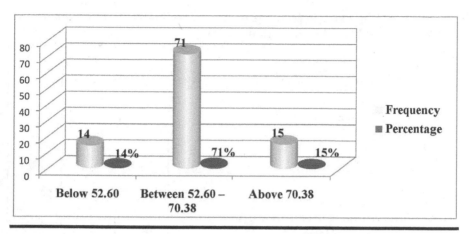

Figure 6.2 Students' overall perception on online education.

Source: (Authors' depicted)

Table 6.3 Percentage of the Perception of Undergraduate Students' on Online Education (Item-Wise)

Item No.	Statements	SA	A	N	DA	SD
1	Online education supports continuous learning.	18 %	43%	18%	17%	4%
2	We can see a lack of discipline in online education.	12 %	48%	21%	16%	3%
3	Through online education, learners can learn anywhere and anytime.	30%	42%	12%	13%	3%
4	Online education squeezes our creative thinking.	7%	33%	29%	22%	9%

(Continued)

Table 6.3 (Continued) **Percentage of the Perception of Undergraduate Students' on Online Education (Item-Wise)**

Item No.	Statements	SA	A	N	DA	SD
5	Online education is a flexible learning process.	12%	44%	20%	23%	1%
6	It is an expensive education system because in this process, we need to buy computers or mobile devices.	44%	36%	10%	8%	2%
7	Through online education, we can learn at our own pace.	24%	58%	6%	11%	1%
8	Through online education, learners feel isolated.	20%	41%	21%	16%	2%
9	Through online education, we can get feedback very quickly.	15%	38%	23%	19%	5%
10	As it is a new process, learners hesitate to use online education.	13%	48%	27%	11%	1%
11	In this pandemic situation, online education is the best alternative for learning.	42%	44%	5%	7%	2%
12	Online education requires strong self-motivation skills.	16%	49%	16%	17%	2 %

Table 6.3 (Continued) Percentage of the Perception of Undergraduate Students' on Online Education (Item-Wise)

Item No.	Statements	SA	A	N	DA	SD
13	Online education increases your technological skills.	32%	39%	12%	15%	2%
14	For this type of education, we need to be efficient with computers or mobile devices.	38%	50%	7%	4%	1 %
15	In this pandemic situation, online education saves us time.	32 %	46%	13%	8%	1%
16	Through online education, we can't take examinations so easily.	25%	42%	23%	9%	1%
17	Through online education, we can choose a variety of programs and courses.	22%	47%	18 %	13%	0 %
18	A good internet connection is necessary for online education.	67%	27%	3%	2%	1%
19	This type of education can easily be carried out at any season of the year.	26 %	56%	4%	13%	1%

(Continued)

Table 6.3 (Continued)   Percentage of the Perception of Undergraduate Students' on Online Education (Item-Wise)

Item No.	Statements	SA	A	N	DA	SD
20	Online education cannot offer human interaction.	12%	42%	13%	30%	3%

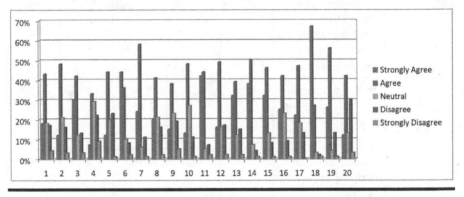

Figure 6.3   Percentage of the Perception of Undergraduate Students' toward Online Education (Item-Wise).

Source: (Authors' depicted)

through this method, learners feel isolated, and 18% disagree. Fifty-three of UG students agreed that through this method, learners can get feedback very quickly, and 24% disagree. Sixty-one percent of UG students agreed that since it is a new method, learners hesitate to use online education, and 12% disagree. In response to item 11, 86% (86 students) of UG students agreed that in this pandemic situation, online education is the best alternative, and 9% (9 students) disagree. In answer to item 12, 65 % (65 students) of UG students agreed that this method requires strong self-motivation, and 19% (19 students) disagree. Seventy-one percent (71 students) of UG students agreed that this method increases learners' technology skills, and 17% (17 students) disagree. Eighty-eight percent (88 students) of UG students agreed that to use this method, learners need to be efficient with computers and mobile devices, and 5% (5 students) disagree. Seventy-eight percent (78 students) of UG students agreed that in the pandemic situation, online education saves our time, and 9% (9 students) disagree. In response to item 16, 67% (67 students) of UG students agreed that through this method, we cannot take examinations so easily, and 10% (10 students) disagree. In response to item 17, 69% (69 students) of

UG students agreed that through online education, learners can choose a variety of courses and programs, and 13% (13 students) disagree. In response to item 18, 94% (94 students) of UG students agreed that good internet connection is very much necessary for this method, and 3% (3 students) disagree. For item 19, 82% (82 students) of UG students agreed that this type of education can be carried out any season of the year, and 14% (14 students) disagree. In reaction to item 20, 54% (54 students) of UG students agreed that through this method, we cannot offer human interaction, and 33% (33 students) disagree.

6.7.2 Testing of H_{02}

6.7.2.1 Gender (Male and Female)

In the case of undergraduate male and female students, the df is 98, as per the result in Table 6.4. Consequently, a t-test with a value of 1.98 or above is significant at the 0.05 level. At the 0.05 and 0.01 levels, the difference in the perceptions of undergraduate male and female students is not significant because the computed value of t, 0.15, is lower than the table values 1.98 and 2.63 (0.15 < 1.98 & 2.63). Resultantly,

Table 6.4 The Distribution of t-Tests for Different Variables

Variables	N	Mean	SD	S_{ED}	Mean Difference	df	t	Level of Significance	
UG Male Students	50	61.62	9.695	1.79	0.26	98	0.15	0.05 & 0.01	Not Significant
UG Female Students	50	61.36	8.096						
UG Rural Students	57	61.88	7.015	1.91	0.9	98	0.47	0.05 & 0.01	Not Significant
UG Urban Students	43	60.98	10.958						
UG 4th Semester	55	58.00	7.567	1.64	7.76	98	4.73	0.05 & 0.01	Significant
UG 6th Semester	45	65.76	8.579						

Here,

N means total number of sample
SD means standard deviation
S_{ED} means standard error of difference
df means degree of freedom

during COVID-19, there was no significant difference in the perceptions of under-graduate male and female students about online education. Although male students' mean scores are slightly higher than female students' mean scores, there is no true difference in undergraduate students' perceptions of online Education over the COVID-19 period. Our finding is quite dissimilar to the earlier studies carried out by Bisht et al. (2022) and Sarkar et al. (2021) found that female students accepted online learning more rapidly, were more flexible in their e-learning education, and thought online assignments were easier compared to male students. This may happen because all the undergraduate students (both male or female) have realized the importance of online education, that it is the best alternative way of receiving educational services during the lockdown in the COVID-19 period.

6.7.2.2 Locality (Rural and Urban)

As per Table 6.4, the df of undergraduate rural and urban students is 98. Thus, a t-test with a value of 1.98 or above is significant at 0.05 level. The difference between the perceptions of undergraduate rural and urban students is not significant because the estimated value of t, 0.47, is lower than the table value 1.98 (0.47 < 1.98). That is to say, for the period of COVID-19, there was no considerable difference in the perception of undergraduate rural and urban students on online education. This is in contrast to the findings of Bast (2021), where students in urban areas responded to online schooling far better than those in rural areas, and Sarkar et al. (2021) found that rural university students have less access to the internet, which could explain why rural students have a lower favorable or positive perception than urban students. It is due to the fact that, though rural and urban students live in a different geographical area and socioeconomic background, in the case of getting online education, they benefitted similarly during the pandemic in receiving class lectures. Online education is an imperative way for availing educational services and resources.

6.7.2.3 Semester of Study (Fourth and Sixth)

According to Table 6.4, in connection with undergraduate fourth and sixth semester students, the df is 98. Since the calculated value of t, 4.73, is greater than the table value, a t-test with a value of 1.98 or more is significant at 0.05 level. When the estimated value of t, 4.73, exceeds the table value 1.98 and 2.63 (4.73 > 1.98 and 2.63) at 0.05 and 0.01 levels, the difference between the perception of undergraduate fourth and sixth semester students is significant at both 0.05 and 0.01 levels. It means, there is a considerable variation in perception on online education between undergraduate fourth and sixth semester students over the COVID-19 period. The mean score of sixth semester students is higher than that of the fourth semester students' mean score. The sixth semester students are at the final stage of graduation; their maturation level is high. So they refined their perception about an online approach in the initial stage of the graduation level. The key reasons for this difference are their maturity level, proficiency in gadget usage, and mental preparation for higher education (postgraduate).

6.7.3 Testing H_{03}

6.7.3.1 Stream (Arts, Science, and Commerce)

Table 6.5 indicates that the computed F-value (4.343) for 2 and 97 df is greater than the critical value of F (3.09) at the 0.05 level of significance. It is clear that the calculated value of F is greater than 3.09 at 0.05 level, not in 0.01 level (F =4.82). It displays that there is a considerable variance in perceptions of online education among undergraduate students depending on their streams. The researchers expected that there should have been some difference regarding their streams, and it is discovered here. The key reason may be the more pro-conventional intention of higher secondary level students in arts division; they are less dependent on online or e-learning resources, and they can manage from offline textbooks. On the other hand, science and commerce students are more reliant on the internet or e-learning throughout the higher secondary level. The undergraduate commerce students have realized the importance of online education better than the students of other streams. Put differently, the perception of undergraduate commerce students is higher than their counterparts during the pandemic situation (Table 6.6 and Figure 6.4).

Table 6.5 For Streams, the Results of One-Way ANOVA

Sources of Variance	df	Sum of Squares	Mean Square	F	Level of Significance	
Between Groups	2	642.647	321.323			
Within Groups	97	7176.343	73.983	4.343	0.05	Significant
Total	99	7818.990				

Table 6.6 The N, Mean, and SD of Undergraduate Arts, Science, and Commerce Students on Online Education

Stream	N	Mean	SD
Arts	56	62.59	6.66
Commerce	5	69.40	12.10
Science	39	58.90	10.46
Total	100	61.49	8.89

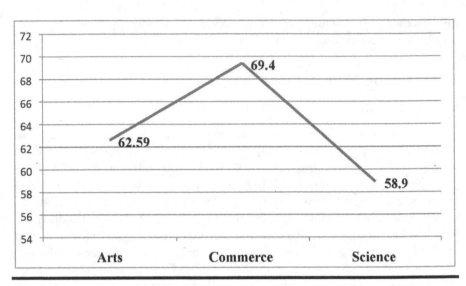

Figure 6.4   Mean score of streams.

Source: (Authors' depicted)

6.7.3.2 Caste (General, OBC, SC, and ST)

The estimated F-value (1.853) is lower than the critical value of F (3.98 & 2.70) for 3 and 97 df at 0.01 and 0.05 levels of significance, according to Table 6.7. It appears that there are no major differences in perceptions regarding online education among undergraduate students based on their castes. Simply, the caste has no effect on the outcome of online education. It is also found that the perception of SC undergraduate students on Online education is higher than their counterparts (Table 6.8 and Figure 6.5). Because they join the classes or activities with mobile devices or computers, the outcome does not matter on which categories of people are operating those devices. Otherwise, they are not able to pursue their education during the lockdown. This is the reason behind this non significance in the result.

Table 6.7   Castes: Results of One-Way ANOVA

Sources of Variance	df	Sum of Squares	Mean Square	F	Level of Significance	
Between Groups	3	428.058	142.686		0.05 & 0.01	Not Significant
Within Groups	96	7390.932	76.989	1.853		
Total	99	7818.990				

Table 6.8   The N, Mean, and SD of Undergraduate General, OBC, SC, and ST Students on Online Education

Stream	N	Mean	S.D
General	34	61.24	11.026
OBC	42	60.00	6.832
SC	14	66.36	8.139
ST	10	61.80	8.189
Total	100	61.49	8.887

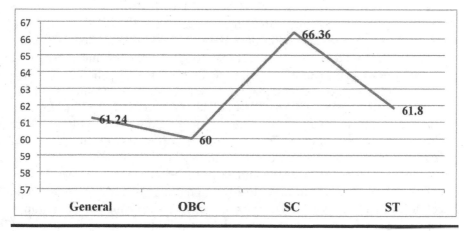

Figure 6.5 Mean score of caste.

Source: (Authors' depicted)

6.8 Conclusion

Human beings are the most intelligent creatures of God. They are always trying to discover a new way to adapt since their inception to date. Since the beginning of 2020, the world has been suffering from the COVID-19 pandemic tremendously. Although most of the affected countries declared a complete lockdown, it was not possible for people to be stuck in one place. Daily life, including education, was also affected enormously. Researchers and educators came forward to mitigate the crisis; they figured out some alternatives to continue their services. Thus, the scale of online education was boosted in an unprecedented high. Currently, most of the higher education systems are dealing with online education. We demonstrated in this chapter that undergraduate students' perceptions of online education differ significantly. The level of the overall perception of UG students is rational, which means students have neither a high perception nor a low perception of online education. But when we analyze the result on several variables, differences are explicitly noticeable in their perceptions in terms of semester and disciplines or streams. Learners were more enthusiastic to apply online education as their means of education. But day after day, the lockdown has become flexible, and conditionally some parts of essential activities are going to be normal. The studies carried out by Abbasi et al. (2020) in Pakistan; Agormedah et al. (2020) in Ghana; Agung et al. (2020), Nugroho et al. (2020), and Syofyan et al. (2020) in Indonesia; Blizak et al. (2020) in Algeria; and Sarkar et al. (2021) in Bangladesh revealed that students have a negative perception of online learning and education. However, studies conducted by Astani et al. (2010) in the USA and Dhawan (2020), Kaur and Bishnoi (2014), Pasha and Gorya (2019), Muthuprasad et al. (2020), and Menon et al. (2021) in India discovered favorable or positive perceptions of online learning and education. Further, the studies of Bali and CLiu (2018) from the Indonesian Open University, Taiwan branch, and Thanavisuth (2021) in Thailand found that students have a positive perception of both online and physical modes of learning. Bast (2021) found that students in urban regions were much more responsive to online education than those in rural ones. Keeping the results in mind, the researchers are compelled to think that when everything will be normal as well the education system, they suggest that it would be very effective for the government to adopt an online education method in higher education along with an offline method or traditional education system. However, educators urge not to convert the traditional education system to online mode. The findings of this paper reveal that learners were ready to embrace online education as their best alternatives during the lockdown. So students have already adapted to an online education system since the COVID-19 crisis stared; they have managed to continue their studies regularly. Many of them, capable or weak, were not interested or did not know about online education, but during and after the pandemic, the students showed enthusiasm toward online education. All the stakeholders currently claim the impact of such online learning experiences. To say it differently, online education has turned into an essential element of academia in the age of the new normal. Therefore, academics, researchers, policy makers, and above all, the government should come forward with effective actions to utilize such impressions of online education in eradicating illiteracy.

References

Abbasi, S., Ayoob, T., Malik, A., & Memon, S. I. (2020). Perceptions of students regarding E-learning during COVID-19 at a private medical college. *Pakistan Journal of Medical Sciences, 36*(COVID19-S4).

Agormedah, E. K., Henaku, E. A., Ayite, D. M. K., & Ansah, E. A. (2020). Online learning in higher education during COVID-19 pandemic: A case of Ghana. *Journal of Educational Technology and Online Learning, 3*(3), 183–210.

Agung, A. S. N., Surtikanti, M. W., & Quinones, C. A. (2020). Students' perception of online learning during COVID-19 pandemic: A case study on the English students of STKIP Pamane Talino. *Soshum: Jurnal Sosial dan Humaniora, 10*(2), 225–235.

Astani, M., Ready, J. K., & Duplaga, A. E. (2010). Online course experience matters: Investigating students' perceptions of online learning. *Issues in Information Systems, 11*(2), 14–21. https://doi.org/10.48009/2_iis_2010_14-21

Bali, S., & Cliu, M. (2018). Students' perceptions toward online learning and face-to-face learning courses. *Journal of Physics: Conference Series, 1108*(012094), 1–7. https://doi.org/10.1088/1742-6596/1108/1/012094

Bast, F. (2021). Perception of online learning among students from India set against the pandemic. *Frontiers in Education*, 18 August. https://doi.org/10.3389/feduc.2021.705013

Bhagat, K. K., Wu, L. Y., & Chang, C. Y. (2016). Development and validation of the Perception of Students Towards Online Learning (POSTOL). *Educational Technology & Society, 19*(1), 350–359.

Bisht, R. K., Jasola, S., & Bisht, I. P. (2022). Acceptability and challenges of online higher education in the era of COVID-19: A study of students' perspective. *Asian Education and Development Studies, 11*(2).401–414. http://doi.org/10.1108/AEDS-05-2020-0119

Blizak, D., Blizak, S., Bouchenak, O., & Yahiaoui, K. (2020). Students' perceptions regarding the abrupt transition to online learning during the COVID-19 pandemic: Case of faculty of chemistry and hydrocarbons at the university of Boumerdes- Algeria. *Journal of Chemical Education, 97*(9), 2466–2471.

Budhwar, K. (2017). The role of technology in education. *International Journal of Engineering Applied Science and Technology, 2*(8), 55–57.

Dhawan, S. (2020). Online learning: A panacea in the time of COVID-19 crisis. *Journal of Educational Technology Systems, 49*(1), 5–22. https://doi.org/10.1177/0047239520934018

Ghandforoush, P. (2013). A study of perceptions of online education among professionals. *IADIS International Conference e-Learning*, 463–465. https://eric.ed.gov/?id=ED562275

Ghavifekr, S., & Rosdy, W. A. W. (2015). Teaching and learning with technology: Effectiveness of ICT integration in schools. *International Journal of Research in Education and Science (IJRES), 1*(2), 175–191.

Jena, K. P. (2020). Impact of pandemic COVID-19 on education in India. *International Journal of Current Research, 12*(7), 12582–12586. https://doi.org/10.24941/ijcr.39209.07.2020

Kaur, J., & Bishnoi, A. (2014). Investigating the ways through evaluation practice in higher education: The value of learner's need. *International Journal of Engineering and Computer Science, 3*(12), 9560–9563.

Koul, P. P., & Bapat, J. O. (2020). Impact of COVID-19 on education sector in India. *Journal of Critical Reviews, 7*(11), 3919–3930.

Manna, M., & Mondal, K. B. (2017). *The Emerging Issue of Forest Degradation in Purulia District*. Retrieved from www.researchgate.net/publication/332171152_THE_EMERGING_ISSUE_OF_FOREST_DEGRADATION_IN_PURULIA_DISTRICT

Menon, K. U., Gopalakrishnan, S., Unni, N. S., Ramachandran, R., Baby, P., Sasidharan, A., & Radhakrishnan, N. (2021). Perceptions of undergraduate medical students regarding institutional online teaching-learning programme. *Medical Journal Armed Forces India, 77*(1), S227–S233. https://doi.org/10.1016/j.mjafi.2021.01.006

Muthuprasad, T., Aiswarya, S., Adity, K. S., & Jha, K. G. (2020). Students' perception and preference for online education in India during COVID-19 pandemic. *Social Sciences & Humanities Open, 3*(1). https://doi.org/10.1016/j.ssaho.2020.100101

Naik, G. L., Deshpande, M., Shivananda, D. C., Ajey, C. P., & Manjunath Patel, G. C. (2021). Online teaching and learning of higher education in India during COVID-19 emergency lockdown. *Pedagogical Research*, *6*(1), em0090. https://doi.org/10.29333/pr/9665

Nugroho, R. A., Basari, A., Suryaningtyas, V. W., & Cahyono, S. P. (2020, September). University students' perception of online learning in COVID-19 pandemic: A case study in a translation course. In: *2020 International Seminar on Application for Technology of Information and Communication (iSemantic)* (pp. 225–231), IEEE.

Pasha, A., & Gorya, J. (2019). Student preference and perception towards online education in Hyderabad city. *International Journal of Trend in Scientific Research and Development (IJTSRD)*, *3*(3), 656–659. https://doi.org/10.31142/ijtsrd22876

Pokhrel, S., & Chhetri, R. (2021). A literature review on impact of COVID-19 pandemic on teaching and learning. *Higher Education for the Future*, *8*(1), 133–141. https://doi.org/10.1177/2347631120983481

Raja, R., & Nagasubramani, C. P. (2018). Impact of modern technology in education. *Journal of Applied and Advanced Research*, *3*(1), 33–35. https://doi.org/10.21839/jaar.2018.v3iS1.165

Sarkar, S. S., Das, P., Rahman, M. M., & Zobaer, M. S. (2021). Perceptions of public university students towards online classes during COVID-19 pandemic in Bangladesh. *Frontiers in Education*, *6*, 703723. https://doi.org/10.3389/feduc.2021.703723

Shrestha, S., Haque, S., Dawadi, S., & Giri, A. R. (2022). Preparations for and practices of online education during the COVID-19 pandemic: A study of Bangladesh and Nepal. *Education and Information Technologies*, *27*, 243–265. https://doi.org/10.1007/s10639-021-10659-0

Sun, Q. A., & Chen, X. (2016). Online education and its effective practice: A research review. *Journal of Information Technology Research*, *15*, 157–190. https://doi.org/10.28945/3502

Syofyan, S., Permatasari, D., Hasanah, U., Armin, F., Yosmar, R., Wahyuni, F. S., & Lailaturrahmi, L. (2020). Student and faculty perceptions related to online learning during the COVID-19 pandemic in Indonesia. *Pharmacy Education*, *20*(2), 302–309. https://doi.org/10.46542/pe.2020.202.302309

Thanavisuth, C. (2021). Students' perceptions of online learning during the COVID-19 pandemic: A study of undergraduate students from an international university, Thailand. *AU Virtual International Conference Entrepreneurship and Sustainability in the Digital Era*, *2*(1), 382–387. Retrieved from www.assumptionjournal.au.edu/index.php/icesde/article/view/5775

Chapter 7

Impact Assessment of the Pandemic on India's Digital Payment Ecosystem

Mahak Sethi and Dr. N. S. Bohra

Contents

DOI: 10.1201/9781003328438-7

7.1 Introduction

The digital payment system in India has fostered a paradigm shift in the economy. From primarily being a cash-obsessed economy, the country has paved its way toward becoming a cashless society. The "Assessment of the progress of digitization from cash to electronic report 2020" by the Reserve Bank of India (RBI) stated that the value of digital payments to gross domestic product (GDP) augmented to 862% in from 2018 to 2019 in comparison to 660% in from 2014 to 2015, making the digital payment shift in India clearly predictable. The rolling out of the Digital India program in 2015 led to the introduction of a myriad of innovative systems, resulting in a drastic switch from paper to electronic payment modes that eventually led to increased emphasis on customer-oriented initiatives and cross-border recognition (Angamuthu, 2020). Since then, the Government of India (GOI) is serviceable at numerous levels to achieve expeditious movement in curbing the residents' dependence on cash (Garg & Panchal, 2017). In the Interest of providing a comprehensive and impermeable delivery of services to Indian inhabitants, GOI has dedicated efforts by encouraging Indian banks to undertake electronic payments to bring a broad ambit of its economy under the digital umbrella (Rooj & Sengupta, 2020). The unfolding of new mobile and digital payment technologies like peer-to-peer (P2P) applications, electronic wallets, and quick response (QR) codes have led to innovation in payment methods that have eventually repositioned customers from traditional payment methods to contactless payments. Not only has GOI has made diverse digital payment systems available at the disposal of all sections of society, but also, extensive training and monetary incentives are furnished to equip and encourage people to operate these systems to eliminate unambiguity in financial transactions, truncate tax evasion, and upgrade societal well-being (Patil et al., 2017). Moreover, the adoption of online payments has made transactions effortless due to their ease of use and the convenience of carrying out transactions 24-7 and at any place, unlike cash payments where one has to first withdraw cash from the account followed by making cash payments for goods and services at shops and various other places. The process further continues with the shopkeeper or the service provider going to the bank to deposit the cash that was received from respective customers. This process is of course an old and time-consuming process for both the customer as well as the shopkeeper. But with the revolutionization of the payment system, the process has been shortened to just a few seconds. The utilization of smartphones for payments through applications or web pages is the new grail and would prosper in coming times (Hassan & Meraj, 2019). With automation in the payment process, neither the customer nor the shopkeeper is required to visit the bank. However, digital illiteracy in the Indian Economy turns out to be one of the stumbling blocks to Digital India (Mahajan, 2019). Lack of knowledge and awareness, fear of loss of money, and risk of hacking emerge as a couple of impediments confronting GOI (Baghla, 2018). Despite that, India stands to be one of the enormous and swiftly booming economies for digital patrons, with 560 million internet subscribers in 2018 after China, reported McKinsey Global Institute.

7.2 Objective of the Study

This chapter attempts to study the digital revolution in India. A review of the last decade of the digital payment system in India is conducted to explore and analyze the trends in the digital payment ecosystem in India after 2010. The chapter analyzes the impact of COVID-19 on India's digital payment ecosystem and deliberates the trends during the pre-COVID-19 and post-COVID-19 eras.

7.3 Background

The Payment and Settlement Act of 2007 regulates the payment and settlement systems in India. It has defined digital payments as an electronic fund transfer mechanism wherein the user instructs the bank to debit or credit the funds through electronic means such as ATMs, point of sale transfers, etc. Since both the parties involved use the digital mode to complete the transaction, no hard cash is involved. This is a new trend, triggering a new evolution in India's economic culture (Sivathanu, 2019). Under the digital payment system, the transactions are governed by a defined set of rules, procedures, standards, instruments, institutions, and technologies, wherein the settlement takes place via transfer of monetary value electronically (Kumar, 2019).

7.3.1 Modes of Digital Payments in India

The digital payment ecosystem in India has encountered a cascade of innovation in the last decade, which is evident in the area of retail payments with the proliferation of web-based payments technologies and near-field communications—or "NFC"—applications (Gupta & Asha, 2018). Making a payment through debit cards, credit cards, e-wallets, etc. is on the verge of becoming conventional, and there's no turning back. Some of these payment modes are highly acceptable throughout the world while others have relatively low acceptability (Gupta & Asha, 2018). This section presents a small note on the various modes of digital payments in India.

	DP Mode	Description
1	Banking cards	Popularly known as plastic money, banking cards include debit cards and credit cards, which are secured by a personal identification number (PIN), wherein payments are processed by entering a one-time password (OTP) sent to the registered contact details of the user.
2	AEPS: Aadhaar Enabled Payment System	This system enables users to carry out payment transactions such as cash deposits and withdrawals and facilitates balance inquiry through Aadhaar verification via the customer's fingerprint or iris image scanner.
3	USSD Banking: Unstructured Supplementary Service Data banking or *99# Banking	The registered phone number of the customer is used for checking one's balance, sending money, changing the MPIN, etc. Neither a smartphone nor an internet connection is required to use this service.
4	UPI: Unified Payments Interface	A 24-7 functional system that merges various banking facilities, uninterrupted fund routing, and merchant payments under one aegis. Multiple bank accounts of the users can be enabled in one application, such as Google Pay, Bharat Interface for Money (BHIM), Paytm, PhonePe, etc.
5	E-wallets	A virtual wallet that requires a smartphone and a stable internet connection wherein the wallet (Jio Money, MobiKwik, M-Pesa, etc.) is linked to the customer's credit card or debit card to carry out payment transactions.
6	POS: point-of-sale terminal	Hardware terminal that reads the magnetic strips embedded in credit cards and debit cards that allow the transfer of money immediately upon the user entering the PIN in the POS terminal.
7	NEFT: National Electronic Fund Transfer System	One-to-one electronic fund-transfer system operating in hourly batches that enable remitters or originators (with or without a bank account) to carry and process payments.
8	RTGS: real-time gross settlement System	Real-time fund transfer system wherein the transactions are settled immediately upon processing without bunching or netting with other transactions— i.e., on gross basis.

	DP Mode	Description
9	IMPS: Immediate Payment Service	Safe and economical 24-7 bank-to-bank electronic payment service provided by the National Payments Corporation of India (NPCI) that allows instant interbank money-transfer facility across India.
10	ECS: Electronic Clearing Service (Debit/Credit)	Automated and efficient remittance system for payments repetitive in nature (monthly, quarterly, half-yearly, or yearly), wherein transfer takes place on providing an ECS mandate to the bank branch.
11	Mobile banking	Enables users to carry out banking transactions over a mobile phone in the presence of a secure internet connection. Only licensed banks in India that have a physical presence and are under the supervision of RBI are allowed to offer mobile banking services.

7.3.2 Evolution of the Digital Payment Ecosystem in India

The pre-internet era envisioned cash as a widely established payment option in India. The ease of using cash made it pervasive among Indian residents (RBI, "Assessment of the progress of digitization from cash to Electronic"). The cash to gross domestic product (GDP) ratio of the Indian economy is higher than many countries of the world, thereby making it crucial to downsize the economy's dependence on cash. Transitioning a cash-dependent economy to a digital one necessitates a concerted effort to enlarge a network of critical mass that deals with cashless transactions (Mukhopadhyay, 2016). Figure 7.1 depicts the evolution of the digital payment ecosystem in India and highlights the historic milestones of India's journey toward digitalization. The first step toward a digital system was taken during the 1990s, when banks introduced the electronic clearing service (ECS) credit scheme to facilitate payments routine and continuous in nature, such as interest, dividends, salaries, etc. It was in the late 1990s when the electronic fund transfer (EFT) system was introduced, whereby account holders could transfer funds electronically to other account holders of any other participating bank. However, in the current scenario, the general public does not have access to this system.

The issuance of debit cards and credit cards by the central bank assisted customers with a debit/credit card in availing banking services during or after formal banking hours. As per RBI's report on the trend and progress of banking in India, 858.2 million debit cards and 47.1 million credit cards were in circulation in the FY 2018–2019. Traditionally, transactions related to the forex market and debt securities were processed and cleared among the banks, which caused contracting parties risk. The RBI was the central authority to carry out these transactions (Nath, 2008). In April 2001, the Clearing Corporation of India Limited (CCIL) was founded with the ultimate aim to enhance the transaction settlement process and to perform clearing and settlement functions relating to government securities, the

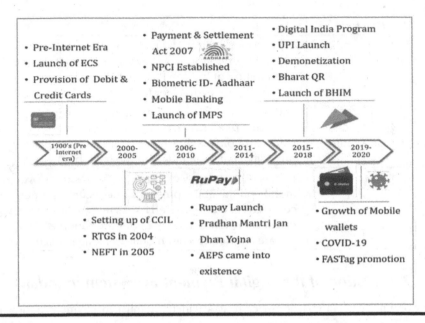

Figure 7.1   **Evolution of Digital Payment Ecosystem in India.**

(*Source:* By author based on review)

money market, and the foreign exchange market by banks, financial institutions, and primary dealers. The banking sector was facing cutthroat competition as new domestic and foreign banks continued to enter. The central bank continued to drive innovations for making payments convenient and speedy with the introduction of the RTGS in 2004 for settling interbank payments (Kelkar, 2004). EFT was later replaced by a more reliable one-to-one fund transfer system—the NEFT system—in November 2005. This system offered unique features like simplifying one-way transfers to Nepal, accepting cash for originating transactions, confirming credit date/time to beneficiaries' accounts, etc. Technological advancements have played a paramount role in increasing the volume and value of ECS, NEFT, and RTGS transactions. The Indian banking sector has evolved as a result of tech evolution, which has resultantly enriched customer service experience and has fastened banking activities (Gupta et al., 2018). To ensure a safe, secure, sound, efficient, approachable, recognized, and legitimate payment mechanism in India, the Payment and Settlement Systems (PSS) Act was implemented in 2007, which came into force on August 12, 2008 after receiving the president's assent on December 20, 2007 (Reserve Bank of India). To further standardize the retail payments system (RPS), the National Payments Corporation of India (NPCI) was established to coordinate various retail payments under one umbrella and to bring greater efficiency in RPS while simultaneously expanding the outreach of innovative payments systems to ensure customer accessibility. To boost the momentum of digital inclusion in the country, the world's largest biometric identification program—Aadhaar—was scaled in 2008 coupled with the establishment of the Unique Identification Authority of India (UIDAI) to provide a distinctive identification number to every Indian resident. Today the use of Aadhaar is not only limited to identification purposes but also has extended to the provision of government subsidies to the general public and the verification of other identification documents such as voter IDs, passports, etc. (Banerjee, 2016). Aadhaar stands to be a primary identity document in India with 1.25 billion Indian residents being enrolled in the same (UIDAI Press Release, 2019). The digital payments in the Indian economy witnessed an upward movement in 2008, when mobile banking guidelines were issued by RBI for licensed banks since then the journey of mobile banking has been fueled by both developments in mobile technology and advancement in business. A report by Mckinsey Global Institute 2019 enunciated the proliferating application of mobile phones by pronouncing the fact that the residents downloaded more than 12 billion applications and had 1.2 billion mobile phone subscriptions in 2018. Mobile accounting, mobile brokerage, and mobile financial information services are the critical mobile banking functions that enable customers to conduct a financial transaction with the help of a mobile phone (Priya et al., 2018). As NEFT and RTGS services were accessible only during formal banking hours, consequently, the banking industry was confronting the challenge of transferring funds on a real-time basis and carrying out 24 × 7 × 365 interbank transactions. To address and resolve this issue concerning mobile payment systems, NPCI in 2010 effectuated a pilot study wherein SBI, BOI, UBI, ICICI, Yes Bank, Axis, and HDFC Bank were the participating banks. Resultantly, a robust and real-time fund-transfer system—IMPS—was launched in November 2010 (National Payments Corporation of India). Later in 2012, it was realized that Indian banks were incurring a high cost of affiliation with international card associations such as Visa and Mastercard. Thus, card payments using debit and credit cards issued by domestic banks were routed through network switches situated outside the country and involved hefty charges. Banks had to pay around Rs 500 crores to Visa and Mastercard for settling the card payments (Seetha, 2014). Eventually, to resolve this concern, India's first global payment network—RuPay—was launched by NPCI in 2012. Keeping in view RBI's vision of financial inclusion, the Pradhan Mantri Jan-DhanYojana (PMJDY) was announced on August 15, 2014, with the idea of providing basic banking facilities to unbanked sections of society. PMJDY, to a large extent, has fulfilled the RBI's vision of financial inclusion by facilitating the poor and marginalized section of society to have a bank account with a minimum or zero balance (Barik & Sharma, 2019). To bolster fewer cash transactions and fasten India's financial-inclusion movement, NPCI launched a simpler, secure, and user-friendly platform known as AEPS. AEPS empowered users to avail fundamental financial services at point-of-sale terminals (POS) or micro automated teller machines (ATMs) by providing Aadhaar verification via fingerprint. Neither debit cards nor any documents are required to conduct the transaction. It only uses the Aadhaar number, bank name, issuer identification number (IIN), and fingerprint to access the bank account (Barik & Sharma, 2019). The rolling out of the Digital India program in 2015 to transform India into a digitally empowered society and knowledge economy accelerated the growth of the digital payment system in India. This initiative was directed to achieve growth in three key areas—viz digital infrastructure, transparency in financial processes, combating corruption in facilitates extending to beneficiaries, sound governance, and enriched financial inclusion, among other subobjectives of the program. The digital divide in remote areas, engendered by lesser literacy rates, lower income and economic status, and deficient health awareness led to the exploitation of this segment. Therefore, the GOI scaled the Digital India program to outreach its agenda of financial inclusion along with the Skill India program (Nedungadi et al., 2018). The adoption of digital payment modes saw a strenuous progression in 2016 with the institution of UPI. The UPI system helped in merging and accessing different bank accounts with a single application that facilitated $24 \times 7 \times 365$ money transfer services. The flow and stacking up of undisclosed black money was increasing at a rapid rate in India, and at the same time, the circulation of counterfeit notes was intensifying; therefore, the Indian government decided to demonetize Rs 500 and Rs 1,000 currency notes to be treated as a legal tender in 2016. As almost 86% of cash in circulation was to be replaced by new currency notes, the Indian economy witnessed long queues outside banks and ATMs for a quite long period (Dash, 2017). Amid demonetization in 2016, the adoption of digital payment modes saw an upward trend as people from all walks of life started to use mobile wallets, UPI, and mobile banking services. The payment and settlement systems witnessed a growth of 55.7% and 24.8% in transaction volume and value for the period 2016–2017, which was recorded to be 49.4% and 9% in the period 2015–2016. The volume of electronic payments for the same period increased from 84.4 % to 89% (Annual Report, RBI, 2017). The value of transactions carried out through mobile wallets amid this phase was witnessed to be the highest among all other modes (Aggarwal & Gupta, 2019). Although, the central objective of the same was not to strengthen the digital payment ecosystem; however, it had a huge impact on the volume and value of digital payment transactions in India for that period (Sobti, 2019). NPCI jointly worked with International Card Schemes (ICS) and continued to drive innovations in the digital payment ecosystem with the launch of Bharat QR in 2016—the world's first compatible and interoperable quick response (QR) code acceptance solution. It was an integrated payment system in India whereby funds can be transferred from one source to another by providing a common interface between RuPay, Mastercard, Visa, and American Express—i.e., the transaction can be easily carried out irrespective of the payment network. The launch of the BHIM app—a UPI-based application allowing peer-to-peer transfers on mobile phones—further contributed to the increased adoption of digital payment modes in India (Pal et al., 2018). Since the inception, the number of BHIM app downloads for Android accounted for 155.14 million and 2.94 million for iOS as of October 3, 2020 (NPCI). As India was moving ahead on the digital path, e-wallets gained tremendous acceptance in the country due to their ease of use and convenience (Singh et al., 2017). Attractive deals, discounts, and cashback offers given by mobile wallet applications lured customers toward these apps (Mittal & Kumar, 2018).

The world economy was enormously affected and faced an unprecedented challenge when the novel coronavirus (COVID-19) unfurled in multiple folds from China to other parts of the world. The Indian stock market witnessed the most significant drop in history (Kumar et al., 2020). The stringent lockdown guidelines and fear of recession among residents eventually led to the downfall of Sensex by 3,934.72 points and Nifty by 1,135 points as of March 23, 2020 (*First post*, March 23, 2020). At this point, the DP system in India observed a downward trend with a decline of 30 percent in the transaction value. It was discovered that the coronavirus could be easily transmitted by cash; therefore, the government and regulators encouraged payments using digital modes like IMPS, NEFT, RTGS, UPI, etc. so that the use of physical cash could be minimized. Such efforts by the government, along with the revocation of nationwide lockdown, indicated recoveries in the DP transactions on different platforms (KPMG's report on the impact of COVID-19 on digital payments in India, 2020). Other areas like the education industry, online grocery stores, and online pharmacies observed a positive impact due to the increased adoption of digital payments during the lockdown period (Jain et al., 2020). The GOI is still keeping up with its efforts to further encourage digital payments in India. FASTag—an automated electronic toll-collection device—has been made compulsory for availing toll discounts by India's road transport and highways ministry, which enabled users to pay for toll charges directly from a prepaid wallet or a bank account linked with the FASTag (Livemint, August 25, 2020).

7.3.3 Factors Advocating the Growth of Digital Payments in India

The digital transactions in India witnessed growth in single digits before 2010, after which it increased to 28% from 2010 to 2016 on account of the introduction of secure and faster payment mechanisms like UPI. The demonetization era accelerated the growth rate to 56% in the period 2016–2017, after which the COVID-19 pandemic has further contributed to the growth of digital payments in India. By 2024–2025 all these factors are jointly expected to generate a revenue of Rs 2,937 billion compared to Rupees 1,982 billion in the period 2019–2020. (The Indian Payments Handbook, PwC, 2020). This segment entails the list of determinants that have positively contributed to the growth of digital payments in India.

a. Increased number of smartphones and internet users: Reasonable smartphone prices, cheap internet data rates, and the accessibility of smartphones and several applications in regional languages have altogether accounted for growing usage of smartphones in India (India Cellular & Electronics Association, 2020). The users are compounding at a rapid rate, and currently, the economy has 700 million internet users and 600 million smartphone users that are growing by 25 million per quarter, making the connectivity base of the Indian economy stronger than ever (Economic Times, 2021) These demographics have enlightened the way for the prosperity of digital initiatives and adoption rates of digital payment modes in India.

b. Technological advancements: Technological advancements have laid the foundation for digital empowerment in India by reshaping the banking philosophy. The emergence and adoption of new and innovative technologies such as ECS, ATMs, NEFT, and RTGS to cater to the changing needs of Indian users have led to the digitalization of the Indian banking sector (Prasad & Prasad, 2019). The evolution of such technologies during the last two decades has set the grounds for booming digital payment transactions in India.

c. Improved infrastructure: The development of banking and IT infrastructure in India has proven to be a crucial factor for the growth of digital payments. The schedule commercial bank branches have grown at a CAGR of 6% in the last decade. The ATMs and POS terminals have similarly compounded at an annual growth rate of 10% and 26% for the same period. Setting up these branches and facilities in rural and semi-urban areas have not only accounted for the growth of digital payments but also have significantly bolstered the government's initiative of financial inclusion (Journey in the Second Decade of the Millennium, RBI, 2020).

d. Increased digital awareness after demonetization and COVID-19: The demonetization of 500 and 1,000 rupee notes by the government of India has spurred the acceptance of online payments since the cash crunch in the economy forced people to adapt to new ways of carrying out transitions (Padiya & Bantwa, 2018). Similarly, the COVID-19 pandemic made online payments the new normal since people started favoring home deliveries over physical-store visits. All these factors have together increased digital awareness among residents.

e. Perceived ease of accessibility: The perceived ease of carrying out transactions anytime and anyplace is one of the quintessential benefits derived from electronic payments. The convenience of undertaking transactions 24-7 and speedy and hassle-free operations coupled with ease of use and flexibility are predominant factors promoting the growth of digital payments (Singh et al., 2018)

7.3.4 Privacy and Security Measures in Digital Payments

The long-term growth of the digital payment system in India is directly correlated with the security factor associated with respective digital payment modes. This growth would be sustained only when users have sufficient trust in the security and privacy measures of electronic payment modes, the unavailability of which would directly hinder future development (Pal et al., 2017). The perceived absence of security is one of the most prominent reasons for the refusal to use the technology. Thus, it becomes imperative for electronic payment service providers to cater to the security needs of their users by building trust through website and risk-assessment techniques (Singh et al., 2017) In order to mitigate the risks associated with digital payments, the Reserve Bank of India (RBI) has been continuously issuing guidelines concerning the technical audit of prepaid payment instrument issuers so as to ensure the secure and efficient functioning of the retail payment systems (RBI Notification on Security and Risk Mitigation measures, December 09, 2016).

7.4 Methodology

This chapter analyzes the comprehensive growth of digital payments in India, coupled with the growth of selected categories during the last decade. The value of transactions for UPI, IMPS, NEFT, RTGS, BHIM, and card payments has been critically analyzed to determine the adoption level of these services during the period under study. Secondary data for the review period has been retrieved from reports published by the RBI and statistics released by the NPCI. A deep analysis of corporate reports, viz KPMG and Mckinsey, has also been conducted for reviewing the literature.

7.5 Data Analysis and Interpretation

This section analyzes and presents the trends in the DP ecosystem in India from the period 2010–2011 to 2020–2021. Since the digital payment system of India is very broad and outspread on that account, the chapter studies the popularly used digital payment indicators in India such as card payments, NEFT), RealRTGS, BHIM, UPI, and IMPS. The value transacted through these modes is critically interpreted to ascertain and elucidate the patterns in the DP system in India in the last decade.

7.5.1 Card Payments

The value of transactions settled through card payments has shown a sizeable growth during the last 10 years, which could be considered as a proxy for the less frequent use of cash payments in India. As depicted in Figure 7.2, the values transacted through credit cards augmented from 755 billion in 2010 to 6.3 trillion in 2021.[1] The same period also witnessed a steep increase in the value of debit card payments from 357 billion to 6.6 trillion. The value of credit card and debit card transactions has increased at a CAGR of 23.64% and 33.93%, respectively from the period 2010–2011 to 2020–2021. The innovations in the digital payment system such as mobile banking, e-wallets, PMJDY, the launch of RuPay cards, etc. have contributed to the increased use of plastic money in India. A sudden rise of 107% in the use of debit cards was noticeable in the period 2016–2017; an undeniable reason

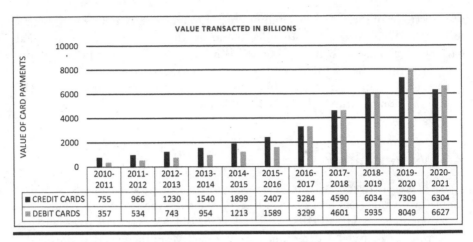

Figure 7.2 Value of Card Payments.

(*Source:* Reserve Bank of India [RBI])

accounting for this growth is the demonetization of 500 and 1,000 rupee currency notes. Although the rudimentary objective of demonetization was not to magnify and boost the digital payment revolution in India, it did have a powerful impact on the same.

7.5.2 *Immediate Payment Service (IMPS), Unified Payments Interface (UPI), Bharat Interface for Money (BHIM)*

The volume and value of transactions executed through IMPS, UPI, and BHIM have increased substantially in the review period. The volume of transactions carried out through IMPS grew from 1.02 million in September 2013 to 384.88 million in September 2021. IMPS payments are favored by users because of their real-time nature and flexibility of accessibility (Timilsina, & Rao, 2019). The value and volume of digital payments through IMPS have swelled at a CAGR of 95% and 102% for the period 2014–2015 to 2019–2020 (see Figure 7.3). The volume of transactions carried out through UPI and BHIM augmented from 1.99 million and 1.85 million in December 2016 to 3654.30 and 7522.56 million in September 2021. UPI emerged as an improvement over other payment systems such as cards and online payment systems as it was both a pull-based and push-based mobile system where payment requests could be initiated by the merchant and the customer has to approve and pay the requested amount (Gochhwal, 2017). UPI payments witnessed a major boost due to the emergence of UPI-enabled applications such as Paytm, BHIM Pay, Google Pay, etc. The speed, efficiency, and safety of the

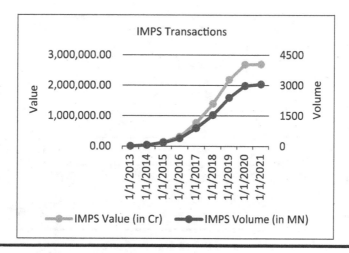

Figure 7.3   Volume and Value of IMPS Transactions.

(*Source:* National Payments Corporation of India [NPCI])

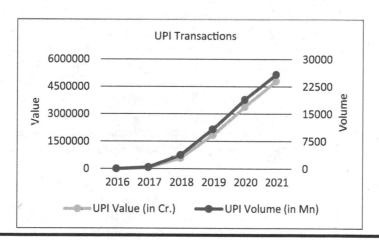

Figure 7.4   Volume and Value of UPI Transactions.

(*Source:* National Payments Corporation of India [NPCI])

transactions gathered consumers' and merchants' trust, which ultimately led to an exponential increment in the transaction volume with a CAGR of 256% from the period 2017–2018 to 2019–2020 (see Figure 7.4). For the same period, the UPI transacted value grew at a CAGR of 290%. The volume and value of BHIM transactions have also witnessed a thriving growth with a CAGR of 61% and 56% for the period 2017–2018 to 2019–2020 (see Figure 7.5).

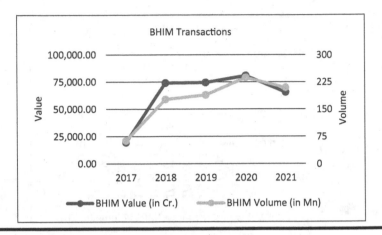

Figure 7.5   Volume and Value of BHIM Transactions.

(*Source:* National Payments Corporation of India [NPCI])

Digital payments in India were escalating rapidly until January 2020, when the novel coronavirus began to spread in India and other parts of the world. As observable in Figures 7.6, 7.7, and 7.8, it was in April when IMPS, UPI, BHIM transactions were spotted at their lowest points for 2020, with 122.47 million, 999.57 million, and 4.4 trillion transaction volume individually. This ultimately led to a reduction in expenditure, fall in employment, delay of routine fixed expenses, and reduction in disposable income of the population (KPMG's report on Impact of COVID-19 on digital payments in India, 2020). Notwithstanding, when the lockdown requirements were made less stringent, consumers started to explore e-commerce websites for their purchase needs, and deferred payments were released, which ultimately led to an increase in disposable income. Eventually, the volume and value of IMPS, UPI, BHIM transactions started to take an upturn. As of December 2020, the volume of IMPS, UPI, and BHIM transactions stand at 355.69 million, 2.2 trillion, and 24.71 million respectively.

7.5.3 National Electronic Fund Transfer System (NEFT) and Real Time Gross Settlement System (RTGS)

During the initial stages of digitalizing India, the RBI scaled electronic products like ECS and EFT, which were decentralized in nature and catered to only a few areas. In the later stages, the vision of RBI shifted to enabling centralized pan-India payment solutions wherein settlement could be done at a central location and users could be serviced throughout India. The vision led to the evolvement of RTGS and NEFT (RBI). NEFT and RTGS have been the key contributors to the digital payment segment in India. The major contribution in India's digital payments is of the

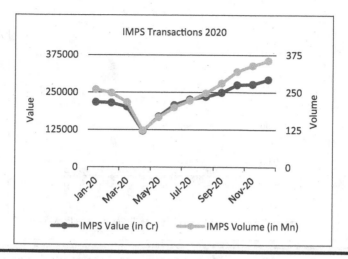

Figure 7.6   Volume and Value of IMPS Transactions for the year 2020.

(*Source:* National Payments Corporation of India [NPCI])

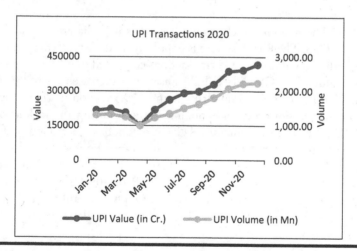

Figure 7.7   Volume and Value of UPI Transactions for the year 2020.

(*Source:* National Payments Corporation of India [NPCI])

NEFT and RTGS segment (Rastogi & Damle, 2020). The RTGS system has witnessed stable growth in both value and volume as presented in Figure 7.9. The volume of RTGS transactions accounted for 49.3 million in 2010 and stands at 159.2 million as of March 2021, which clearly portrays the increased adoption of RTGS. On the other hand, the NEFT transaction volume has also depicted a similar pattern, with 132.3 million transactions in 2010 to 3092.8 million transactions as of

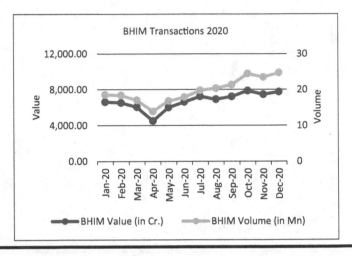

Figure 7.8   Volume and Value of BHIM Transactions for the year 2020.

(*Source:* National Payments Corporation of India [NPCI])

March 2021. The majority of electronic payments in India are executed through NEFT and RTGS. The RTGS system is popularly used for high transaction values, and resultantly, the value of RTGS transactions compared to NEFT is substantially more. The value of RTGS and NEFT transactions increased from 484.8 trillion and 9.4 trillion in 2010 to 1.3 quadrillion and 229.5 trillion in 2020 respectively. On account of the slowdown of economic activity during the lockdown period and COVID-19 phase, the value of RTGS transactions depicted a dip of 3.3% in 2020 compared to 2019, and the value of NEFT transactions witnessed a negligible growth of 0.6% in 2020. For the period 2010–2011 to 2019–2020, the volume of NEFT and RTGS transactions grew at a CAGR of 40% and 13%, respectively. As per RBI, the NEFT facility was available through 225 banks as of March 2021 through 175,283 branches, and the RTGS facility was available through 227 banks via 175,947 branches.

7.5.4 Impact of COVID-19 on Digital Payments in India

The disruptive aftermath of COVID-19 accompanied by a nationwide lockdown led to the lowest statistics in the history of the Indian economy ever since the trade liberalization of 1990 (Kumar et al., 2020). This segment compares and contrasts the unprecedented consequences on various modes of digital payments during the pre-COVID-19[2] and post-COVID-19 phase.[3] The fluctuations in the value and volume of transactions carried out via debit cards and credit cards, IMPS, UPI, BHIM, NEFT, and RTGS during the COVID-19 era are depicted in Figure 7.10.

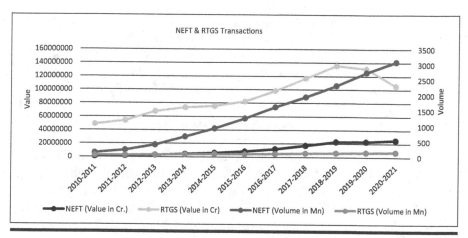

Figure 7.9 **Volume and Value of NEFT & RTGS Transactions.**

(*Source:* Reserve Bank of India [RBI])

a. Card payments: The COVID-19 pandemic had a propitious impact on card payments in India. In the pre-COVID-19 phase, the transactions carried out through credit cards and debit cards were valued at 6 trillion and 5.9 trillion, respectively. It was stated that the health risks associated with cash payments were relatively higher; therefore, the same resulted in a short-lived shift to contactless payments (Jonker et al., 2020). Consequently, the value of transactions carried out through credit cards and debit cards in FY 2019–2020 rose by 21.13% and 18.62% respectively. In the period 2020–2021, the usage of debit cards and credit cards declined by 10.44% and 13.75% respectively. As stated by Jonker et al., 2020, people might return to their preferred payment methods once the repercussions of COVID-19 on their health and daily life fades away. Hence, the post-COVID-19 phase witnessed a downward trend in card payments.

b. IMPS, UPI, and BHIM: IMPS, UPI, and BHIM transactions have portrayed a similar pattern during the COVID-19 era. During the pre-COVID-19 phase,[4] the value of IMPS, UPI, and BHIM transactions was documented to have a steady growth. The same period recorded an average annual growth rate of 3.8% and 9.56% for IMPS and UPI sequentially. The value of BHIM transactions, on the other hand, observed a negative growth rate of 0.54% for the same period on account of lower usage in comparison to UPI and IMPS. Amid the post-COVID-19 phase, an immediate downturn of 40%, 27%, and 26% in the value of IMPS, UPI, and BHIM transactions was stimulated due to the nationwide lockdown imposed in March 2020. The average annual growth rate (AAGR) for IMPS and UPI for the period 2019–2020 reduced to 3.61% and 6.89% in comparison to the pre-COVID-19 AAGR. The value of BHIM transactions for the same period augmented to 1.98%. The second wave of coronavirus left a catastrophic effect on the Indian economy. Consumer-buying behavior to spending habits have been revolutionized as far as digitalization is concerned since people favored home deliveries rather than physically visiting the stores (Raza & Nikhat, 2021). Eventually, during the post-COVID-19 phase of 2020–2021, since the economy was already habituated with the new ways of work and life, the second wave did not have a drastic effect on the digital payment segment, and a negligible downtrend of 0.99%, 0.12%, and 0.23% is witnessed in average annual growth rate for IMPS, UPI & BHIM. In totality, UPI outperformed all modes with an exceptional growth rate of 103% in transaction volume and 98.87% in transaction value from September 2020 to September 2021. On the other hand, IMPS and BHIM transaction values augmented by 30.34% and 4.26% sequentially for the same period.

c. NEFT and RTGS: During the pre-COVID-19 phase, the volume of NEFT and RTGS transactions stood at 23.1 trillion and 1.3 trillion, respectively. Soon after the spread of COVID-19—i.e., during FY 2019–2020—the volume of the latter exhibited a growth of 18.35% and 10.32%. On the other hand, a contradictory trend is witnessed in the RTGS transaction value, where a decline of 3.3 % is observed during the same period. On account of the economic slowdown during the post-COVID-19 phase, the large--value corporate transactions facilitated by RTGS declined. Resultantly, a downfall of 19.5% in RTGS transaction value is noticeable in FY 2020–2021. Subsequently, NEFT transactions witnessed a rise of 12.7% during the same period.

The transaction value of debit cards and credit cards significantly increased for the period 2019–2020. The volume and value of IMPS, UPI, and BHIM transactions exhibited a steep downtrend between September 2019 to September 2020.]

Comprehensively, a positive impact is observed on the Indian economy in terms of digitalization since the groundbreaking challenges dispensed by the pandemic led to the increased adoption of digital payment modes in India. Overall, a total growth of 26.2% in the transaction volume of the payment system is documented for the period 2020–2021 (Annual Report Publications, RBI).

7.6 Discussions

The DP landscape of India has been transforming vigorously in recent times, powered by developments in information and communication technology. There's an immediate need to migrate from paper-based payment systems to paperless or electronic-based payment systems since they are more economical, time-saving, and convenient. Also, there is a high potential for India to become a cashless society, and

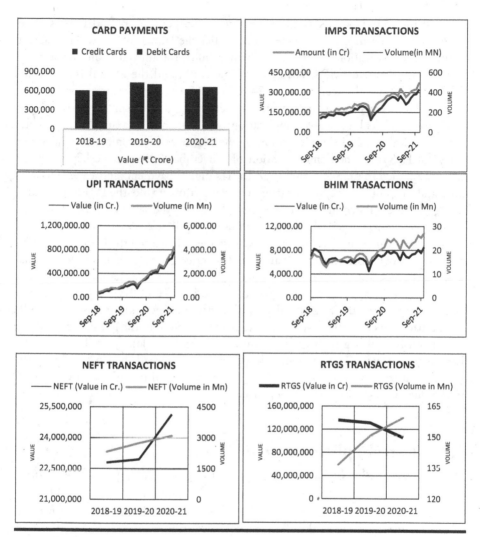

Figure 7.10 Digital Payments during pre-COVID-19 and post-COVID-19 phase.

(*Source:* Reserve Bank of India [RBI] and National Payments Corporation of India [NPCI])

only a dedicated effort will help in successfully achieving that goal (Sontakke & Shekhar, 2018). Historic breakthroughs that have fueled the pace of the evolution of the DP ecosystem of India involve the initiation of ECS and EFT (1990s); the issuance of debit cards and credit cards, the institution of Clearing Corporation of India Limited (CCIL) in 2001 to improve the efficiency in the settlement process; the launch of RTGS (2004) and NEFT (2005) systems to facilitate fund transfer process; the foundation of National Payments Corporation of India (NPCI) to boost and standardize retail payments in India; the launch of the world's largest biometric-identification program, Aadhaar (2008); the introduction of real-time fund transfer system IMPS (2010); PMJDY, AEPS, and the Digital India initiative by GOI; and the scaling up of 24 × 7 × 365 day fund transfer service UPI (2016). The trends in evolution were further changed with small yet significant initiatives, such as UPI-enabled applications, the launch of Bharat QR, the growth of mobile wallets, and the promotion of the National Electronic Toll Collection (NETC) FASTag. The demonetization of November 2016 was perhaps a major catalyst that led to dramatic growth in India's digital payment landscape. The volume and value of transactions relating to the instruments like the IMPS, UPI, and BHIM have exhibited an impressive growth during the review period; however, these instruments witnessed a major downfall in April 2020 due to economic slowdown, after which the instruments have regained their growth. Despite the economic slowdown, the growth in value of UPI transactions is phenomenal and has surpassed expectations. In comparison to 2019, the UPI transacted value has shown a whopping growth of 84%. Contrary to which, IMPS and BHIM transacted values depicted a growth of 22% and 8%, respectively, for the same period. Overall, digital payments in India have witnessed positive growth in the last decade and are continuously evolving with further innovations and developments driven by the Indian government. The pandemic, however, has disturbed their pace of growth, which is clearly noticeable by a declining average annual growth rate in UPI and IMPS during the post-COVID-19 phase.

7.7 Future Implications

This chapter has valuable implications for academic scholars and research practitioners since it acknowledges the direction for future studies in numerous fields. The factors accountable for the growth of digital payments in India have proven to be of paramount importance; therefore, researchers can further study the relationship between these factors and digital payment evolution in India. Further, a comparative analysis of different developing and developed countries can be conducted to administer the digitalization of respective economies, and subsequently, the determinants that have contributed to the same can be compared to determine necessary measures that developing economies may take to magnify their pace of digitalization.

Notes

1. The data for the review year 2021 has been taken till 30th September 2021.
2. FY 2018-19 is considered as the pre-covid phase

3. FY 2019-20 & 2020-2021 is considered as the post covid phase
4. The period September 2018 to August 2019 is considered as the pre-covid phase & September 2019 to August 2020 & September 2020 to August 2021 are considered as the post-covid phase for IMPS, UPI & BHIM to have greater accuracy in analyzing the recent statistics.

References

Aggarwal, M., & Gupta, M. 2019. Demonetization: Move towards cashless economy. *Finance India*, 33(3): 639–654.

Angamuthu, B. 2020. Growth of digital payments in India. *NMIMS Journal of Economics and Public Policy*, 5(4).

Annual Report, Reseve Bank of India (RBI). 2017. Retrieved from: www.rbi.org.in/Scripts/AnnualReportPublications.aspx?Id=1209

Assessment of the progress of digitisation from cash to electronic. 2018. *The Reserve Bank of India (RBI)*. Retrieved from: www.rbi.org.in/Scripts/PublicationsView.aspx?id=19417

Baghla, A. 2018. A study on the future of digital payments in India. *IJRAR-International Journal of Research and Analytical Reviews*, 5(4): 85–89.

Banerjee, S. 2016. Aadhaar: Digital inclusion and public services in India. *World Development Report*: 81–92.

Barik, R., & Sharma, P. 2019. Analyzing the progress and prospects of financial inclusion in India. *Journal of Public Affairs*, 19(4): 1–6. http://doi.org/10.1002/pa.1948

Contribution of smartphones to digital governance in India. July 2020. A study by India Cellular & Electronics Association (ICER). Retrieved from: https://icea.org.in/wp-content/uploads/2020/07/Contribution-of-Smartphones-to-Digital-Governance-in-India-09072020.pdf

Dash, A. 2017. A study on socio-economic effect of demonetization in India. *International Journal of Management and Applied Science*, 3(3): 13–15.

Digital India: Technology to transform a connected nation. 2019. *McKinsey Global Institute*. Retrieved from: www.mckinsey.com/business-functions/mckinsey-digital/our-insights/digital-india-technology-to-transform-a-connected-nation

Garg, P., & Panchal, M. 2017. Study on introduction of cashless economy in India 2016: Benefits & challenges. *IOSR Journal of Business and Management*, 19(4): 116–120. http://doi.org/10.9790/487X-190402116120

Gochhwal, R. 2017. Unified payment interface—An advancement in payment systems. *American Journal of Industrial and Business Management*, 7(10): 1174–1191. http://doi.org/10.4236/ajibm.2017.710084

Gupta, S. D., & Asha. 2018. Digital payments revolution in India. *Digitalization*, Delhi, Maharaja Agrasen University Publications, 137–139.

Gupta, S. D., Raychaudhuri, A., & Haldar, S. K. 2018. Information technology and profitability: Evidence from Indian banking sector. *International Journal of Emerging Markets*, 13(5): 1070–1087.

Hassan, M., & Meraj, Q. F. 2019. Digital financial services: Initiatives and progress with reference to banking industry: Evidence from India. In *Proceedings of 10th International Conference on Digital Strategies for Organizational Success*, 968–974. http://doi.org/10.2139/ssrn.3319894

Impact of Covid-19 on digital payments in India. 2020. *KPMG*. Retrieved from: https://assets. kpmg/content/dam/kpmg/in/pdf/2020/08/impacting-digital-payments-in-india.pdf

Jain, A., Sarupria, A., & Kothari, A. 2020. The impact of COVID-19 on E-wallet's payments in Indian economy. *International Journal of Creative Research Thoughts*, 8(6): 2447–2454. http://doi.org/10.13140/RG.2.2.13584.02562

Jonker, N., Cruijsen, C., Bijlsma, M., & Bolt, W. 2020. Pandemic payment patterns. *DNB Working Papers 701*, Netherlands Central Bank, Research Department. http://doi. org/10.2139/ssrn.3760322

Journey in the Second Decade of the Millennium, Payment and Settlement Systems in India. 2020. Retrieved from: https://rbidocs.rbi.org.in/rdocs/Publications/PDFs/PSSBOOK LET93D3AEFDEAF14044BC1BB36662C41A8C.PDF

Kelkar, V. 2004. India: On the growth turnpike. *The First Ten K R Narayanan Orations*, 125–151.

Kumar, A. 2019. Digital payment and its effects in Indian business. *Iconic Research and Engineering Journals*, 2(12).

Kumar, S., Maheshwari, V., Prabhu, J., Prasanna, M., Jayalakshmi, P., Suganya, P., & Jothikumar, R. 2020. Social economic impact of COVID-19 outbreak in India. *International Journal of Pervasive Computing and Communications*, 16(4): 309–319. http://doi.org/10.1108/IJPCC-06-2020-0053

Mahajan, N. 2019. Digital India: Empowering to rural economy. *Journal of Social Sciences & Multidisciplinary Management Studies*, 2(3): 37–43.

Mittal, S., & Kumar, V. 2018. Adoption of mobile wallets in India: An analysis. *IUP Journal of Information Technology*, 14(1): 42–57.

Mukhopadhyay, B. 2016. Understanding cashless payments in India. *Financial Innovation*, 2(1): 27. http://doi.org/10.1186/s40854-016-0047-4

Nath, G. C. 2008. Role of Clearing Corporation in Indian financial market development. *Macroeconomics and Finance in Emerging Market Economies*, 1(2): 307–311. http://doi. org/10.1080/17520840802253140

Nedungadi, P. P., Menon, R., Gutjahr, G., Erickson, L., & Raman, R. 2018. Towards an inclusive digital literacy framework for digital India. *Education+ Training*, 60(6): 516–528. http://doi.org/10.1108/ET-03-2018-0061

Overview of Payment Systems in India, Payment and Settlement Systems. *Reserve Bank of India (RBI)*. Retrieved from: www.rbi.org.in/scripts/PaymentSystems_UM.aspx#mainsection

Padiya, J., & Bantwa, A. 2018. Adoption of E-wallets: A post demonetisation study in Ahmedabad City. *Pacific Business Review International*, 10(10).

Pal, A., Dattathrani, S., & De, R. 2017. Security in Mobile Payments: A Report on User Issues. Indian Institute of Management, Banglore (IIMB). Retrieved from: www.iimb. ac.in/sites/default/files/inline-files/iimb-csitm-security-issues-in-mobile-payment.pdf

Pal, J., Chandra, P., Kameswaran, V., Parameshwar, A., Joshi, S., & Johri, A. 2018. Digital payment and its discontents: Street shops and the Indian government's push for cashless transactions. In *Proceedings of the 2018 CHI Conference on Human Factors in Computing Systems*, 1–13. http://doi.org/10.1145/3173574.3173803

Patil, P. P., Dwivedi, Y. K., & Rana, N. P. 2017. Digital payments adoption: An analysis of literature. In *Conference on e-Business, e-Services and e-Society Springer*, Cham, 61–70. http://doi.org/10.1007/978-3-319-68557-1_7

Prasad, E. H., & Prasad, G. B. 2019. Digital payments in Indian banking sector: A study. *Review of Professional Management*, 17(1): 84–91. http://doi.org/10.20968/rpm/2019/ v17/i1/145653

Priya, R., Gandhi, A. V., & Shaikh, A. 2018. Mobile banking adoption in an emerging economy. *Benchmarking: An International Journal*, 25(2): 743–762. http://doi.org/10.1108/BIJ-01-2016-0009

Rastogi, A., & Damle, M. 2020. Trends in the growth pattern of digital payment modes in India after demonetization. *PalArch's Journal of Archaeology of Egypt/Egyptology*, 17(6): 4896–4927.

Raza, M. D., & Nikhat, R. 2021. Impact of coronavirus on consumer behaviour. *SPAST Abstracts*, 1(1).

Rooj, D., & Sengupta, R. 2020. A multivariate bayesian vector autoregression analysis of digital payment systems and economic growth in India. *Macroeconomic Stabilization in the Digital Age*, 108.

Seetha, A. 2014. RuPay: The Indigenous electronic card payment scheme. *AISECT University Journal*, 3(6).

Singh, B. P., Grover, P., & Kar, A. K. 2017. Quality in mobile payment service in India. In *Conference on e-Business, e-Services and e-Society*, Springer, Cham, 183–193. http://doi.org/10.1007/978-3-319-68557-1_17

Singh, G., Kumar, B., & Gupta, R. 2018. The role of consumer's innovativeness & perceived ease of use to engender adoption of digital wallets in India. In *2018 International Conference on Automation and Computational Engineering (ICACE)*, IEEE, 150–158. http://doi.org/10.1109/ICACE.2018.8686875

Singh, N., Srivastava, S., & Sinha, N. 2017. Consumer preference and satisfaction of M-wallets: a study on North Indian consumers. *International Journal of Bank Marketing*, 35(6): 944–965. http://doi.org/10.1108/IJBM-06-2016-0086

Sivathanu, B. 2019. Adoption of digital payment systems in the era of demonetization in India. *Journal of Science and Technology Policy Management*, 10(1): 143–171. http://doi.org/10.1108/JSTPM-07-2017-0033

Sobti, N. 2019. Impact of demonetization on diffusion of mobile payment service in India. *Journal of Advances in Management Research*, 16(4): 472–497. http://doi.org/10.1108/JAMR-09-2018-0086

Sontakke, K. A., & Shekar, V. 2018. A study of advance payment and settlement systems in India: An overview. *Finance India*, 32(3).

The Indian Payments Hanbook 2020–2025. 2020. *PwC*. Retrieved from: www.pwc.in/assets/pdfs/consulting/financial-services/fintech/payments-transformation/the-indian-payments-handbook-2020-2025.pdf

Timilsina, S., & Rao, C. A. 2019. A comparative study of NEFT and IMPS as retail payments instruments in India. *Think India Journal*, 22(14): 9672–9681.

Press Releases and News Articles

Boost to digital payments: Govt makes FASTag mandatory for availing discount on toll, August 25, 2020, *Livemint*. Retrieved from: www.livemint.com/news/india/boost-to-digital-payments-govt-makes-fastag-mandatory-for-availing-discount-on-toll-115983 60256587.html, accessed on September 15, 2021.

India's growing data usage, smartphone adoption to boost Digital India initiatives: Top bureaucrat, October 26, 2021, *Economic Times*. Retrieved from: https://economictimes.indiatimes.com/news/india/indias-growing-data-usage-smartphone-adoption-to-boost-digital-india-initiatives-top-bureaucrat/articleshow/87275402.cms, accessed on October 30, 2021.

Notification on Security and Risk Mitigation measures, December 09, 2016, *RBI*. Retrieved from: http://cashlessindia.gov.in/files/rbi-notification-security-and-risk-mitigation-measure-technical-audit-of-prepaid-payment-instrument-issuers.pdf, accessed on October 15, 2021.

Now 125 crore residents of India have Aadhaar, 2019, *Ministry of Electronics & IT, UIDAI Press Release*. Retrieved from: https://uidai.gov.in/images/Press_Release_Dec_2019_English_1.pdf, accessed on October 15, 2021.

Sensex ends day's session tanking over 3,900 points, Nifty plunges 1,135 points; Axis Bank, IndusInd, Bajaj Finance among top losers, March 23, 2020, *First Post*. Retrieved from: www.firstpost.com/business/stock-market-today-live-updates-share-market-latest-news-bse-sensex-nifty-coronavirus-trading-halted-45-minutes-8177821.html, accessed on September 28, 2021.

Bibliography

National Payments Corporation of India (NPCI). Retrieved from: www.npci.org.in, accessed on October 20, 2021.

Reserve Bank of India (RBI). Retrieved from: www.rbi.org.in, accessed on October 20, 2021.

Chapter 8

Evaluation of Crypto Assets and Their Adoption in the Business World: A Global Perspective of the COVID-19 Pandemic

Maumita Ghosh and Moumita Banerjee

Content

DOI: 10.1201/9781003328438-8

8.1 Introduction: Background and Driving Forces

Information and communication technology (ICT) has an immense contribution in our everyday lives and provides newer and quicker ways to interact and gain access to information through telecommunication, which in turn enhances the quality of human life. Though it is widespread and sophisticated in developed countries, it is no longer a luxury for developing countries. By leapfrogging older generations of technology, developing countries are catching up to digitalization fast, which suits the needs of their user communities. One of the sectors that benefits extensively from digitalization is the monetary and business sector (Perkins, 2020).

Money has existed in economic activities in many forms through the ages. It exists because it serves various economic functions such as a medium of exchange of goods and services, value storage, and a unit of account. Money has changed its form from precious metals like gold, copper, and silver that have intrinsic value to a fiat money system where instead of intrinsic value, an object derives its value by some government decree. If a government is sufficiently powerful and credible, it can declare an object, even simple paper, as money. Depending on the government decree, this simple paper (money) can be used in various economic activities such as settling debts, buying goods, or paying taxes (Perkins, 2020).

In the monetary sector, the evolution of banks and other financial institutions plays a pivotal role in to providing an alternative to the physical exchange of tangible currency between two parties. Here the bank plays the role of intermediary, who accomplishes the valid transfer of value between parties who are not in physical proximity. In a modern era, the electronic exchange of money is widely accepted, along with the fear of certain difficulties such as lack of trust between parties. Electronic money transfer can also lead to lack of scarcity as a digital file can be copied many times over by keeping the exact information as its predecessor. The use of electronic payment services involves a huge amount of data about the individual's financial transactions and personal information.

One of the remarkable pathways to digital transformation in the monetary sector that provides an alternative way to the traditional electronic payment system is cryptocurrency. Cryptocurrencies—such as Bitcoin (BTC), Ethereum (ETH), Litecoin, Binance Coin (BNB), etc.—provide an alternative transaction in the financial sector. In the last few years, cryptocurrency has taken the world by storm. The overall market cap of these digital currencies has swelled to $3.3 trillion in November 2021 according to Coin Gecko pricing (CoinGecko, n.d.). A cryptocurrency is a digital or virtual currency that uses cryptography for security. A cryptocurrency is difficult to counterfeit because of this security feature. A defining feature of a cryptocurrency, and arguably its most endearing allure, is its organic nature; it is not issued by any central authority, and therefore, it is theoretically immune to government intervention and/or manipulation. Cryptocurrencies have their advantages and disadvantages both (Raphael Auer, 2020). The foremost benefit that makes cryptocurrencies exceptional is that they make it easier to transfer funds between two parties through the use of public and private keys for security purposes, and these fund transfers are done with minimal processing fees, although the threat of hacking is the biggest threat of cryptocurrency system of payments. For example, in Bitcoin's short history, the company has been subject to over 40 thefts, including a few that exceeded US$1 million in value (Perkins, 2020). However, despite the potential risks, many observers still look at cryptocurrencies as hope that a currency can exist that preserves value, facilitates exchange, is more transportable than hard metals, and is outside the influence of central banks and governments.

An increasing number of companies worldwide have created a new business phenomenon and new types of trading—transactions by investing in cryptocurrencies. Here comes the question whether the system of investing and trading in cryptocurrencies has faced any challenge during the present COVID-19 crisis. The pandemic posed a great challenge to the world economy. The global scientific and business community believes that the world economy faces some unprecedented crises that will lead to large drop in 2021, as it faced in the first quarter of 2020. Therefore, it is also important to look how cryptocurrencies behave in this situation.

So this study would highlight two main pillars: a comparative analysis among the price movements of the top four crypto assets based on their market capitalization and the importance of cryptocurrency in the business world during the COVID-19 pandemic.

8.2 Objectives of the Study

This study aims to do the following:

1. To analyze the behavior of investors based on the price movements of some selected crypto assets and to analyze whether there is a growing interest in adopting crypto assets in the business sector worldwide amid the surge of COVID-19
2. To analyze the behavior of investors based on the relationship among the prices of some of the cryptocurrencies under study
3. To understand whether the popular crypto asset Bitcoin has entered small and medium enterprises

8.3 Theoretical Background

An asset is a strong safe haven if it is negatively correlated with another asset on an average, and an asset is a strong hedge if it is negatively correlated with another asset during an economic downturn (Bouri et al., 2017). During the first wave of the COVID-19 pandemic in 2020, dynamic correlations and regression results showed that the two major cryptocurrencies, Bitcoin and Ethereum, emphasized their short-term safe-haven characteristics for stocks (Mariana et al., 2020).

One study analyzed the impact of macroeconomic variables on the Indian stock market (Gurloveleen & Bhatia, 2016). The correlation between these two coins and the S&P 500 turned negative during 2020 while the correlation was positive before the pandemic. According to Van Wijk, there is a significant influence by the Dow Jones index on Bitcoin prices (Van Wijk, 2013). The effects of COVID-19 on the stock performance of blockchain-based companies have been studied in comparison to non-blockchain based companies, where cumulative abnormal returns showed that the stock prices of blockchain based companies recovered losses slower than non-blockchain companies (Kordestani et al., 2021). He used a sample of S&P Global 1200, the real-time tradable global equity index, to examine the impact of the COVID-19 announcement on March 11, 2020, on stock returns and volatilities. The result of the study showed that the performance of both non-blockchain and blockchain stocks worsened after the announcement of COVID-19 pandemic. In the last few months, several authors studied the influence of the COVID-19 crisis on the cryptocurrency market. Mnif et al. (2020) studied the influence of the pandemic on the behavioral pattern of two major cryptocurrencies, Bitcoin and Ethereum. They used a multifractal detrended approach, a magnitude of a long memory index and a generalized Hurst exponent, and found that the pandemic had a positive impact on the efficiency of the crypto market. The study revealed that Bitcoin was more efficient before the crisis while Ethereum was more efficient after the outbreak of COVID-19. Yarovaya (2020) examines the response and recovery of four broad-class financial assets—14 equity indices (comprising American, European, French,

Portugal, and Japanese stock indices); precious metals; 10-year benchmark bonds; and cryptocurrencies—using a quantile unit root test (Yang, 2020). They found that in very high periods of shock, almost all of the previous equity indices demonstrated a high potential for recovery, reiterating their safe-haven characteristics. Cryptocurrency exhibited unexpected results in the study. Ethereum offered a scope for post shock recovery toward long-term equilibrium while Bitcoin and Litecoin offered some hope in short-term lower levels of shock only. Akyildirim et al. (2020) examined the impact of the pricing of Bitcoin on traditional exchanges like Chicago Mercantile Exchange (CME) and Chicago Board Options Exchange (CBOE).

Elon Musk, CEO of Tesla Motors, may be considered as the real piper for cryptocurrencies as crypto prices shot up when Tesla announced that it had invested $1.5billion in Bitcoin and when they decided to accept Bitcoin as payment for their electric cars. Now, our center of interest is what the true nature of the high volatility of cryptocurrencies is. New York University professor Nouriel Roubini considered Bitcoin a "pseudo asset" that is pumped by huge manipulation.

We conceived the idea of our present study based on the previously mentioned research papers of various eminent scholars.

Now, we are introducing the central theme of our study.

8.4 Part A

8.4.1 Cryptocurrency

It is prudent to understand first what cryptocurrencies are. As mentioned, in their basic form, cryptocurrencies are digitally encrypted tokens that can be transferred between two parties without the need for centralized regulation. Instead, users of the system confirm payments using certain protocols. Bitcoin and other cryptos are created through a process named "mining." Miners use considerable computational power to authenticate transactions that have taken place on the Bitcoin blockchain. Each Bitcoin at its basic form is a computer file that can be stored in a digital wallet application on a smartphone or computer. People can send Bitcoin or a part of it to others' digital wallets and vice versa. Every single transaction is recorded in a list called "blockchain." There are no intermediaries, so they can be directly transferred to the digital wallet of the receiver.

Table 8.1 shows the latest value of the market capitalization of top cryptocurrencies.

Bitcoin is the world's largest cryptocurrency by market capitalization. Its supply is limited to 21,000,000 and has a current circulation of 18,590,300. Since Bitcoin has a fixed supply, it ensures the increase in value over time unlike government-issued currencies.

Table 8.2 shows the ranking of the global adoption of cryptocurrencies country-wise, adjusted for purchasing power parity (PPP). Vietnam tops the ranking, India ranks second, and Pakistan is in third position.

Table 8.1 Market Capitalization of Top Cryptocurrencies

Crypto Assets	Market Cap
Bitcoin (BTC)	$708,391,038,222
Ethereum (ETH)	$320,155,988,350
Solano (SOL)	$32,384227,836
USD Coin (USDC)	$50,876,147,296
Dogecoin (DOGE)	$18,359,366,936
Cardano (ADA)	$33,808,132,441
Ripple (XRP)	$29,109,760,342
Tether (USDT)	$77,981,906,225
Binance Coin (BNB)	$62,515,174,943
Terra (LUNA)	$20,286,927,088

Source: (Data from Coingecko.com, 4th Feb, 2022)

8.4.1.1 Bitcoin

Bitcoin, the first crypto, was invented during the 2008 world financial crisis, and since then it has become the world's largest and most valuable cryptocurrency. For a long period of time, Bitcoin remained in the shadows, but in 2017, it gained prominence when its price increased from $777.76 to $19,497.40 in the same year (source: Coin Market Cap). There is no standard level of BTC price. The prices of Bitcoin vary depending on how much cryptocurrencies are traded on different exchange platforms. According to Coin Market Cap data on March 6, 2018, BTC was traded at $10,958 on Bitfinex, $11274.83 on HitBTC and $10938.94 on GDAX. Though there are variations in the price levels, the variations are not that large. Prices of BTC are independent of different trading platforms as they are not synchronized. The factors that affect this varying nature of BTC price are as follows:

8.4.1.2 Size of the Market

The Bitcoin price in different trading exchange platforms is determined in the same way the goods prices are determined through price mechanism in the goods market. If the demand for Bitcoin increases on the exchange but the supply is limited, the price of Bitcoin will go up according to the law of demand and supply.

Table 8.2 Country-Wise Ranking of Global Adoption of Cryptocurrencies

Country	Index Score	Overall Index Ranking	Ranking for Individual Weighted Metrics Feeding into Global Crypto Adoption Index		
			On-Chain Value Received	On-Chain Retail Value Received	P2P Exchange Trade Volume
Vietnam	1.00	1	2	4	3
India	0.37	2	3	2	72
Pakistan	0.36	3	12	11	8
Ukraine	0.29	4	5	6	40
Kenya	0.28	5	28	41	1
Nigeria	0.26	6	10	15	18
Venezuela	0.25	7	22	29	6
United States	0.22	8	4	3	109
Togo	0.19	9	42	47	2
Argentina	0.19	10	17	14	33
Colombia	0.19	11	23	27	12
Thailand	0.17	12	11	7	76
China	0.16	13	1	1	155
Brazil	0.16	14	7	5	113
Philippines	0.16	15	9	10	80
South Africa	0.14	16	16	18	62
Ghana	0.14	17	37	32	10
Russian Federation	0.14	18	6	8	122
Tanzania	0.13	19	45	60	4
Afghanistan	0.13	20	38	53	7

(Data from Chainalysis, The 2021 Global Crypto Adoption Index)

8.4.1.3 Exchange Volume

Since all the coins that are being mined are fixed, the volumes are limited. BTC solely depends on what price an individual is willing to pay to buy a Bitcoin and what the other person is ready to pay for it. Once the upper and lower limits are identified, the price transaction takes place between the individuals in an exchange, and the price is decided thereafter. Buyers are obviously interested in obtaining Bitcoin at the lowest price possible while sellers are interested in obtaining the highest price as possible.

8.4.1.4 Average Estimate Pricing

Based on the transaction history on a popular exchange, most prices are calculated on an average estimate or at a recently traded price. Due to the transaction fee charged by most exchanges, the investors should keep in mind that the actual cost of Bitcoin is likely to be higher in an exchange beyond the inaccuracies built into a price tracker. The correct price of any cryptocurrency is dictated by large traders known as "whales" and public sentiments. Since exchanges are heavily influenced by one or two deep pockets and pricing is still largely speculative, this further contributes to the inconsistency in prices.

The influence of the COVID-19 pandemic on cryptocurrency, more specifically on Bitcoin, as it is the most transacted crypto, has been studied by several researchers in the last few months. The study by Mnif et al. (2020) considered five cryptocurrencies to investigate herding biases during the COVID-19 crisis. The finding of the study distinctly said that the COVID-19 pandemic had a positive impact on the efficiency of the cryptocurrency market. The study investigated whether the crypto market is a safe haven. A study argues that during the first wave of the COVID-19

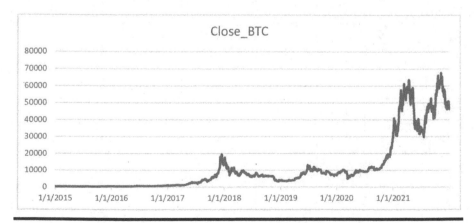

Figure 8.1　Price volatility of Bitcoin (BTC) over time.

(*Source:* Daily data taken from Coin Market Cap during the period January 1, 2015, to December 31, 2021)

crisis, gold and oil, as typical global commodities, could have been diversifiers (Vukovic, 2021). The study developed a COVID-19 global composite index that measured the COVID-19 pandemic time-variant movements on each day. The study used OLS (ordinary least squares), quantiles, and robust regressions to check whether the COVID-19 crisis has had any significant direct influence on the crypto market. "A study on Cryptocurrency in India" by Mubarak and Manjunath (2021) investigated the investment risks in both Bitcoin and gold.

The rise of Bitcoin investments coincided with the pandemic and lockdowns when economies were struggling to remain afloat. In this downturn, funds began to move out of stock markets rapidly and pouring into cryptocurrency and gold. In Figure 8.1, trend of the daily closing prices of Bitcoin has been shown during the period 1st January 2015 to 31st December 2021. The volatility of the Bitcoin prices can be speculated from this trend.

8.4.1.5 Ethereum

Ethereum is the world's second largest cryptocurrency based on market capitalization, which hit an all-time high on November 3, 2021, as per the popular crypto exchange platforms (CoinMarketCap). The years 2015 and 2016 marked the foundation of Ether tokens, which helped it gain acceptance post-Bitcoin. In Figure 8.2, the trend of the daily closing prices of Ethereum has been shown during the period 1st January 2018 to 31st Dec 2021. The volatility of the Ethereum prices can be speculated from this trend.

8.4.1.6 Tether

Tether (USDT) is the third largest crypto asset (CoinMarketCap), though it is very different from Bitcoin and other virtual coins. While other cryptocurrencies often fluctuate, Tether was designed to be pegged to the dollar; that's why it is known as

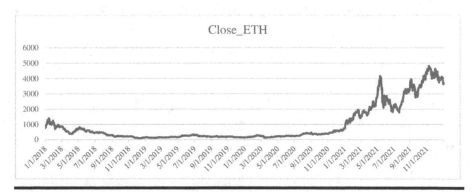

Figure 8.2   Price volatility of Ethereum (ETH) over time.

(*Source:* Daily data taken from Coin Market Cap during the period January 18, 2018, to December 31, 2021)

Figure 8.3 Price volatility of Tether (USDT) over time.

(*Source:* Daily data taken from Yahoo Finance during the period January 1, 2018, to December 31, 2021)

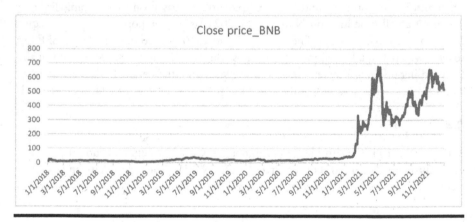

Figure 8.4 Price volatility of Binance (BNB) over time.

(*Source:* Daily data taken from Yahoo Finance during the period January 1, 2018, to December 31, 2021)

a stable coin (as shown in Figure 8.3). But it is not always the case, which in the past has spooked investors due to the wobbles in its value.

8.4.1.7 Binance

According to recent data (Coin Gecko), BNB is the fourth largest crypto asset as per market cap. Its trading options are more limited in the US economy and is currently under regulatory investigation in the country. The Binance platform is complex and confusing, and no built-in digital wallet is available. It recommends Trust wallet, which has a good reputation, but due to its regulatory and security issues, there may be some problem with BNB transfers. Crypto investors of all skill levels are likely to experience a steep learning curve with this crypto asset. The trend of the daily closing prices of Binance has been shown in Figure 8.4 for the time period 1st January 2018 to 31st December 2021 where significant volatility of the Binance prices can be observed from March 2021.

8.4.2 Data and Methodology

A comparative study to examine the interrelationships among different crypto-currencies has been conducted, for which we have chosen top four crypto assets according to their ranking based on their market capitalization. The selected crypto currencies are Bitcoin (BTC), Ethereum (ETH), Tether (USDT), and Binance (BNB). The daily transaction data of each of these selected cryptocurrencies has been taken from the Coin Market Cap website. The daily data on closing prices, open prices, high prices, and low prices of each selected crypto currency were taken. The study period for Bitcoin was January 1, 2015, to December 31, 2021. The study period for Ethereum, Tether, and Binance was February 1, 2018, to December 31, 2021. We mainly intended to analyze the relationships among the closing prices of these cryptocurrencies. To analyze the price movements of the selected five crypto assets and their association, if any, a popular statistical software, Stata, has been used, where various econometric tools like the augmented Dickey-Fuller test and the Johansen co-integration test have been used.

To analyze whether business firms are interested in adopting cryptocurren-cies in their portfolio, this study has been carried out by borrowing data from the Reserve Bank of India's platform, Coin Market Cap Exchange, the Statista Data platform, and data from Yahoo Finance.

8.4.3 Result and Discussion

8.4.3.1 Augmented Dickey Fuller Test

A new type of revolution in both economics and econometrics started since the mid-1980s, known as the "unit root and cointegration revolution" (Rao, 1994). According to Engle and Granger (1987), an important requirement of the station-arity of time series data is that the means and variances of the variables should have well-defined constants and remain independent of time. It is a recognized fact that most of the financial series are nonstationary or random walk data that contain a unit root at raw level. Granger and Newbold (1974) documented that using a nonstationary series for analysis lead to a situation of spurious statistical output. The presence of the unit root in the series shows a bias and inaccuracy in the other statistical tests. To avoid it, several unit root tests like Dickey-Fuller's DF test and ADF test (Dickey & Fuller, 1979); Phillips–Perron test (Phillips, 1988); KPSS test (Kwiatkowski, 1992); and the less frequently used ADF-GLS test (Elliot, 1996) and NGP test (N.G, 2001) can be used. The ADF test gives a reliable result for unit root testing in case of time series data with a large number of observations. The PP test and KPSS test are suitable for very short time series data. Moreover, the ADF test is the most commonly used unit root test because of its simple construction and feasibility (Arltova & Fedorova, 2016).

The ADF test involves the Dickey-Fuller regression model augmented by including m lag of the dependent variable to correct any serial correlation in the disturbance term. If Y_t is the time series to be tested for the unit root, then the following model can be estimated, and the null hypothesis H_N: $\delta=0$ can be tested by using a tau-statistic:

$$\Delta Y_t = \alpha + \delta Y_{t-1} + \sum_{i=1}^{m} \beta \Delta Y_{t-1} + U_t \tag{8.1}$$

(U_t is a white noise error term.)

It is important to determine the number of different terms in the ADF regression equation, for which we have applied the selection of order criteria test (varsoc), which reports the FPE (Final Prediction Error); AIC (Akaike's Information Criteria); Schwarz's Bayesian information criterion (SBIC); and HQIC (Hannan and Quinn information criterion) for selecting the lag order. The decision rule is that we will select the order of lag corresponding to the lowest value of AIC, FPE, HQIC, and SBIC.

According to the varsoc table, AIC, FPE, and SBIC values are lowest at lag 2 for the variables BNB, ETH, and BTC, while they are lowest at lag 4 in the case of Tether. Hence, ADF tests were conducted for the previous variables at respective lags.

Table 8.3   Examining Nonstationarity of Data

Variables	5% Critical Level	t-Statistic	t-Statistic at 1st Difference	p-value	Null Hypothesis	Result
Bitcoin	−3.410		−20.973	0.0000	Rejected at 1st difference	Variable is stationary at 1st difference
Ethereum	−3.410		−28.204	0.0000	Rejected at 1st difference	Variable is stationary at 1st difference
Tether	−3.410	−5.627		0.0000	Rejected at level	Variable is stationary at level
Binance	−3.410		−28.204	0.0000	Rejected at 1st difference	Variable is stationary at 1st difference

(Author's own calculation)
Unit root test result

In Table 8.3, the analysis of unit root testing suggested that the time series data of the close prices of Bitcoin, Ethereum, and Binance are nonstationary at level and stationary at 1st difference, while Tether is stationary at level.

8.4.3.2 Johansen Co-Integration Test

Johansen (1988) provided a simple test to examine the presence of a co-integrating relationship or long-run relationship between the variables. The Johansen co-integration test variables should be nonstationary at level but stationary at first difference. The ADF test result shows that the close prices of the crypto asset Tether (USDT) are stationary at level, while the Bitcoin, Ethereum, and Binance series are nonstationary at level and stationary at first difference. Hence, we have taken three variables—Bitcoin, Ethereum, and Binance—and conducted the Johansen co-integration test to examine the long-run relationship among the price movements of these three cryptocurrencies.

We conducted the test in two phases. The first phase is during COVID-19 (Table 8.4) and the second phase is prepandemic (Table 8.5). In the first phase test, we have taken daily data of Bitcoin, Ethereum, and Binance during pandemic years 2020 and 2021 (January 1, 2020, to December 31, 2021), and in the second phase, we have taken daily data on Bitcoin, Ethereum, and Binance prices from 2018 to 2019 (January 1, 2018, to December 31, 2019).

Maximum rank column tells the order or rank of co-integration among the variables.

For rank = 0,
Null Hypothesis (H_N): There is no co-integration or 0 co-integration relationship.
Alternative Hypothesis (H_A): There is co-integration.

Table 8.4   Co-Integration Result during Pandemic Phase

Maximum Rank	Trace Statistic	5% Critical Value
0	48.0175	29.68
1	18.2737	15.41
2	1.6888	3.76

(Authors' own calculation)
Test result 1

Maximum Rank	Max Statistic	5 % Critical Value
0	29.7438	20.97
1	16. 5849	14.07
2	1.6888	3.76

Test result 2

Table 8.5 Prepandemic Phase

Max Rank	Trace Statistic	5% Level of Significance
0	36.6037	29.68
1	12.6005	15.41
2	3.5606	3.76

(Authors' own calculation)
Test result 1

Max rank	Max statistic	5 % critical value
0	24.0032	20.97
1	9.0399	14.07
2	3.5606	3.76

Test result 2

Here, the decision rule is that if the trace statistic value is higher than the 0.05 critical value, then we can reject H_N and conclude that there is co-integration between the variables. The test result shows that the trace statistic value is 48.0175, which is higher than the 5% critical value 29.68. Hence, we will reject null and say that there is co-integration or a long-run relationship among the Bitcoin, Ethereum, and Binance prices.

Since we could reject H_N, we have to go for the next rank.

For rank = 1,
H_N: There is a maximum of 1 co-integration relationship.
H_A: There is more than 1 co-integration relationship.

Here, the decision rule is same. If the trace statistic value is higher than the 0.05 critical value, then we can reject H_N and conclude that there is at most 1 co-integration relationship between the variables. The result shows that trace statistic value is 18.2737, which is higher than 0.05 critical value. So H_N is rejected and we will move to rank 2.

For rank = 2,
H_N: There are a maximum of 2 co-integration relationships.
H_A: There are more than 2 co-integration relationships.

The decision rule is the same as before, and we found from the test result that the trace statistic value, which is 1.6888, is less than the 0.05 critical value of 3.76. Hence, we can accept H_N and conclude that there are 2 co-integration relationships among the variables or there are 2 co-integrating equations.

Test result 2 also shows the same movement in the value of max statistic, and it is double confirmed that a long-run relationship exists among the close prices of Bitcoin, Ethereum, and Binance.

From the previous empirical output of the co-integration test (Table 8.5), the trace statistics and max statistics are both less than the 5% critical level, and we can conclude that there is 1 co-integration relationship among the variables.

So from the results of both the phases, it is found that the prices of one of these cryptocurrencies are driven by the prices of the other. If there is any shock to any one of them, then it will immediately be transformed to the other. From an investor's perspective, constructing a portfolio entirely based on cryptocurrencies may be risky. Since closing prices have a long-run relationship, if an investor wants to invest in Bitcoin, it is necessary to study the closing prices of other cryptocurrencies as well. For example, when there is a price drop in Ethereum, it will be reflected in Bitcoin, indicating a collapse of the correlation structure between Bitcoin and Ethereum, and investors should distance themselves from crypto assets.

8.5 Part B

8.5.1 Bitcoin Adoption in Various Business Sectors

With various developments occurring on the crypto market and many countries pushing for digital payments during the COVID-19 pandemic, more and more people have started to wonder how big the adoption is of Ethereum, Bitcoin, and other cryptocurrencies worldwide. Many new users have turned to cryptocurrency in order to send and receive remittances, preserve their savings in the face of currency devaluation, and to make business transactions. Such transactions have grown even as central banks in countries like India, Nigeria, etc. have banned access between banks and crypto exchanges (Business Today, 2021).

8.5.1.1 Bitcoin in Large Business: A Global Perspective

The rising demand for Bitcoin surged the Bitcoin price by more than 200% in 2020. This explosive price pump has caused a drastic shift in the relationship between investor-held Bitcoin (illiquid) and trader-held Bitcoin (liquid). In 2020, the number of retailers accepting Bitcoin surpassed 100,000 according to the latest industry figures (Local Bitcoins, 2021).

Several major firms, viz Tesla, Square, Burger King, Coca-Cola, etc.—have purchased hundreds of millions of dollars' worth of cryptocurrency in recent years (Haqqi, 2021). Crypto could enable access to a liquidity pool and new capital through traditional investments that have been tokenized. Here are some examples.

Tesla Motors is an American Company that is best known for its electric vehicles. Based on a price of $58,919 on March 31, 2021, the company owned $2.48

billion worth of Bitcoin. According to the company's first-quarter update of 2021, it earned a record profit from selling some of its Bitcoin holdings more than selling cars. As of June 30, 2021, Elon Musk's Tesla showed a net digital asset value of $1.311 billion in its Q2 unaudited balance sheet (Table 8.6).

The table of cash flow statements of Tesla (Table 8.7) shows that the only time the company sold its Bitcoin was in Q1 for $272 million. Elon Musk tweeted on June 13, 2021, that the company sold only 10% of its BTC holdings to prove the easy liquidity of Bitcoin without moving markets (Jain, 2022).

Table 8.6 Balance Sheet (Unaudited)

Assets	30-June-2020	30-Sep-2020	31-Dec-2020	31-March-2021	30-June-2021
Current assets	8,615	14,531	19,384	17,141	16,229
Cash and cash equivalents	1,485	1,757	1,886	1,890	2,129
Accounts receivable, net Inventory	4,018	4,218	4,101	4,132	4,733
Prepaid expenses and other current assets	1,218	1,238	1,346	1,542	1,602
Total current assets	15,336	21,744	26,717	24,705	24,693
Operating lease vehicles, net	2,524	2,742	3,091	3,396	3,748
Solar energy systems, net	6,069	6,025	5,979	5,933	5,883
Property, plant and equipment, net	11,009	11,848	12,747	13,868	15,665
Operating lease right-of-use assets	1,274	1,375	1,558	1,647	1,734
Digital assets, net	-	-	-	1,331	1,311
Goodwill and intangible assets, net	508	521	520	505	486
Other noncurrent assets	1,415	1,436	1,536	1,587	1,626
Total assets	38,135	45,691	52,148	52,972	55,146

(Data from Tesla)
In million US$

Table 8.7 Statement of Cash Flows (Unaudited)

Cash Flows from Investing Activities	Q2 2020	Q3 2020	Q4 2020	Q1 2021	Q2 2021
Capital expenditures	546	1,005	1,1511	1,348	1,505
Purchases of solar energy systems, net of sales	20	16	13	12	10
Purchase of intangible assets	-	5	5	-	-
Receipt of government grants	-	-	122	6	-
Purchases of digital assets	-	-	-	1,500	-
Proceeds from sales of digital assets	-	-	-	272	-
Business combinations, net of cash acquired	-	13	-	-	-
Net cash used in investing activities	566	1,039	1,047	2,582	1,515

(Data from Tesla)
(Million US$)

8.5.1.2 Square

Square, currently Block Inc., is an American digital payment and financial services company based in San Francisco, California. In 2020, Square made a $170 million investment in Bitcoin (Bursztynsky, 2021). The sum is relatively small but is noteworthy in the initial stage of investment. Cash App, which allows to save and invest in Bitcoin is now owned by Square. Jack Dorsey, CEO of Square, has spent the last five years fascinated with cryptocurrency and supported the development of Bitcoin Lightning Network and Bitcoin developers through a unit called Square Crypto.

In October, 2021, Dorsey announced that his company Square is considering a Bitcoin-mining system. His goal is to make crypto mining more accessible as much as possible so that it would be easier for small businesses and independent proprietors to take credit card payments. He also said that Jesse Dorogusker (hardware lead at Square) and his team will begin studying the technology and process necessary to take this project on. In December 2021, he rolled out lightning-based tipping and promised NFT (nonfungible token) avatar integration. He is going to turn Square into an entire blockchain and cryptocurrency company. He has two businesses currently, small business checkout systems and consumer apps, both of which have a larger user base. In recent years, revenue from these two businesses has grown massively. Dorsey is looking for real opportunities to improve the experiences of existing customers with crypto.

8.5.1.3 Burger King

In 2020, Burger King Venezuela (the fast-food giant) declared that it will adopt a variety of cryptocurrency including Bitcoin. They will do it in partnership with Crypto buyer. Crypto buyer is a company that manages the conversion of crypto to fiat currency.

The burger chain rewarded members of its Royal Perks Loyalty Program who spent $5 on the website, app, or in the store between November 1 and November 21, 2021. Most customers were rewarded with Dogecoin, worth about 27% according to Coin Market Cap. The offer was open only for US residents. Most customers were rewarded with Dogecoin worth about 27%. The fast-food chain gave away a total of 200 Ethereum, 2 million Dogecoin, and 20 Bitcoin. Few customers got a full Ethereum or a full Bitcoin. Burger King was partnered with a Robinhood, an online brokerage firm, to give away these digital currencies to a handful of winners. According to the company, cryptocurrency is a hot topic in recent times. The company always wants to reward their loyal guests with exciting offers that are unique and culturally relevant. Cryptocurrency is difficult to understand, but in the current pandemic, when investors are bending toward crypto, the company wanted to introduce the asset to their guests in a way that was accessible and digestible.

8.5.1.4 Coca-Cola

In 2020, Coca-Cola Amatil, a Coca-Cola distributor, announced a collaboration with Centrapay, a digital assets platform, to accept Bitcoin as a payment option in the Asia-Pacific region (Handagama, 2020). Over 2,000 vending machines across Australia and New Zealand have let their customers buy a Coke with Bitcoin. Transactions are conducted via the Sylo Smart wallet and Centrapay, which have about 250,000 users. The Sylo Smart app is to be downloaded on customers' smartphones, and Bitcoin is to be added to their wallets, where a QR code should be scanned to purchase Amatil products. According to Dorian Johannink, Sylo cofounder and business manager, Sylo allows customers to purchase digital assets in the real world (a Coke token though) and use it to purchase products. According to Jerome Faury, CEO of Centrapay, the initiative has already been demonstrated in Australia and New Zealand, and it will be targeting the US market with some world-first innovations.

8.5.1.5 Crypto in Global Small Businesses

The growth of the crypto industry has been explored in new research released by small business invoicing and accounting firm Skynova. Skynova conducts a large number of surveys on its client base to identify the adoption of crypto as payment among small businesses. The recent study found that nearly 32% of US small business owners accept cryptocurrencies as payment options. The small business employees were surveyed on whether or not they wanted to be paid in various forms of cryptocurrencies. Based on the completed questionnaires from more than 580 owners and managers, the researchers found a +/–3%margin of error with a 95% confidence interval. Moreover, the study revealed the order of preference for customer payments:

Bitcoin (58%)
Bitcoin Cash (36%)
Ethereum (35%)
Litecoin (28%)
Binance Coin (24%)

As multiple businesses accept more than one crypto type, the percentages have exceeded 100%. The survey also listed what or whom were the primary drivers for founders and managers to embrace crypto payments:

The two major payment companies, PayPal and Mastercard, have adopted cryptocurrency (59%). Thirty-two percent of social media influencers with huge followings on Twitter, YouTube, and Telegram have adopted cryptocurrency, while 34% of current media report and cover the crypto industry. Thirty-seven percent of customers demand for cryptocurrency funds as payment options, while 50% of innovative companies are making big crypto buys.

The survey revealed that the reason for adopting crypto in small and medium-sized businesses was to stay ahead or just keep pace with competitors who already accepted various kinds of blockchain-based bucks. The adoption of crypto is no doubt, in the short term at least, becoming less of a competitive advantage and more of a competitive survival.

8.5.1.6 Bitcoin in Small Business: An Indian Perspective

It causes much inconvenience when a grocery store or a small business does not offer choices of payment options. The "cash only" method ends up frustrating customers, and that is why most small businesses have started accepting cashless payments. Bitcoin users are now expecting to have a Bitcoin mode of payment along with the other modes of online payments (Local Bitcoins, 2021). According to a Chainalysis report, the Bitcoin trade volume in India by the end of December 2020 grew dramatically over $60 million every day.

Moreover, a small yet growing set of businesses in the formal as well as informal economy in India is also increasingly accepting crypto tokens like Bitcoin,

Ethereum, Solana, etc. in exchange for goods and services amid the rising popularity of the digital asset (*The Economic Times*, 2021). Lokesh Verma, the founder of Devilz Tattooz, who owns and operates three studios in New Delhi, has been a long-term believer as well as investor in crypto assets. He started accepting them as payment options in March 2021 after he got enormous requests from his younger clients.

The acceptance and adoption of Bitcoin has increased in the country after the Supreme Court overturned a decision by RBI on crypto in 2018 that prohibited banks from dealing with cryptocurrency exchanges. Studies showed that Bitcoin trades were worth over $60 million every day by the end of December 2020. LocalBitcoins, one of the most secure peer-to-peer Bitcoin marketplaces, interviewed a few small business owners in India to understand how it worked for them so far. They got the following responses:

8.5.1.7 Company Name: Ahmev India (www.ahmev.com)

Owner: Manish Garg

Ahmev, an online fashion store and New Delhi–based label, brings sustainable and eco-friendly handmade wear to the global market. The company was established in 2019 and started accepting Bitcoin payment from the very beginning because the other payment modes like bank transfers or PayPal were slow and pricey. With Bitcoin, the transaction charges are low and transfer was instant. Small business demands liquidity, and the Bitcoin payment benefits by making instant transfers. Moreover, it ensures customers transaction security and global payment flexibility. Bitcoin has helped the company to perform in the highly competitive fashion industry. According to Manish Garg, Ahmev stores Bitcoin as a future investment. It uses profits from other sales to manage liquidity to run the business. Hence, price volatility in Bitcoin doesn't bother them as they don't trade Bitcoin.

8.5.1.8 Company Name: Exceed Enterprise Pvt Ltd (Surat, Gujrat, https://exceedenterprise.business.site/)

Owner: Nirmal Patel

The company is a Gujrat-based leading service provider, distributor, and supplier of industrial electrical, electronic, mechanical, and instrumentation materials, which started accepting Bitcoin payments in 2017. It helps the business to receive international payments fast and securely.

8.5.1.9 Company Name: Netilly | Digital Marketing Agency (Delhi, netilly.com)

Owner: Kuldeep Koul

Netilly is India's leading digital marketing agency specializing in social media marketing, content writing, community management, branding, pay for click, search engine optimization, etc. It started accepting Bitcoin in 2017 because of its convenience and instant cross-border payments. The owner found Bitcoin as the safest hedge against inflation in current times. The company manages Bitcoin price fluctuations while accepting payment by converting Bitcoin to stable coins like USDT.

8.5.2 Effect of the COVID-19 Pandemic on Bitcoin (BTC) Price

The governments around the world have flooded global markets with money created by central banks in response to the risk of economic collapse due to COVID-19. But increasing the money supply has eroded its value and led people to look for alternate inflation-resistant assets to hold. In this scenario, Bitcoin has evolved as a hedge against such looming inflation and poor returns on other assets.

Bitcoins (BTC) price reached an all time high, despite its volatility, in 2021 (shown by the dotted line in figure 8.5). It reached a new all-time high, over $68,000, on November 10, 2021. BTC has seen a lot of ups and downs in the said year, including a drop toward $30,000 in January and July. According to experts, this new high does not mean that its fluctuations will subside completely; rather, they expect it to happen more. BTC price in 2020 (shown by ash-colored line in Figure 8.5) took an upward trend from the month of September.

8.6 Limitation and Scope for Further Research

This comparative study among four chosen crypto assets in Part A has been done for a limited time period due to lack of data. We intend to choose the time period of the study to be from 2015 to 2021. Different websites have been analyzed, but we have found Bitcoin data only from 2015, while complete Ethereum data was found

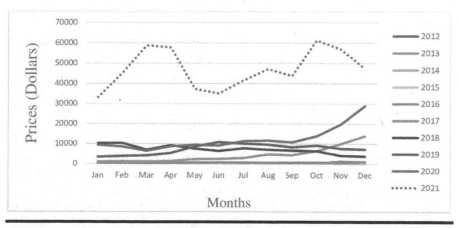

Figure 8.5   Trends of BTC prices over the years (Statista).

from 2017 to 2021. There were certain days in 2016 where we found missing data for Ethereum. The complete data on Binance and Tether was found from mid-2017. Hence, for the co-integration tests, we fixed our study period from January 1, 2018, to December 31, 2021.

We are keen to do further research on this area and include more companies that are entering the crypto market, and the research period might be extended as well.

8.7 Conclusion

This study revealed that the investors should use a portfolio approach to evaluate individual investment on cryptocurrencies based on their close prices and interrelationships with the other crypto prices and returns. According to a survey conducted in the US last year, it has been revealed that almost 36% of small and midsized companies in the country are using crypto assets for a host of operational transactional purposes, while 59% of those companies purchased them for their own use (TOI, 2021). It has been found that up to 40% of customers who use crypto as payment options are new customers of the companies, and the amount of their purchases is twice than those of credit card users. Many companies are finding growing interest among clients and vendors who want to engage by using crypto. Our findings suggest that in the face of economic meltdowns, cryptocurrencies have proven to be remarkably resilient. Bitcoin, being a highly valued asset in 2020 and 2021, is continuing to witness itself as the longest bull run in the business world.

But when discussing the merits of crypto assets, one must understand that these currencies do not possess any intrinsic value. Stocks, bonds, and gold possess some intrinsic value as mentioned previously. Stock provides partial ownership of a company that produces goods and services. Bonds are considered as a steady source of income, and gold, being a precious metal, has an inherent value. But cryptocurrencies are purely nonproductive assets that are traded because there is demand for them. Those who would like to invest in these currencies should know that they are speculating rather than investing because the movement in crypto asset prices are mainly driven by public sentiments and investments by large traders. Although during the COVID-19 pandemic, the growth of crypto market has been enormous, it would become challenging for monetary regulators to step in and aid a wounded economy.

In India cryptocurrencies were under the scanner for some time in 2018. The then Union Finance Minister said, "The government does not recognize Cryptocurrencies as legal tender or coin and will take all measures to eliminate the use of these cryptoassets in financing illegitimate activities or as part of its payment system." After, the Cryptocurrency and Regulation of Official Digital Currency Bill of 2021 sought to prohibit all private cryptocurrencies in India but allowed for certain exceptions to promote the underlying technology and its uses. But so far it is not clear that what kind of regulation the Indian government is going to impose on these currencies. Regarding the budget of 2022, the announcement by the finance minister of the introduction of the digital rupee the by Reserve Bank of India gave a big boost to the digital economy.

Additionally, the budget also proposed an imposition of a tax of 30% on income from virtual assets like cryptos. The investors and coin exchangers in the crypto market believe that the government moving to tax them may provide them with clarification as well as a sense of enthusiasm for the further acceptance of this asset class. We are concluding our research in an optimistic way, considering the fact that the government itself is moving toward setting up its own digital rupees (Business Today, 2021).

References

Akyildirim, Erdinc, Shaen Corbet, Paraskevi Katsiampa, Neil Kellard, and Ahmet Sensoy. 2020. "The Development of Bitcoin Futures: Exploring the Interactions Between Cryptocurrency Derivatives." *Finance Research Letters* 34: 101234. http://doi.org/10. 1016/j.frl.2019.07.007.

Arltova, M., and D. Fedorova. 2016. "Selection of Unit Root Test on the Basis of Length of the Time Series and Value of AR (1) Parameter." *Statistika* 96(3): 47–64.

Banerjea, A. 2021. "Digital rupee to launch in 2022–2023 using blockchain; to be issued by RBI: FM in Budget 2022". BusinessToday. Feb 01. www.businesstoday.in/union-budget-2022/news/story/digital-rupee-to-launch-in-2022-23-using-blockchain-to-be-issued-by-rbi-fm-in budget-2022-321060-2022-02-01.

Bouri, Elie, Naji Jalkh, Peter Molnár, and David Roubaud. 2017. "Bitcoin for Energy Commodities Before and After the December 2013 Crash: Diversifier, Hedge or Safe Haven?" *Applied Economics*: 1–11. http://doi.org/10.1080/00036846.2017.1299102.

Bursztynsky, Jessica. 2021. CNBC. Feb 23. https://www.cnbc.com/2021/02/23/square-buys-170-million-worth-of-bitcoin.html.

Deepika. 2021. Are There Any Small Business Owners in India that Accept Bitcoin? Local Bitcoins. Feb 05. https://blog.localbitcoins.com/are-there-any-small-business-owners-in-india-that-accept-bitcoin-163842841131.

Dickey, David A., and Wayne A. Fuller. 1979. "Distribution of the Estimators for Autoregressive Time Series with a Unit Root." *Journal of the American Statistical Association* 74(366): 427. http://doi.org/10.2307/2286348.

Elliott, G., Rothenberg, T. J. and Stock, J. H. 1996. "Efficient Tests for an Autoregressive Unit Root." *Econometrica* 64(4) (July, 1996): 813–836.

Engle, Robert F., and C. W. J. Granger. 1987. "Co-Integration and Error Correction: Representation, Estimation, and Testing." *Econometrica* 55(2): 251. http://doi.org/10.2307/ 1913236.

Granger, C. W. J., and P. Newbold. 1974. "Spurious Regressions in Econometrics." *Journal of Econometrics* 2(2): 111–120. http://doi.org/10.1016/0304-4076(74)90034-7.

Gurloveleen, K., and B. S. Bhatia. 2016. "An Impact of Macroeconomic Variables on the Functioning of Indian Stock Market: A Study of Manufacturing Firms of BSE 500." *Journal of Stock & Forex Trading* 05(01). http://doi.org/10.4172/2168-9458.1000160.

Handagama, Sandali. 2020. Coin Desk. https://www.coindesk.com/markets/2020/06/11/ coca-cola-distributor-offers-bitcoin-payment-options-for-aussie-vending-machines/.

Haqqi, Ty. 2021. 15 Biggest Companies that Bitcoin. Yahoo Finance. February 18. https:// finance.yahoo.com/news/15-biggest-companies-accept-bitcoin-165115491.html.

Jain, S. 2022. "Did Elon Musk sell his Bitcoin? No. Tesla CEO explains why his company sold 10% of its holding." *Financial Express*. https://www.financialexpress.com/market/ did-elon-musk-sell-his-bitcoin-no-tesla-ceo-explains-why-his-company-sold-10-of-its-holding/2241096/.

Johansen, S. 1988. "Statistical Analysis of Cointegration Vectors". *Journal of Economic Dynamics and Control* 12: 231–254.

Kordestani, A., N. Pashkevich, P. Oghazi, M. Sahamkhadam, and V. Sohrabpour. 2022. "Effects of the COVID-19 Pandemic on Stock Price Performance of Blockchain-based Companies." *Ekonomska Istrazivanja* 35: 3206–3224. https://doi.org/10.1080/13316 77X.2021.1986676.

Kwiatkowski, D., Phillips, P.C.B., Schmidt, P. and Shin, Y. 1992. "Testing the Null Hypothesis of Stationary Against the Alternative of a Unit Root." *Journal of Econometrics* 54(1–3): 159–178.

Mariana, C. D., I. A. Ekaputra, and Z. A. Husodo. 2020. "Are Bitcoin and Ethereum Safe Havens for Stocks During the COVID-19 Pandemic?" *Finance Research Letters* 38(3): 101798. http://doi.org/10.1016/j.frl.2020.101798.

Mittal, A. & Manikandan, A. 2021. "Cryptocurrency payments slowly gain ground in India." *The Economic Times.* https://economictimes.indiatimes.com/tech/technology/cryptocurrency-gains-ground-as-a-payment-method-in-india/articleshow/86732844.cms.

Mnif, E., A. Jarboui, and K. Mouakhar. 2020. "How the Cryptocurrency Market Has Performed During COVID 19?" A Multifractal Analysis of Finance Research Letters 36: 101647.

Mubarak, M. and Manjunath, H. 2021. "A Study on Cryptocurrency in India". *ResearchGate* 8: 435–444.

News, Business, and Cryptocurrency News. 2021. "Wondering What You Can Buy with Cryptocurrency in India? Read This—Times of India." *The Times of India.* https:// timesofindia.indiatimes.com/business/cryptocurrency/wondering-what-you-can-buy-with-cryptocurrency-in-india-read-this/articleshow/85390355.cms.

N.G, S. and Perron, P. 2001. "Lag Length Selection and the Construction of Unit Root Tests with Food and Power." *Econometrica* 69(6) (November, 2001): 1519–1554.

Ossinger, J. 2021. Crypto World Hits \$3 Trillion Market Cap as Ether, Bitcoin Gain. Bloomberg. https://www.bloomberg.com/news/articles/2021-11-08/crypto-world-hits-3-trillion-market-cap-as-ether-bitcoin-gain

Perkins, David W. 2020. "Cryptocurrency: The Economics of Money and Selected Policy Issues." Congressional Research Service (CRS Report). R45427: Version 3. UPDATED: 1–27.

Phillips, P.C.B. and Perron, P. 1988. "Testing for a unit root in a time series regression." *Biometrika* 335–346.

Rao, B. "Cointegration for the Applied Economist". *Economics and Finance* (R0). Published by Palgrave Macmillan London. ISBN: 978-1-4039-9614-5. XIX, 260.

Raphael A., Giulio C. and Jon F. 2020. "Covid-19, cash, and the future of payments." *BIS Bulletin* 3: 1–7.

Vukovic, D., Maiti, M., Grubisic, Z., Grigorieva, E.M., and Frommel, M. 2021. Covid-19 Pandemic : Is the Crypto Market a safe Haven? The impact of the First Wave. *Sustainability* 13(15): 1–17.

Wijk, D. van. "What can be expected from the Bitcoin." (2013). Thesis.

Yang, Y. and Zhao, Z. 2020. "Quantile nonlinear unit root test with covariates and an application to the PPP hypothesis". *Econometric Modelling* 93: 728–736.

Yarovaya L., Matkovskyy R., Jalan A. "The effects of a 'black swan' event (COVID-19) on herding behaviour in cryptocurrency markets: Evidence from cryptocurrency USD, EUR, JPY and KRW markets." *Journal of International Financial Markets, Institutions and Money* 75(4): 101321. DOI:10.1016/j.intfin.2021.101321.

Chapter 9

Social Media and the COVID-19 Pandemic: Boons and Banes

Rajashree Chaurasia and Udayan Ghose

Content

DOI: 10.1201/9781003328438-9

9.1 Introduction

We are all too familiar with the term "social media" as we use a multitude of such applications on a daily basis, like Twitter, Facebook, WhatsApp, Reddit, Weibo, LinkedIn, etc. Social media refers to the collection of interactive applications that are used to share ideas, thoughts, opinions, information, interests, etc. through the Internet. In this rapidly changing digital era, social media has become an essential means of communication among us and also a major source of information about the latest happenings around us. This has been made possible not only with the advent of affordable smartphone technology but also with an economical and fast internet connection. According to (Hanlon & Bullock, 2021), a whopping 4.55 billion active social media users exist as of October 2021, compared to 4.48 billion in July 2021 (Kemp, July 2021; Kemp, Oct 2021) and 4.2 billion users in January 2021 (Statista Anon., 2021). There is an increasing trend (the annual average increase being approximately 10%) every few months as more and more people are connecting through social media, of all age groups, either through smartphones or via other means. The top five social media platforms (see Figure 9.1) are Facebook, YouTube, WhatsApp, Instagram, and Facebook Messenger as of July 2021 (Hanlon & Bullock, 2021). Mobile users alone constitute about two-thirds of the world's total population, and every unique internet user spends around two hours every day on seven different social media platforms every month on average (Hanlon & Bullock, 2021).

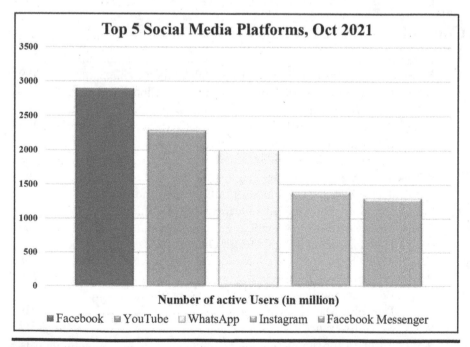

Figure 9.1   The top five social media platforms worldwide as of October 2021 (Statista, Anon., 2021).

Generally speaking, social media has had an immense impact on the global population, which is both good and bad. A plethora of research articles can be found online that present the positive and/or negative effects of social media in varied fields of study, ranging from behavioral sciences to politics. Often, one can find articles where cyberbullying or trolling has led to the deterioration of the mental health of individuals. Rumormongering, hate speeches, social media ranting, leaking private information, etc. are only some of the abuses in social media. At the same time, social media is effectively being used to expand the reach of several businesses, connect individuals over great distances, share information and updates, market products, learn online, etc. However, in this review, we will focus on the good and bad influences of social media with regard to the current pandemic situation being faced by the global population.

In December 2019, the world experienced a never-before-seen crisis in the form of a mutated coronavirus that is called SARS-CoV-2 (severe acute respiratory syndrome coronavirus 2), which caused humans to suffer from flulike symptoms similar to the 2003 outbreak of the SARS (severe acute respiratory syndrome) virus. Just like SARS, SARS-CoV-2 is a *Betacoronavirus* that causes a viral lung infection in humans. And just like SARS, this virus originated in China, but unfortunately, and unlike SARS, it spread so terribly across the globe that it quickly attained the status of a pandemic from an epidemic. The disease associated with this new virus is termed COVID-19 (coronavirus disease 19) by the WHO (World Health Organization, Anon., 2021) and is much more infectious and transmissible than SARS. As of January 1, 2022, the worldwide tally for coronavirus cases is more than 288 million and counting (Worldometer, Anon., 2022). The worldwide tally for deaths from COVID-19 is more than 5.45 million as of January 1, 2022 (Worldometer, Anon., 2022). Figure 9.2 shows the cumulative COVID-19 case count per million population on a global scale as of December 31, 2021 (Our World in Data, Anon., 2022). The virus is still mutating, and a new variant called Omicron has recently been identified in South Africa, which is being said to be much more infectious and transmissible (Bloomberg, 2021) than the deadly Delta variant that is still wreaking havoc around the globe. Figure 9.3 displays the percentage of Omicron COVID-19 cases out of the total number of sequences analyzed biweekly as of December 31, 2021 (Our World in Data, Anon., 2022) on the world map. Figure 9.4 shows the rapid rise in the share of this highly transmissible variant out of the sequences analyzed biweekly for the UK, USA, Canada, India, Germany, France, Denmark, and South Africa from October 18, 2021, to December 27, 2021 (Our World in Data, Anon., 2022).

The destructiveness of this pandemic called for various containment and social distancing policies to be strictly enforced, and nationwide lockdowns that lasted many months at a stretch were put in place to reduce transmission and infection. According to a news article (Sandford, 2020), by the beginning of April 2020, more than 3.9 billion people were ordered to stay at home in 90 countries, which amount to half of the world's population being on lockdown. These curfews included preventing people from traveling locally and internationally, closing all public places, restricting public transport, restricting any type of public gathering, closing all

Cumulative confirmed COVID-19 cases per million people, Dec 31, 2021
Due to limited testing, the number of confirmed cases is lower than the true number of infections.

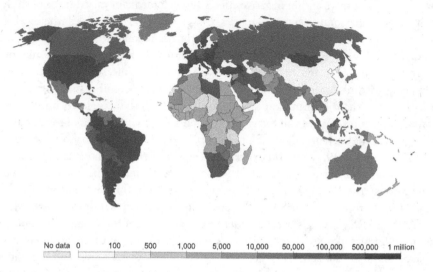

No data 0   100   500   1,000   5,000   10,000   50,000   100,000 500,000 1 million

Source: Johns Hopkins University CSSE COVID-19 Data   CC BY

Figure 9.2   World map displaying the cumulative COVID-19 confirmed cases as of January 1, 2022 (Our World in Data, Anon., 2022).

Share of SARS-CoV-2 sequences that are the omicron variant, Dec 31, 2021
Share of omicron variant in all analyzed sequences in the preceding two weeks.

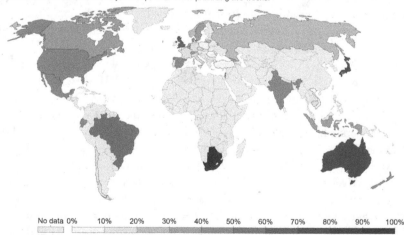

No data 0%   10%   20%   30%   40%   50%   60%   70%   80%   90%   100%

Source: CoVariants.org and GISAID   CC BY
Note: This share may not reflect the complete breakdown of cases, since only a fraction of all cases are sequenced. Recently-discovered or
actively-monitored variants may be overrepresented, as suspected cases of these variants are likely to be sequenced preferentially or faster than
other cases.

Figure 9.3   World map showing the share of the Omicron variant in the biweekly analysis of Sars-CoV-2 sequences as of December 31, 2021 (Our World in Data, Anon., 2022).

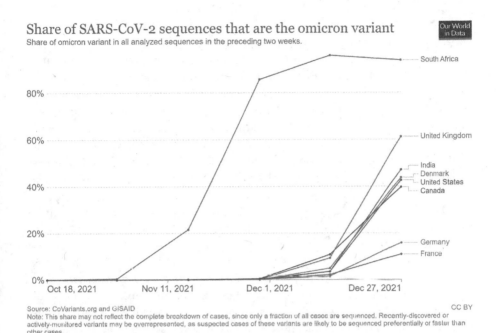

Share of SARS-CoV-2 sequences that are the omicron variant

Share of omicron variant in all analyzed sequences in the preceding two weeks.

Source: CoVariants.org and GISAID

Note: This share may not reflect the complete breakdown of cases, since only a fraction of all cases are sequenced. Recently-discovered or actively-monitored variants may be overrepresented, as suspected cases of these variants are likely to be sequenced preferentially or faster than other cases.

CC BY

Figure 9.4   The rapid increase in the percentage of Omicron variant out of the analyzed sequences from October 18, 2021, to December 27, 2021, on a biweekly basis for South Africa, the UK, India, Denmark, the USA, Canada, Germany, and France (Our World in Data, Anon., 2022).

educational institutions and government offices, closing corporate organizations, etc. As a result of these lockdowns and due to COVID-19, social media usage increased tremendously for a multitude of reasons.

Social media platforms provided instant updates and important information from official accounts of government organizations, departments, and personnel. It also provided firsthand experiences from people suffering from COVID-19 through videos, messages, blogs, images, etc. Medical professionals were also able to help more people through social media by giving guidance, trashing rumors and myths associated with this disease, teleconsultations, spreading awareness, encouraging people to vaccinate, etc. But with information emerges misinformation and rumormongering, discrimination, fear, and panic. Anything bad usually tends to spread faster than anything good in such scenarios because people are stuck inside their homes, and their only sources of information being social and mass media, they believe bad news more fervently.

Social media has a vast and global reach, and such as the rate of infection, the spread of information is also exponential in nature. This is both good and bad in the sense that if accurate information is responsibly shared, it can prepare and help people in numerous ways. On the other hand, it can cause chaos if false or misleading information is circulated without much thought. Therefore, in such emergencies, information needs to be regulated and well accounted for before being disseminated to the masses. During the current pandemic, too, we have encountered numerous cases of good and bad information disseminating throughout the masses. Reliable information coming from authorized personnel is very important so that there is no void left for misinterpretation. But many times, we see that the government or the authorities give vague or incomplete answers to questions posed, making it easier for the masses to make their assumptions in an attempt to fill that void, giving rise to rumor. Many such rumors spread like wildfire through the people on such sensitive issues as vaccination effectiveness, social distancing policies, wearing of masks, preventive measures, possible treatments, etc.

Data from social media platforms can also be used for analysis and mining trends and patterns. A lot of research has been done in this field using various data-mining techniques like classification and clustering, as well as machine learning and deep learning algorithms. Useful insights have been gained from such analyses in varied application areas. However, breach of privacy, data-ownership issues, and misuse of data are some of the pitfalls. Many research publishing organizations have made all data and research articles open access to expedite the battle against COVID-19. This is a favorable move as it has helped researchers across the world to access research articles, genomic data, information on clinical trials, etc. Remote collaboration among researchers has also increased through video conferencing using social media platforms.

Social media platforms are also being used for sharing thoughts and opinions through group discussions on various platforms. Support groups during the pandemic grew in large numbers, which offered various kinds of assistance to the general public like consultations with medical professionals, basic amenities, medicines and other pharmaceutical supplies, ambulance services, lab-testing information, vaccination sites, moral support, etc. People came together to help each other out in this time of crisis, which inculcated a sense of brotherhood. However, we also saw thousands of cases of cyberbullying, fraud, trolling, discrimination, etc. Individuals with malicious intent took advantage of the crisis, and many cases of financial and services fraud came to light when victims of such fraud shared their experiences and warned others through social media. Many were trolled or bullied for speaking about vaccinations, government policies, guidelines issued, social distancing, and wearing masks, while others were discriminated against based on their choices and opinions.

Social media also helped the government in enforcing social distancing guidelines and other COVID-19 protocols that were put in place to reduce the chances of transmission. Where these protocols were being violated, people posted images and videos of such incidences and other lapses on various social media platforms that went viral within a short frame of time. This led to the sensitization of the people as well as the authorities toward following the COVID-19 protocols more effectively and ensuring that others follow the protocols too.

Social media was also used by researchers and the government alike to gauge the mindset of the general public through surveys and polls posted on different platforms. Questionnaires regarding the effectiveness of policies and guidelines, the vaccination status and health of individuals, COVID-19 diagnostic tests, reporting of symptoms, etc. were posted, and data from these and other surveys were used to analyze public opinion, which further assisted in the formation of new policies and methods of enforcement.

Social media was extensively used to advertise and market products and services effectively across business sectors. During COVID-19, lockdowns and movement restrictions resulted in several industries like restaurants, bars, cafés, spas, salons, hotels, gyms, shopping districts, malls, amusement parks, etc. closing down temporarily or permanently due to many reasons. The economy suffered huge losses, and only businesses that were able to change their marketing and manufacturing strategies have been able to survive and expand. Businesses that switched to social media for advertising not only their products and services but also to communicate their reliable news, information, and contribution during the pandemic were able to retain the trust of their existing consumers and expand their customer base. The closure of schools, colleges, universities, and other training institutions has also resulted in a shift from face-to-face communication and teaching to virtual online teaching and learning. Social media became a great tool for communication between students and their faculty, researchers and their collaborators, teachers and learners, and businesses and their consumers.

In the following sections, we will be looking at all these aspects and more in detail. In section two of this chapter, we will be discussing the positive impact of social media in this pandemic situation concerning some of the important research that has been done to mine useful insights as well as other ways in which social media has benefitted mankind during COVID-19. In section three, we will also look at the negative aspects of social media in detail, and lastly, in section four, we will discuss how, in the future, social media may be utilized in a controlled manner to aid us in such crises, at the same time, minimizing its negative effects.

9.2 Positive Impact of Social Media during COVID-19

In Tsao et al. (2021), 81 studies concerning the usage of social media from the beginning of the pandemic in 2019 to November 2020 were studied, and some central themes categorizing these articles were identified. Survey of public opinions, infodemics, mental health, COVID-19 trends prediction, investigation of government response to the pandemic, and evaluation of health information quality in educational videos were the major areas that these articles were classified under. In Goel and Gupta (2020) and Wajahat Hussain (2020), a brief overview of the advantages and disadvantages of social media's impact on COVID-19 was given. In this section, we will throw light on how social media has been put to good use

Figure 9.5 Major areas of positive social media impact during the pandemic.

in helping us fight this pandemic. The following subsections discuss in detail each of the major areas where social media has had a positive influence (see Figure 9.5).

9.2.1 Positive Dissemination of Information at a Global Scale

Social media platforms have helped the general public in sustaining communication with their loved ones to cut loneliness and boredom during the pandemic. The global and faster reach of the social media platforms have aided in the rapid dissemination of accurate information regarding COVID-19 protocols, symptoms, and other related information about the COVID-19 disease; preventive measures; management of symptoms; home quarantine; etc. For instance, an infographic was circulated via Twitter and WeChat on the principles of airway management focusing on infection control for staff and patient safety (Chan et al., 2020). The infographic became viral, and many countries requested translations and context-specific modifications that helped thousands of healthcare professionals manage symptoms and infection spread.

In a study on digital crisis interaction (Volkmer, 2021), the importance of social media influencers as a means of communicating vital information through the network has been presented. The study has been conducted in 24 countries, and it has been found that these influencers who participated in this global survey tend to have a good number of followers on average. Top-level influencers who have a following of more than a million users are pursued by major companies for marketing purposes. Market research organizations hire top, middle, and nano influencers for different purposes. Likewise, during the pandemic, too, these influencers have been instrumental in communicating information about government policies, guidelines, protocols, COVID-19 restrictions, the need for vaccination, as well as such issues relating to emotional health within their network of followers. The governments of the UK, Finland, Indonesia, Australia, India, etc. have included social media influencers to encourage compliance with public health directives and restrictions (Volkmer, 2021). Not only influencers but also regular social media users with a small community also hold the power to spread information. These users share images or videos with their immediate community, which can reach a large number of people through "cascading" interactions. Cascading interactions mean that information travels from one set of followers to other communities and then others, still, due to continuous connections (Volkmer, 2021).

Since the start of the pandemic, people took to social media to discuss their symptoms and worries and share their experiences and advice. A large number of WhatsApp groups were created to help the needy in every possible way. For instance, in India, during the peak of the deadly second wave of the pandemic in 2020, as the official channels of assistance yielded under the pressure of too many calls for help, victims and their families frantically started sending out appeals and SOS messages on Twitter, WhatsApp, Facebook Messenger, or any other social media platform they could use. Responders acted quickly, arranging for hospital beds, medicines, blood plasma, oxygen cylinders, and concentrators, providing meals and other essential services (Saluja, 2021). Individuals who were infected with COVID-19 also shared their experiences on YouTube, Instagram, Facebook, etc. from home quarantine and other government quarantine facilities and hospitals. Healthcare professionals who were constantly working on the front posted many videos about the disease and its spread, methods of managing the symptoms at home, the importance of maintaining social distancing and wearing masks, etc., reducing the stigma and busting some myths around this new disease. Sharing procedures about treatment, personal protection equipment, or even proposals for impartial allocation in scarce medical resource settings became the new standard (González-Padilla & Tortolero-Blanco, 2020).

Sharing scientific information, research articles, results of a clinical trial, etc. are very much essential in times of a health crisis. Social media has increased the downloads and citations of research articles on COVID-19 and the coronaviruses.

The abundance of data from social media platforms has helped researchers develop machine learning techniques to train neural network models for effective and efficient prediction, knowledge mining, and analysis. Publishing companies have made all such research articles open access for all, which has further accelerated research in this direction. Articles related to the pandemic have seen reduced peer-review timelines, which have dropped from months to days or weeks. The possibility of arranging collaborative research projects, surveys, and multicenter studies has multiplied during the pandemic. Recruitment to many clinical trials has been promoted via Twitter, Facebook, WhatsApp, etc. Figure 9.6 shows the most popular types of content that were shared by millennials and Gen Z (Generation Z or Zoomers) around the globe over social media platforms according to a large-scale online survey conducted between late 2020 and

Figure 9.6   The most popular content shared by millennials and Gen Z around the globe during the pandemic (based on Anon., 2022).

early 2021 (Anon., 2022). Reliable scientific articles and information topped the charts with about 44% of the respondents sharing responsibly via social media handles.

Responsible sharing of all kinds of reliable and accurate information has therefore aided many in dealing with the afflictions of this crisis we are facing. By strengthening such channels of communication, we can aim to effectually curtail future catastrophes of such nature.

9.2.2 Psychological and Other Support

During the lockdown, people had limited means of communication with friends and family. The lack of physical contact caused increased levels of anxiety among the general public. The only solace was through social media applications like WhatsApp, Weibo, Facebook Messenger, etc., which allowed the population to connect with their loved ones virtually. This, in turn, helped many people overcome stress and negative emotions during the pandemic (Zhong, Jiang et al., 2020; Cheng et al., 2020; Saha et al., 2020).

Social media gave us the capability to share experiences with family and friends to help us fight both physical and emotional separation (Lisitsa et al., 2020; Saltzman et al., 2020). At the same time, it also reminded us that we're all in this together, thereby creating a sense of unity among society. For example, those who could not be there with their loved ones in this crisis due to travel restrictions and other factors got help through social media for their family members who needed assistance. Many, like the elderly, people with disabilities, working parents who could not get childcare facilities, children who lost their parents to the pandemic, and those who lost their jobs and businesses, were experiencing challenging circumstances. Communities joined forces to support such individuals by crowdfunding and sharing fundraisers with large audiences through social media. As many people were facing challenging situations during the pandemic, cases of depression, stress, and anxiety increased manifold. Professional psychological guidance was also available through video-conferencing on various platforms like Zoom, Google Meet, Skype, WhatsApp, etc. People found moral and emotional support through social media groups in addition to other needs during the crisis, which helped them overcome some of the negative emotions. Social media can also be used for peer-based crowd-sourcing for offering solutions to psychological anxiety and depression related to COVID-19 (Drouin et al., 2020). Figure 9.7 presents a global snapshot of a large-scale as-is survey (Kemp, July 2020) indicating how digital media has helped people cope with pandemic-related challenges. The report also includes other reports about COVID-19.

Hence, social media provided not only emotional help and moral support but also supplied basic amenities like food, water, emergency services, financial help, medications, transportation, ambulance, life support, care services, etc.

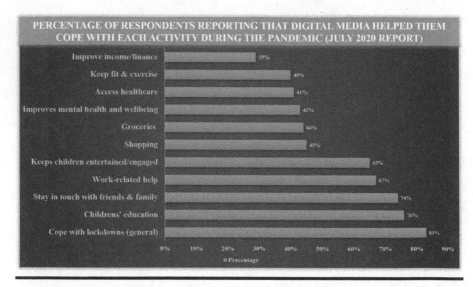

Figure 9.7 **How digital media helped people cope with the pandemic-related challenges (based on Kemp, July 2020).**

9.2.3 Prediction of COVID-19 Trends and Characteristics

According to Li et al. (2020), web searches and social media data regarding the COVID-19 outbreak peaked almost two weeks before the actual peak of daily infections in China. In the study conducted by Li et al. (Li et al., 2020), the authors present a possible way of predicting COVID-19 trends using social media posts and internet search data from Weibo, Baidu Index, and Google Trends. They performed a correlation analysis on searches and posts with the terms "coronavirus" and "pneumonia" and showed that there was a strong lag correlation of 8–12 days for lab-confirmed cases and 6–8 days for suspected cases. In another study (Huang et al., 2020), Huang et al. conducted a data-mining analysis on the Weibo social media platform in China to mine the epidemiological characteristics of lab-confirmed and suspected cases of COVID-19. They observed that most of the patients that sought help through social media in China at the beginning of the outbreak were mostly the elderly who showed symptoms of fever and chest opacities in chest tomography (CT) scans. They also noted that the distance of these families from their designated hospitals was large, and due to the stringent lockdown enforced in China, they tried seeking assistance through social media. Liu et al. (Liu et al., 2020) also used posts from Sina Weibo to analyze the characteristics of patients with COVID-19. They found that old age, scattered distribution, and low blood-oxygen levels are aspects that can help health professionals to detect patients with COVID-19 who have a weak diagnosis. Their study advocates that information from social media can be all-inclusive, instantaneous, and instructive in diagnosing COVID-19. Peng et al. (Peng et al., 2020) studied Weibo posts using spatiotemporal, kernel density, and regression analyses. They observed three stages of primary COVID-19 transmission in Wuhan—scattered cases, community spread, and full-fledged epidemic. They further noted that more than half of the help seekers on Weibo were elderly people, which confirms that the elderly were a high-risk group during the epidemic in China.

Several such research studies have since been carried out, which analyze social media data in numerous ways to predict several aspects of the pandemic (Figure 9.8). In Golder et al. (2020), like the study of Huang et al. (Huang et al., 2020), Golder et al. have analyzed Twitter data to predict the outbreak in the UK. Their method was based on a previous study done for the USA by Klein et al. (Klein et al., 2020) using Twitter posts. Both studies point to the fact that social media posts can be a good indicator of possible outbreaks with a heads-up of about one to two weeks before official counts. Similarly, Weibo posts have been used to detect the possible rise in infected cases up to 14 days ahead of official records (Shen et al., 2020). In O'Leary and Storey (2020), O'Leary et al. present a model to forecast the number of infections and deaths in the USA based on the number of Google searches, tweets on Twitter, and Wikipedia page views. Qin et al. (Qin et al., 2020) have used a Social Media Search Index (SMSI) for cough, fever, chest distress, coronavirus, and pneumonia to predict the number of cases using the subset selection method. Their findings suggest that SMSI can be detected 6–9 days earlier than the fresh suspected cases. In another recent study (Yousefinaghani et al., 2021) focusing on the USA and Canada, the authors used Twitter and Google Trends

Figure 9.8   Social media content analysis reveals that COVID-19 case trends can be predicted with sufficient accuracy up to two weeks in advance.

data after employing filters for symptoms and preventive measures to comprehend the delay between the warning signs and actual epidemic waves. They were able to detect up to 83% of initial waves 7 days before the actual outbreak for Canada and 100% of initial waves about 2–6 days beforehand for the USA. They were also able to identify up to 78% of second waves in the USA states that had not previously experienced an initial wave, 7–14 days in advance. In addition, they reported that fever and cough were the most significant symptoms in detecting cases in the US.

Many studies utilize machine learning and deep learning techniques to mine important insights regarding the COVID-19 pandemic from social media messages and posts. In one such study (Mackey et al., 2020), the authors used unsupervised machine learning techniques for the classification of symptoms and experiences via messages on Twitter. During the peak of the first and second waves of the pandemic, when caseloads increased to many lakhs worldwide, testing for COVID-19 was not possible for numerous people due to testing kit shortages, long queues, and other restrictions and protocols. In the absence of such testing confirmation, accurate estimates of infected cases were not done, which resulted in a lot of under-reporting. The authors of this study hope that such data-mining analyses of social media posts can help inform the authorities of a probable outbreak in the future as a form of "infoveillance." In (Chew et al., 2021), a deep learning hybrid model has been employed on COVID-19 time series data collected from a humongous quantity of Twitter posts to forecast the day-to-day increase in confirmed COVID-19 cases on a global scale. By mining the psychological responses to the pandemic, the authors were able to develop an accurate predictive model. Peng et al. (Peng et al., 2021) have used data of the previous daily incidence and Google Trends search data from 215 nations to predict the number of confirmed cases one week ahead. They have employed many machine learning techniques like random forest regression analysis, classification, and clustering, to accurately predict new infections one week in advance for these 215 countries.

Machine learning and deep learning methodologies show a lot of promise for prediction studies in pandemic situations as a large volume of data in the form of social media posts across various platforms is available to train models for accurate prediction.

9.2.4 Government Policy Enforcement

During this pandemic, social media has been extensively used by both the public as well as government stakeholders and health professionals to disseminate information regarding risks, prevention, social distancing, policies, guidelines, etc. Several global health authorities like the World Health Organization (WHO), National Institute of Health (NIH), and Center for Disease Control (CDC) have official Twitter handles. In a study by Wang et al. (Wang et al., 2021), data mining and dynamic network analysis techniques have been employed to assess Twitter messages during the early stages of the pandemic to investigate crisis communication concerning post categories, interaction adequacy, promptness, conformity, consistency, and synchronization. Sixteen message types have been identified, viz strategies and guidance recommended by health agencies, executive orders, situational information, closure and opening messages of critical services, operations, clarifications, rumor and scam management, volunteering and donations, recruitment, external resources, guidance on other ailments and occurrences, event schedules and agendas, and finally, intelligence gathering. The dynamic network analysis showed amplified levels of connectivity and synchronization among the government and health organizations during the beginning of the pandemic in the USA. Some inconsistencies have also been identified in some categories of messages, but the overall results show that for effective information spread, the role of the government and health agencies is very important in times of crisis when rumors can easily overtake and overshadow reliable information through social media circulation. In a similar study (Sutton et al., 2020), retransmission of Twitter posts by public agencies in the USA has been evaluated for style, content, and context in rapidly changing pandemic situations. They conclude that the general public is likely to retransmit a wide range of practical information regarding the health impacts of COVID-19, protective action measures, and the progress of the pandemic itself. In (Rufai & Bunce, 2020), Rufai and Bunce analyze the role of Twitter in response to COVID-19 when used by Group of Seven (G7) world leaders. They found that eight out of nine G7 leaders had an active Twitter account, and more than 80% of their viral tweets were classified as being informative, about half of which had reliable links to government sources. In (Abd-Alrazaq et al., 2020), various natural language processing (NLP) and supervised machine learning methods were used to classify information related to COVID-19 from Weibo posts into eight categories, viz caution and advice, notifications, donations, emotional support, help-seeking, criticizing, antirumor, and nonsituational. Retransmission of all these categories was also evaluated by looking at many factors and followers. Another study (Merkley et al., 2020) highlights the importance of elites and political party members in Canada in the dissemination of reliable information and in influencing the general public by their social media posts on Twitter. The study indicates that all party members in Canada forcefully stressed the need for social distancing and appropriate hygiene methods, like washing hands frequently and avoiding touching one's face. Additionally, no party-member tweets contained any misinformation or disinformation, and none showed that public concern about COVID-19 was inflated. Basch et al. present in their study (Basch et al., 2020) that YouTube is a highly effective means of communication and mobilization of the people to change their attitudes in order to alleviate community transmission of COVID-19. Videos related to prevention behaviors recommended by the US Centers for Disease Control and Prevention and others gained popularity during the pandemic. These videos were collectively viewed more than 350 million times and had a global reach. Videos related to such preventive behaviors as staying at home, handwashing, avoiding close contact with people, using a face mask, cleaning, disinfection, etc. garnered millions of views worldwide.

The government and health authorities must themselves introduce strong and reliable networks of communication for the effective dissemination of protocols, guidelines, and preventive measures. Social media influencers, elites, political party members, entertainers, and medical professionals having a large following can further accelerate the distribution of important information and, at the same time, can sensitize the community to follow procedures and respect protocols. The government also needs to involve its people in the process of policy and decision-making, more so in times of crisis, so that the people feel that their voices and concerns are being heard.

9.2.5 Gauging Public Attitude

Social media gives us an immense opportunity to directly communicate with the general public and also provides an insight into the attitudes, opinions, and concerns of the people. Figure 9.9 presents the top concerns millennials and Zoomers reported during the pandemic (Anon., 2022). Several studies have been carried out to gauge the public ideology related to the pandemic. Such insights are very useful for building surveillance systems through the monitoring of social media. It also gives the authorities a chance to quell fake news and misinformation. Some of the important research in this direction is discussed briefly as follows.

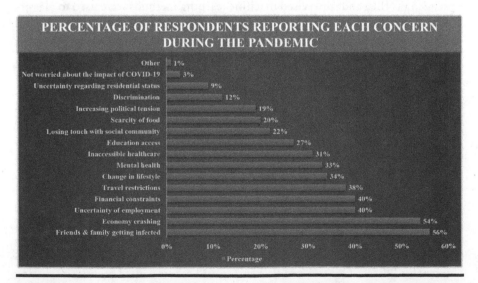

Figure 9.9   The top concerns reported by millennials and Gen Z during the pandemic (based on Anon., 2022).

In (Abd-Alrazaq et al., 2020), Twitter posts have been analyzed using unigrams and bigrams employing sentiment analysis for gauging the concerns of the people during the pandemic. Four major themes were identified, namely virus origins, impact on people, sources of the virus, and mitigation strategies. Their analysis revealed that out of the 12 categories of tweets, 10 showed positive sentiment and 2 (fatalities and racism) showed negative sentiment. Arpaci et al. (Arpaci et al., 2020) studied textual posts on Twitter to understand the trend of public attitude. They found that extensive attention was given to the topics related to the COVID-19 pandemic using evolutionary clustering. They observed that high-occurrence words such as "death," "test," "spread," and "lockdown" suggested that people were fearful of getting sick and of dying due to COVID-19. The results also showed that people agreed to stay at home and follow social distancing protocols due to this fear. In another study on sentiment analysis (Boon-Itt & Skunkan, 2020), the authors applied data mining to Twitter data for topic modeling to identify the most common topics of discussion during COVID-19. The results indicate that three core topics emerged concerning public awareness and apprehension and showed that people had a negative outlook toward the pandemic. Such findings can help the government and health officials to alleviate these concerns among the community and spread greater awareness. A study of sentiment analysis during the lockdown in India (Das & Dutta, 2020) based on mining Twitter messages studied the progression of public opinion concerning the crisis in the country. The results showed a more positive sentiment among people for corpus-level simple emotional analysis and only slightly more positive than negative for the more complex individual-level sentiment analysis. A similar study on topic tracking through Twitter data analysis to gauge the mindset of the public in Italy can be found in (De Santis et al., 2020). An analysis of public opinion in China through the evaluation of Sina Weibo data for topic modeling and retransmission rate of messages on similar formats can be found in (Yin et al., 2020). A study on the gendered impact of COVID-19 (Al-Rawi et al., 2020) from Twitter posts using hashtags #Covid-19 and #Covid19 recognized five main themes, viz fear of infection and death, health concerns, unemployment, and financial issues, admiration for frontline workers, and use of exclusive gendered emojis. The findings indicate that the bulk of emojis was overwhelmingly optimistic in nature among the different genders, but there were also many differences when other topics from the major themes were discussed. One research paper (Chen et al., 2020) particularly focuses on how the Chinese government deployed social media for citizen engagement to understand public concerns and minimize panic, fear, and anxiety. Through dialogic loops, citizens felt positively involved in public affairs, which resulted in strengthening trust between the government and the public. In K (2020), Reddit news and streaming articles have been analyzed using machine learning to classify sentiment into three classes—positive, negative, and neutral. Results showed that 50% of Reddit articles were neutral, 22% were positive, and about 28% were negative. Another study (Gozzi et al., 2020) characterizes media coverage and the collective internet response to the COVID-19 pandemic in four countries—Italy, the UK, the USA, and Canada. This study used Wikipedia pages, YouTube videos, and Reddit posts to confirm the crucial role of social and mass media during health emergencies and showed how collective awareness is largely driven by media exposure. It was also observed that information type and quality may have a grave impact on risk awareness and behaviors, which ultimately affect the evolution of the outbreak. Another study (Jelodar et al., 2020) on similar lines analyzed Reddit posts using deep learning models and NLP for thematic evaluation and highlighting the importance of social media in understanding public opinion. Likewise, a global sentiment analysis based on Twitter data (Lwin et al., 2020) showed that emotions sharply changed from fright to rage over the progression of the pandemic, though sorrow and happiness also emerged.

Hence, social media content can be effectively mined to understand the public attitude of the community. Governments should utilize results from such analyses to address the top-level concerns of the public proactively to avoid unforeseen circumstances stemming from the anxiety and exasperations of its citizens.

9.2.6 Social Media Marketing

The COVID-19 pandemic has forced millions of people to stay at home for long periods since late 2019. The increased exposure to social media platforms during this period and the need to purchase basic amenities from home have led to a shift in how consumers interact with businesses and brands. Several businesses have recently felt the need to change the way their products are promoted and proffered, in order to adjust to the overwhelming demand for safe and contactless home delivery. Amid the government restrictions on public movement and closure of several types of businesses like theaters, malls, spas, gyms, salons, cinemas, restaurants, bars, shopping districts, etc. in the face of rising cases of COVID-19 infections, the economy has suffered huge losses. Numerous companies have endured losses or have closed permanently due to debt or other reasons. Employees have been laid off in many cases, and only those businesses that were able to adapt quickly to changing circumstances have survived. In this situation, social media marketing can help promote these brands to increase sales or product engagement and enhance the customer base at the same time. Social media platforms like Facebook, LinkedIn, Instagram, YouTube, TikTok, WhatsApp, etc. can be effectively and extensively used to target consumers of a particular region and age group based on their interests. According to a global survey (Kemp, Oct 2021), social media platforms have been extensively used for researching brands in various flavors like social networks, messaging boards, microblogs, video blogs, etc. (Figure 9.10). Seventy-two percent of respondents have reported that they have used at least one social media platform to find products and services online and compare, review, and evaluate these brands during the pandemic.

A lot of research has been conducted during the pandemic to study the impact of social media in the marketing domain (Mason et al., 2021; Syaifullah

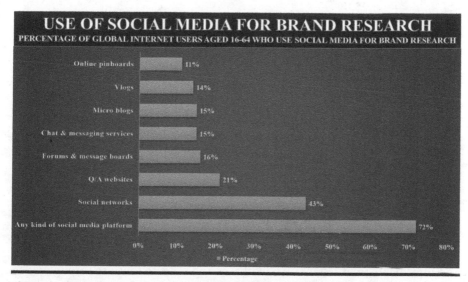

Figure 9.10 Percentage of respondents between 16–64 years of age who used different social media platforms for brand research during the pandemic (based on Kemp, Oct 2021).

et al., 2021; Novitasari, 2021; Hidayati & Yansi, 2020; Patma et al., 2021; Ara Eti et al., 2021). These studies collectively point out that during the pandemic, consumer usage of social media has increased manifold not just for obtaining information and communicating with others but also for finding products and services online and reviewing and purchasing them. In developed and many developing nations, almost all services can be found online. Groceries, medicines and other health supplies, salon services, cleaning and sanitization services, etc. were already available online. However, the COVID-19 pandemic brought many other services to our doorsteps like virtual physician and psychiatric consultations through video calls and conferencing, ready-made and affordable healthy meals for families in need, COVID-19 diagnostic testing, other lab-test services, at-home installation of ICU (Intensive Care Unit) with dedicated healthcare professionals, home delivery of oxygen concentrators, oxygen cylinders, medicines, etc.

Current businesses need to tailor their marketing and advertising strategies to focus on not just increasing sales but also on building and retaining the trust of their consumers during situations of emergency. Brands must enhance their social media presence in such a way that projects empathy and compassion for their employees as well as their customers. A large-scale survey was conducted by (Edelman, 2020) in many countries to study the responsibility brands are expected to display during the pandemic. It was reported that 33% of the respondents stopped using brands that did not respond suitably in response to the crisis people were facing and encouraged others to do so as well. To retain the trust and enhance consumer base, 89%

of respondents felt that businesses need to generate new product lines or tune their existing services so as to help people cope better during the pandemic and offer their services free-of-cost or at marginal prices to high-risk groups, the unemployed, and frontline workers.

There are many take aways for corporations and markets to strengthen their business during the ongoing pandemic. By adapting their advertisements and collaborating with government and relief agencies, businesses can help propagate how they are contributing to the community during the crisis. They can also include important reliable information about the disease and keep their consumers up to date about the latest research, guidelines and protocols, preventive strategies, possible at-home treatments, quarantine instructions, etc. Social media channels are very helpful in this respect especially for businesses that have had to temporarily shut down due to restrictions. For instance, online competitions and events to help people cope with stress, spa, and salon treatments at home by vaccinated professionals, meal creation kits with instructions and ingredients from restaurants, workouts and exercise routines through video from gyms, live virtual theatre play screenings, and concerts, movies and shows released on OTT (over-the-top) platforms, virtual guided tours, etc. can enable community building and provide social assistance to people. Businesses must also be able to operate in a hybrid mode in the future, as well as seamlessly be able to switch between virtual and physical modes in the event of restrictions and permission to open, respectively. According to a global survey (Kemp, July 2020), approximately half of the respondents report that they will be frequently using online facilities for purchasing products and services even after the end of the pandemic (see Figure 9.11).

9.2.7 Technological Paradigm Shift in Education and Research

The closure of educational and other training institutions around the globe has prompted the shifting of focus from face-to-face classroom teaching to virtual classroom teaching via online videoconferencing. While the developed and some developing nations have not encountered major technological infrastructure issues, certain nations and sections of society within developing countries have had to face several challenges in this respect. Even so, this paradigm shift in teaching and learning has paved the way for new avenues. Virtual learning during COVID-19 has been found to be as effective as traditional classroom learning for theoretical and hybrid (both theoretical and practical) courses (Agustinus Palimbong, 2021). Videoconferencing platforms like Zoom, Google Meet, Cisco WebEx, Microsoft Teams, Facebook Live, WhatsApp group video calling, etc. have gained tremendous popularity in education, research, and corporate sectors. Online learning software and apps have also accumulated widespread acclaim due to ease of use and progress tracking features. Learning management systems

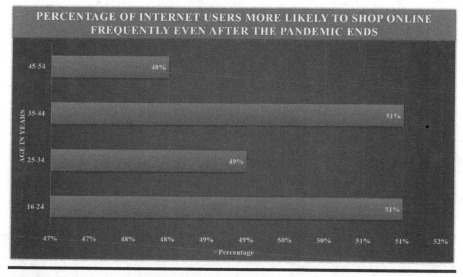

Figure 9.11 Respondents of a global survey report that they expect to purchase products and services online more frequently even after the pandemic ends (based on Kemp, July 2020).

(LMS) are also gaining momentum in the education sector as a formal means of communication between the students and faculty. Online proctoring systems for conducting exams are also being increasingly used in universities and schools. Other technological aspects that have seen tremendous growth during the pandemic are fast internet connectivity providers, touchscreen devices, graphics tablets, cloud storage, and the like. In the absence of a formal LMS, teachers have relied heavily on social media platforms for communicating, teaching, and grading their students. Several studies (Sobaih et al., 2020; Jogezai et al., 2021; Katz & Nandi, 2021; Khan, 2020; Dutta, 2020; Khan et al., 2021; Zarzycka et al., 2021; Adzovie et al., 2020) indicate that platforms like WhatsApp, YouTube, Google Classroom, among others have seen massive growth in educational communication and content. Teachers communicated and shared class content via WhatsApp groups as well as by creating Google Classrooms for courses. Some educators also created YouTube channels for their students. Assignments, exams, and grading of students' test responses were done online through the use of such social media platforms. However, in order to embrace digital education fully, students and teachers have had to get accustomed to working with new technology and software that they might not have been familiar with before the pandemic. Still, online learning has its benefits that have ultimately helped the students to connect to and guide each other in tough times, in addition to taking assistance from the faculty. Social media has been that very tool that the students have already been using and are comfortable with before the pandemic began. Teachers have also shown a positive outlook in using social media for imparting education, not only school and college-level teaching but teaching of any kind have found a place in social media. The pandemic has only caused more and more people to switch to online teaching and learning, be it music, art, crafts, cooking, programming courses, etc. This crisis has also taught the education sector the importance of technology and how to effectively use these tools to impart training.

Similarly, research in many fields has gone online through remote collaboration and communication via videoconferencing. Social media has been used by researchers to advertise upcoming events, conferences, seminars, workshops, calls for papers and chapters, etc. All these events have also adapted to the hybrid or fully online mode where paper presentations, and seminars are given and taken from the comfort of our homes. This has come as a boon to many researchers worldwide, where travel restrictions meant a cancellation of events in physical mode. Research surveys are also conducted online via social media platforms or the circulation of survey questionnaires through social media circles. Online surveys tend to gather a larger number of responses than offline surveys as the reach of online questionnaires is far more than offline surveys as geographical boundaries are not a limitation anymore. Not only this, but most corporations and consultancies have now incorporated a work-from-home policy in order to protect their employees from the risk of infection. Transition to online communication and collaboration is important as technology permits us to easily connect to individuals through a number of different platforms. Online education is here to stay, and it is time that both public and private education sectors realize this fact and prepare themselves and their students for the same.

9.3 Negative Impact of Social Media During COVID-19

With information comes misinformation, which leads to the spread of various negative emotions among the people. Misunderstandings and misinterpretations give rise to rumors that spread rapidly due to the instant and vast global reach of social media platforms, especially WhatsApp, Twitter, Facebook, Instagram, YouTube, etc. Fake news and conspiracy theories fuel anxiety, stress, and depression that create a sense of panic among people. This affects the global sentiment in ways that can cause chaos in the community and destroy the trust people place in their government. The authorities and health organizations should analyze the negative aspects of social media in a bid to improve their communication such that rumors and misinformation have no place to proliferate. In the following subsections, we briefly discuss the damaging role of social media during the current crisis. Figure 9.12 displays the major areas where social media has had a negative impact during the pandemic.

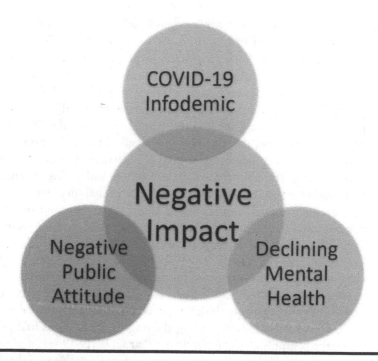

Figure 9.12   Major areas of negative social media impact during the pandemic.

9.3.1 The COVID-19 Infodemic

During the pandemic, besides authentic information, a lot of misinformation and fake news has been circulating through social media channels. This type of situation is known as an infodemic, or information epidemic or information pandemic (WHO, Anon., 2021) and can result in risk-taking behavior, chaos, and loss of trust of the people in health and government authorities. Infodemics also give rise to conspiracy theories and can create panic among the citizens. One such conspiracy birthed due to the infodemic alongside the pandemic was the 5G COVID-19 conspiracy theory. In many countries where 5G was being used, launched, or was on trial runs, a conspiracy theory emerged and quickly spread over social media that 5G was one of the principal causes of coronavirus and also contributed significantly to its transmission. Several audio, video, and image files circulated over the internet linking these two aspects together. In a study (Ahmed et al., 2020) on this conspiracy theory, Twitter content was analyzed through social media graph clustering. Results showed that while 35% of tweets linked both the topics and fueled the conspiracy, 65% of tweets were nonsupporters, and thus, even though the topic garnered high volumes of attention, only some of the users believed in the conspiracy. However, this conspiracy created some panic and radicalization among individuals, and there have been incidences of burning of 5G towers by citizens in some countries out of fear and anger toward the government and health authorities. Another study (Bruns et al., 2020) has analyzed the Facebook CrowdTangle platform for social media analytics to assess the dynamics of this conspiracy into many phases, citing a lot of news and social media articles and posts talking about 5G and COVID-19 and spreading the conspiracy. Another major conspiracy that spread like wildfire was that the pandemic was only a hoax and that the rapid spread of COVID-19 was being exaggerated. To prove the theory, some people went to hospitals to show that hospitals were empty or operating normally. They made videos and uploaded them with the hashtag #FilmYourHospital on YouTube and Twitter (López Seguí et al., 2020). Such conspiracy theories increase the probability that people will disregard government instruction regarding social distancing and other public health intermediations, thus putting themselves and others around them at risk of infection. Advocates of such conspiracy theories were more likely to refuse vaccinations and spread the message that vaccinations were also another scam by the government. Many theories targeted vaccinations saying that the inoculations themselves were manufactured beforehand, and the pandemic situation had been designed specifically to increase the sales of these already developed vaccines. Another frightening conspiracy regarding the origins of the virus had been circulating since the beginning of the pandemic that COVID-19 was a bioweapon and had been engineered by international organizations. It is also said that several countries concocted and spread the lethal coronavirus in Wuhan as part of an economic and psychological warfare against China (Breland, 2020). However, a large number of people from various nations alleged that the virus was man-made as part of a biowarfare program by China against the world (Share Your Story, Anon., 2021; Receive News, Anon., 2020; Feis, 2021).

Many studies have been conducted since the onset of the pandemic that researches the impact of these conspiracies across various social media platforms like Facebook, Twitter, Instagram, WhatsApp, YouTube, etc. across many nations (Brennen et al., 2020; Jones, 2020; Das & Ahmed, 2021; Galhardi et al., 2020; Gallotti et al., 2020; Kouzy et al., 2020; Moscadelli et al., 2020; Rovetta & Bhagavathula, 2020; Uyheng & Carley, 2020). In Islam et al. (2020), a list of rumors, myths, stigma, and conspiracy theories spread by elites, influencers, bots, and ordinary citizens through social media has been given. The pandemic created a lot of stigma around healthcare and other frontline workers out of fear of infection. Healthcare professionals involved in treating COVID-19 in hospitals were discriminated against and harassed in several ways by their neighbors and landlords. Some were even evicted by their landlords from their homes and were physically and emotionally abused and bullied. Elites referred to the virus as the Chinese/Wuhan virus, creating a stigma around people of Chinese origin and Asian descent living in other nations. Chinese students studying abroad were also tormented and harassed. Due to this kind of stigma and fear, people avoided temperature screening at airports and other public places, patients were denied admission in hospitals because they were suspected to be COVID-19 positive, people presented fake COVID-19 negative lab test reports to escape mandatory quarantines and to avoid travel restrictions, etc.

Rumors regarding treatments also spread far and wide as people struggled to alleviate their symptoms at home during home quarantine or due to lack of bed availability in hospitals. Many videos were circulated advertising various natural methods for treating COVID-19 symptoms. Some videos and social media posts also reported that drinking alcohol-based cleaning products could cure or prevent coronavirus infection. Such rumors resulted in disastrous outcomes, and hundreds have lost their lives due to misinformation (Coleman, 2020). In several countries, rumors of nationwide lockdowns during the first wave of the pandemic sparked panic buying so much so that vulnerable groups like the economically weaker sections and the elderly who could not afford to buy groceries, other necessities, and medicines in bulk were not able to get these products because they had gone out of stock (Islam et al., 2021).

Figure 9.13 represents that approximately 85% of internet users feel concerned over the spread of fake news during the pandemic (Anon., 2022). What the world needs in such crises is responsible sharing of reliable information so that such mishaps can be avoided in the future. Government agencies and social media regulations are also needed to limit the spread of fake information and rumors.

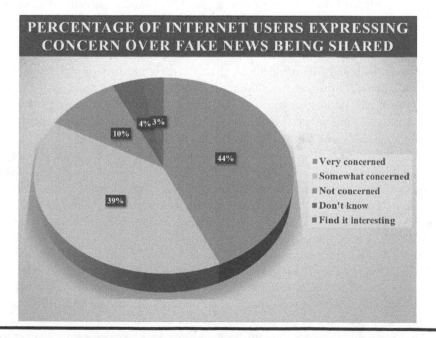

Figure 9.13 **Internet users who express concern over sharing fake news during the pandemic (based on Anon., 2022).**

9.3.2 Deterioration of Mental Health Due to Social Media Exposure

Information overload, disheartening news articles circulating on social media, the coronavirus infodemic, and fake news can cause severe damage to one's psychological health. According to one study, depression and anxiety were the two major mental health disorders that found a prevalence among others during the COVID-19 pandemic (Gao et al., 2020). The declaration of COVID-19 as an epidemic and then later a pandemic sparked a lot of misinformation and negative feeling among the citizens. As social media was the main source of information for people during the lockdowns, many expressed their concerns, encounters, worries, fears, and experiences over social media. In a study of the psychological effects of the epidemic in China (Li et al., 2020) using Weibo data, it was found that the uncertainties and distressing situations created by the disease produced a more negative emotional state of insecurity and mental anxiety than positive feelings. Another study (Ahmad & Murad, 2020) of the impact of social media in Iraq using Facebook data showed that a majority of the people aged between 18 and 35 years were facing heightened mental anxiety. In the USA (Valdez et al., 2020), lockdowns forced the citizens to change their lifestyles, which caused a lot of negative emotion. Mental anxiety also fueled cases of domestic violence, alcohol use, and substance abuse (Capasso et al., 2021). Several similar studies have been carried out (Zhong et al., 2021; Sujarwoto et al., 2021; Haddad et al., 2021; Geirdal et al., 2021; Zhu et al., 2020; Khan et al., 2020) that come to the same conclusions that the mental health of people deteriorated considerably during the pandemic situation. In some extreme cases, depression and anxiety due to fear of stigma, bullying, harassment, cyberbullying, discrimination, and incivility led to suicide. A sharp increase occurred in the number of suicides in India (Pathare et al., 2020; Plus, Anon., 2021; Sahoo et al., 2020; Rana, 2020) during the pandemic, where anxiety and depression were the major driving forces that led people to end their lives. Increased suicide rates were also reported in Nepal, Bangladesh, and China (NewIndianXpress, 2020; Bhuiyan et al., 2020; Lim et al., 2020) due to degraded mental health and adversities faced by people due to the pandemic. Imposed lockdowns amplified domestic violence, closed businesses and educational institutions, increased unemployment, constrained travel, affected the investment sector, endangered the security of financially weaker sections, and burdened governments with colossal debt (Brown, 2020). From February 2020 to April 2020, unemployment in the USA increased to 14.7% from 3.5%, which is a massive jump in such a short period. Economic recession in the US was officially declared in June of that year by the National Bureau of Economic Research (Davidson, 2020). Economic slumps are linked with higher rates of suicide, which in turn may be associated with financial strain due to harsh mitigation strategies during health emergencies (Reger et al., 2020).

Had mental well-being concerns been addressed with priority since the beginning of this health emergency, many of the consequences could have been avoided.

Managing anxiety, depression and panic is essential to managing the transmission of the contagion. Controlling the infodemic is integral to the problem of increased anxiety among the community, which can be mitigated by effective communication with the public and community engagement.

9.3.3 Negative Public Attitude

A sentiment analysis of data from social media platforms can be used to categorize public opinion regarding policies and guidelines for COVID-19 appropriate behavior. Rumors and social stigma also contribute to discrimination, chaos, and negative sentiment buildup. As soon as vaccines for COVID-19 were rolled out, social media platforms were flooded with antivaccination factions trying to discourage people from getting the shot. A machine learning analysis of Facebook content (Sear et al., 2020) studied the antivaccination and provaccination communities at the beginning of the global pandemic and found that the antivaccination faction had garnered a more diverse and more broadly accommodating discussion than their counterparts. Antivaccination communities were very active on social media when the first vaccines were being rolled out for COVID-19. Misinformation about the side effects of the vaccines spread through social media, while some conspiracy theories also emerged regarding the vaccines themselves being fake. People argued that the vaccines were developed first and the pandemic situation was created by pharmaceuticals in collaboration with health authorities and governments to reap profits from the sale of these vaccines. This fear of adverse side effects gave birth to vaccine hesitancy and distrust among people and attracted hostile attitudes wherever these inoculations were made mandatory by governments. Many (Relias Media, Anon., 2021; Wilson & Wiysonge, 2020; Loomba et al., 2021; Karabela et al., 2021; Muric et al., 2021; Mohammed et al., 2021) studies on vaccination intent conclude that due to the spread of misinformation and rumors on social media regarding the safety of coronavirus vaccines, the rate of vaccination dropped significantly. Another negative attitude brought about by the infodemic was the rise of discrimination and stigma around healthcare professionals, other frontline workers, people under quarantine, hospitalized individuals, people of Asian or Chinese descent, etc. due to fear of infection and death from COVID-19. Many social media posts ran the headline of COVID-19 being called the Chinese/Wuhan virus on Twitter, Facebook, Instagram, WhatsApp, etc. (Chang et al., 2020; Budhwani & Sun, 2020; Darling-Hammond et al., 2020). Due to the origin of the pandemic in Wuhan, China, people across the globe blamed the Chinese government and research authorities for leaking the virus from their lab. Hostility against them increased on a global scale that led to racial discrimination of Chinese and Asians living outside their countries. On the other hand, the spread of misinformation about the pandemic being fake or other rumors like brown-skinned or dark-skinned people being more immune to the infection led to a casual attitude among those who believed these rumors. Many cases of flouting protocols of social distancing, refusing to wear masks in public places, hosting large gatherings and parties, etc. were reported on social media as well as mass media and news channels. Antimask, antivaccination, and antilockdown protests were organized in many countries like the USA, the UK, Australia, Canada, Germany, France, Italy, etc., some of which turned violent as well. Some protests and rallies asked for freedom from lockdowns and demanded that their rights be respected. Many of these events were planned and organized through Instagram, Facebook, and Telegram. While some people blamed their governments for not being able to effectively handle the crisis, others held strikes and demonstrations to protest against the restrictions imposed on the general public. Details of all such demonstrations can be found at Wikipedia (Anon., 2021).

There is an immediate need for effective regulation of social media content to identify and filter out misinformation and radical sentiment. Social media platform controllers need to put in place real-time analysis networks so that such negative sentiment does not become widespread.

9.4 Future Prospects and Lessons Learned

Social media has an immense potential and outreach that can be fruitfully utilized in many spheres of crisis situations to better manage these circumstances. It can also be used to help each other out in the immediate community in which we live. Research implications of social media are also vast as massive amounts of varied content is created over such platforms each day. However, we need to investigate the negative aspects just as well because these facets give us valuable lessons so that we may right the wrongs in future emergencies. In the following subsections, we provide a summary of what has been discussed so far, and provide some insights into theoretical, managerial, and social relevance of this review.

9.4.1 Pandemic Management

Social media plays a pivotal role in times of crisis as an immediate and only source of information during government-enforced restrictions on movement and situations of emergency. It is therefore of utmost importance that this information is reliable and accounted for. Lack of credibility and responsibility in a pandemic can quickly replace accurate information with misinformation, rumor, and fake information, which is termed as an infodemic. Infodemic management is crucial to enable good health practices. According to the World Health Organization (WHO, Anon., 2021), infodemic management is the organized use of risk-based and evidence-based examination of and approaches to manage the infodemic and diminish its influence on health behaviors throughout such crises. Infodemics can be managed effectively with four types of activities (WHO, Anon., 2021), viz listening to the apprehensions of the public, fostering risk awareness and professional health assistance, developing resilience to information, and engaging and galvanizing societies to take constructive action. The WHO also provides several credible resources of information on its website (Anon., 2021a) along with an exclusive section on "Mythbusters" to quash every myth/rumor related to COVID-19 (Mythbusters, WHO, 2021). Hashtags that mention and spread conspiracy theories can be targeted to invalidate content having half-truths and disinformation. Social media establishments need to strengthen their efforts to tag or withdraw messages that contain misinformation. Health agencies should solicit the support of social media influencers, elites, entertainers, government officials, and health professionals in spreading accurate and reliable information (López Seguí et al., 2020). Governments must understand the tendencies of rumors, stigma, and conspiracy theories regarding COVID-19 that are circulating through the internet so that they can develop suitable content for risk communication. For example, the WHO has collaborated with major social media organizations like Facebook, Google, Twitter, and YouTube to scrutinize and minimize fake news. The WHO also provides training courses online for infodemic management and holds annual conferences on the topic. WHO has also recently launched an AI (Artificial Intelligence) powered social listening tool called EARS, or Early AI-supported Response with Social Listening (EARS, Anon., 2021) to enable health professionals to respond to the infodemic promptly with real-time analysis of public narratives. It has also been used to build reliable information infrastructure to enable countries to understand public attitudes and opinions.

Propagation of accountable information demands corresponding measures at the ground level (TOI, 2021). For instance, promoting the advantages of getting the coronavirus vaccination has to be reinforced with the provision of inoculations in adequate quantities at the ground level. In cases of a regional scarcity of vaccines, the local community should be notified in advance, which will maintain the trust of citizens in the government structure rather than promoting vaccine hesitancy. In an OECD (Organization for Economic Co-operation and Development) public response article (OECD, 2021), the role of governments in building trust in COVID-19 vaccination has been presented. According to this article, the government needs to proactively disseminate information on immunization policies, modalities, and achievements in a timely fashion across various formats. Further, by fostering transparency and integrity of special advisory bodies, medical research bodies, and community engagement in the development of vaccination strategies, governments can leverage the trust of their citizens in taking the vaccinations to build herd immunity.

In a paper by Eysenbach, (Eysenbach, 2020) four pillars of infodemic management are presented. Accurate facilitation of information translation from one audience to another is the first step in infodemic management, wherein the influencing factors like politics, commercial interests, misunderstanding, and selective reporting should be minimized. The second step or pillar is the fact-checking or refinement of that translated information to accelerate the internal quality improvement process. The third step is then to build and appraise health information from online resources to construct a trustworthy flow of information. Lastly, surveillance and monitoring of information and misinformation on online channels are needed to detect any infodemics.

9.4.2 Social Relevance

The government needs to be more attentive to the emotional well-being of the general population while battling COVID-19. If mental health issues of the public are properly and promptly addressed, many catastrophic situations can be avoided. People will be able to understand their responsibility toward observing government-enforced restrictions and COVID-19 appropriate behavior in a better way. The Chinese government has provided psychological health facilities through diverse channels like mental health hotlines, virtual consultation, online courses, and outpatient consultation (Gao et al., 2020), but more attention should be paid to depression and anxiety. The WHO and its partners have also provided mental health and psychological assistance by developing and disseminating a wide range of material on coping strategies, clinical guidance on neurological manifestations of COVID-19, adaptation of existing pyschosocial tools for COVID-19, and adaptation of essential mental health services during the pandemic (Adhanom Ghebreyesus, 2020). Not only the government and health authorities but we as fellow citizens must also realize our responsibilities toward the well-being of others. Social media peer groups can be created by volunteers and more people need to join such groups not only to receive but also to offer moral and emotional support.

Social media groups and networks need to channelize their efforts in helping their immediate community to offer services and other types of help to the needy. Such groups can also be created and managed by healthcare institutions and the government. For the economic and education sectors, online at-home product delivery, services, and learning has become exceedingly popular during the pandemic. Governments and corporates must prepare to incorporate a hybrid approach and, at the same time, collaborate and transition to social media–led marketing, advertising, communicating, and teaching.

9.4.3 Theoretical Relevance

As discussed in the previous sections, several studies have shown that by employing deep learning and machine learning techniques on social media content, predictions of COVID-19 trends and characteristics can be done up to two weeks ahead of official records. These types of predictive analyses can be used in similar situations in future health emergencies to assess infection rates, fatalities, disease characteristics, etc. Constant monitoring of infectious agents and their emerging strains is essential to predict such epidemics in the future. Epidemiologists and infectious disease experts should not disregard public opinion and personal experiences in their research. Robust online surveys over the most popular social media platforms will offer additional awareness into the disease characteristics and trajectory in situations of case overload and underreporting resulting from limited testing resources. Such insights will prove to be valuable in preparing us in a better way to manage and contain such outbreaks so that they do not spread uncontrollably.

In a nutshell, public health lessons learned for forthcoming infectious disease pandemics involve (Brown, 2020) protecting against research prejudice that may undervalue or overemphasize accompanying risk of disease and death, effective management of infodemics and proper community engagement, reviewing the integrity of terror-based public health movements, and affording complete public disclosure of undesirable effects from uncompromising mitigation strategies to contain the transmission of infection.

9.5 Conclusion

In this review, we have discussed various facets of the positive and negative impact of increased social media usage among the general population on a global scale. The major themes that have been explored as positive influencers are the positive and rapid dissemination of reliable information worldwide, psychological and other forms of assistance, predicting trends and characteristics of the pandemic, gauging public attitude, government policy enforcement, social media marketing, and technological shift in the education and research sector. Social media has helped the governments of nations understand their people better, thereby effectively addressing many of the concerns of the public. Better decision-making by the upper echelons in health organizations and government agencies has been made possible due to the inputs received from analyses of social media content across various platforms. Social media has also been used by these authorities to spread awareness and shun rumors, in collaboration with social media influencers, healthcare professionals, government officials, and the like. In situations where governments failed to manage the steep rise in cases which resulted in a shortage of essential services, oxygen supplies, hospital beds, etc., social media support groups came forward to help handle the crisis. Where businesses were severely impacted due to the strict lockdowns enforced by governments, social media came to the rescue and new-age marketing strategies emerged with full force that utilized these platforms to promote and market their products online. Due to the closure of schools, colleges, and other educational institutions, classroom learning was replaced by videoconferencing and virtual classrooms. Work-from-home policies were adopted by several industries and corporations including the public and private sectors. It has been more than two years into the pandemic since its beginning in late 2019, and a huge technological shift in working policies, learning and imparting education, decision-making, running businesses, research, collaboration, etc. has emerged and is here to stay. In a nutshell, it suffices to say that social media has been vastly supportive in managing the pandemic and has given us a new perspective on how we can manage several aspects of our lives digitally within the comfort of our homes. However, every new technology or idea can be put to good or bad use, and it is only a matter of perspective about how we choose to tap the potential of anything good. In the same manner, the negative impact of social media exposure is inevitable, especially in times of crisis. Major themes that show social media in a negative light during this crisis are the "infodemic," deterioration of mental health of individuals, and negative public attitude. Baseless rumors, myths, misinformation, disinformation, fake news, etc. spread like wildfires through social media networks. Such unreliable information may suppress the actual facts and can cause social stigma, lessen the trust of the people in their governing bodies and health infrastructure, and lead to panic and chaos among the public. Stressful situations coupled with the social media infodemic resulted in anxiety, depression, and psychological deterioration of individuals, in addition to the stigma and discrimination that some myths and rumors caused. The buildup of negative attitude led to strikes and protests, which became violent in some cases.

Even with the depressing consequences that social media exposure has caused during the pandemic, the extent to which social media has and can be utilized to control the crisis far supersedes its negative aspects. Much of the undesirable consequences stem from the infodemic that social media has caused, which can be curtailed through responsible sharing of information by both the people and social media platform managers. If misinformation spread can be quickly replaced by a refutation of the baseless claims and, in turn, reliable information that is also well-accounted for is shared along with the disclaimer, a cascade of negative consequences can be avoided. Further, by studying the vast amounts of social media content using state-of-the-art techniques like machine learning and deep learning, significant insights can be garnered related to public opinion, attitude, and concerns, case trends, disease characteristics, patient characteristics, trends and patterns related to symptoms, patient response to treatment, etc. Such insights are not only helpful in fighting the current state of the pandemic but also in proffering vital lessons to be learned so that such situations can be better managed in the future and the scale of damage can be lessened. Therefore, governments and health organizations across the globe need to understand the importance of social media content and find ways in which its potential can be constructively exploited to address forthcoming crises.

References

Abd-Alrazaq, A., D. Alhuwail, M. Househ, M. Hamdi, and Z. Shah. 2020. Top Concerns of Tweeters during the COVID-19 Pandemic: Infoveillance Study. *Journal of Medical Internet Research* 22, no. 4.

Adhanom Ghebreyesus, T. 2020. Addressing Mental Health Needs: An Integral Part of COVID-19 Response. *World Psychiatry* 19, no. 2: 129–130.

Adzovie, D.E., A.B. Jibril, R.H. Adzovie, and I.E. Nyieku. 2020. E-Learning Resulting from COVID-19 Pandemic: A Conceptual Study from a Developing Country Perspective. In *7th European Conference on Social Media ECSM*. Reading, United Kingdom: Academic Conferences and Publishing Limited, p. 19.

Agustinus Palimbong, M.L. 2021. Survey Online Learning in the Pandemic Time of Covid-19, Case Study at Universitas Kristen Indonesia. *Psychology and Education Journal* 58, no. 2: 6041–6049.

Ahmad, A.R., and H.R. Murad. 2020. The Impact of Social Media on Panic during the COVID-19 Pandemic in Iraqi Kurdistan: Online Questionnaire Study. *Journal of Medical Internet Research* 22, no. 5.

Ahmed, W., J. Vidal-Alaball, J. Downing, and F. López Seguí. 2020. COVID-19 and the 5G Conspiracy Theory: Social Network Analysis of Twitter Data. *Journal of Medical Internet Research* 22, no. 5.

Al-Rawi, A., M. Siddiqi, R. Morgan, N. Vandan, J. Smith, and C. Wenham. 2020. COVID-19 and the Gendered Use of Emojis on Twitter: Infodemiology Study. *Journal of Medical Internet Research* 22, no. 11.

Anon. 2021a. Advice for the Public on COVID-19. *World Health Organization*. Accessed December 26. www.who.int/emergencies/diseases/novel-coronavirus-2019/advice-for-public.

Anon. 2021b. Covid-19 Mythbusters. *World Health Organization*. Accessed December 26. www.who.int/emergencies/diseases/novel-coronavirus-2019/advice-for-public/myth-busters#5g.

Anon. 2022. *Social Media & COVID-19*. Accessed January 24. https://covid19-infodemic.com/.

Ara Eti, I., M.A. Horaira, and M.M. Bari. 2021. Power and Stimulus of Social Media Marketing on Consumer Purchase Intention in Bangladesh during the COVID-19. *International Journal of Research in Business and Social Science (2147–4478)* 10, no. 1: 28–37.

Arpaci, I., S. Alshehabi, M. Al-Emran, M. Khasawneh, I. Mahariq, T. Abdeljawad, and A. Ella Hassanien. 2020. Analysis of Twitter Data Using Evolutionary Clustering during the COVID-19 Pandemic. *Computers, Materials & Continua* 65, no. 1: 193–204.

Basch, C.E., C.H. Basch, G.C. Hillyer, and C. Jaime. 2020. The Role of YouTube and the Entertainment Industry in Saving Lives by Educating and Mobilizing the Public to Adopt Behaviors for Community Mitigation of COVID-19: Successive Sampling Design Study. *JMIR Public Health and Surveillance* 6, no. 2.

Bhuiyan, A.K., N. Sakib, A.H. Pakpour, M.D. Griffiths, and M.A. Mamun. 2020. Covid-19-Related Suicides in Bangladesh Due to Lockdown and Economic Factors: Case Study Evidence from Media Reports. *International Journal of Mental Health and Addiction* 19, no. 6: 2110–2115.

Bloomberg. 2021. Omicron Four Times More Transmissible than Delta in Japan Study. *The Mercury News*. www.mercurynews.com/2021/12/09/omicron-four-times-more-transmissible-than-delta-in-japan-study/.

Boon-Itt, S., and Y. Skunkan. 2020. Public Perception of the COVID-19 Pandemic on Twitter: Sentiment Analysis and Topic Modeling Study. *JMIR Public Health and Surveillance* 6, no. 4.

Breland, A. 2020. Russian Media Outlets Are Blaming the Coronavirus on the United States. *Mother Jones*. www.motherjones.com/politics/2020/02/russian-disinformation-coronavirus/.

Brennen, J.S., F.M. Simon, and R.K. Nielsen. 2020. Beyond (Mis)Representation: Visuals in Covid-19 Misinformation. *The International Journal of Press/Politics* 26, no. 1: 277–299.

Brown, R.B. 2020. Public Health Lessons Learned from Biases in Coronavirus Mortality Overestimation. *Disaster Medicine and Public Health Preparedness* 14, no. 3: 364–371.

Bruns, A., S. Harrington, and E. Hurcombe. 2020. 'Corona? 5G? or Both?': The Dynamics of Covid-19/5G Conspiracy Theories on Facebook. *Media International Australia* 177, no. 1: 12–29.

Budhwani, H., and R. Sun. 2020. Creating Covid-19 Stigma by Referencing the Novel Coronavirus as the "Chinese Virus" on Twitter: Quantitative Analysis of Social Media Data. *Journal of Medical Internet Research* 22, no. 5.

Capasso, A., A.M. Jones, S.H. Ali, J. Foreman, Y. Tozan, and R.J. DiClemente. 2021. Increased Alcohol Use during the COVID-19 Pandemic: The Effect of Mental Health and Age in a Cross-Sectional Sample of Social Media Users in the U.S. *Preventive Medicine* 145: 106422.

Chan, A.K., C.P. Nickson, J.W. Rudolph, A. Lee, and G.M. Joynt. 2020. Social Media for Rapid Knowledge Dissemination: Early Experience from the COVID-19 Pandemic. *Anaesthesia* 75, no. 12: 1579–1582.

Chang, A., P.J. Schulz, S.T. Tu, and M.T. Liu. 2020. Communicative Blame in Online Communication of the COVID-19 Pandemic: Computational Approach of Stigmatizing Cues and Negative Sentiment Gauged with Automated Analytic Techniques. *Journal of Medical Internet Research* 22, no. 11.

Chen, Q., C. Min, W. Zhang, G. Wang, X. Ma, and R. Evans. 2020. Unpacking the Black Box: How to Promote Citizen Engagement through Government Social Media during the COVID-19 Crisis. *Computers in Human Behavior* 110: 106380.

Cheng, P., G. Xia, P. Pang, B. Wu, W. Jiang, Y.-T. Li, M. Wang, et al. 2020. Covid-19 Epidemic Peer Support and Crisis Intervention via Social Media. *Community Mental Health Journal* 56, no. 5: 786–792.

Chew, A.W., Y. Pan, Y. Wang, and L. Zhang. 2021. Hybrid Deep Learning of Social Media Big Data for Predicting the Evolution of COVID-19 Transmission. *Knowledge-Based Systems* 233: 107417.

Coleman, A. 2020. 'Hundreds Dead' Because of Covid-19 Misinformation. *BBC News.* www.bbc.com/news/world-53755067.

Darling-Hammond, S., E.K. Michaels, A.M. Allen, D.H. Chae, M.D. Thomas, T.T. Nguyen, M.M. Mujahid, and R.C. Johnson. 2020. After "The China Virus" Went Viral: Racially Charged Coronavirus Coverage and Trends in Bias against Asian Americans. *Health Education & Behavior* 47, no. 6: 870–879.

Das, R., and W. Ahmed. 2021. Rethinking Fake News: Disinformation and Ideology during the Time of Covid-19 Global Pandemic. *IIM Kozhikode Society & Management Review*: 227797522110273.

Das, S., and A. Dutta. 2020. Characterizing Public Emotions and Sentiments in COVID-19 Environment: A Case Study of India. *Journal of Human Behavior in the Social Environment* 31, no. 1–4: 154–167.

Davidson, P. 2020. It's Official: The US Is in a Recession, Ending Longest Expansion in History. *USA Today.* Gannett Satellite Information Network. www.usatoday.com/story/money/2020/06/08/recession-begins-us-ending-longest-expansion-history/5320335002/.

De Santis, E., A. Martino, and A. Rizzi. 2020. An Infoveillance System for Detecting and Tracking Relevant Topics from Italian Tweets during the Covid-19 Event. *IEEE Access* 8: 132527–132538.

Drouin, M., B.T. McDaniel, J. Pater, and T. Toscos. 2020. How Parents and Their Children Used Social Media and Technology at the Beginning of the COVID-19 Pandemic and Associations with Anxiety. *Cyberpsychology, Behavior, and Social Networking* 23, no. 11: 727–736.

Dutta, D.A. 2020. Impact of Digital Social Media on Indian Higher Education: Alternative Approaches of Online Learning during COVID-19 Pandemic Crisis. *International Journal of Scientific and Research Publications (IJSRP)* 10, no. 05: 604–611.

EARS, Anon. 2021. Who Launches Pilot of AI-Powered Public-Access Social Listening Tool. *World Health Organization*. Accessed December 26. www.who.int/news-room/feature-stories/detail/who-launches-pilot-of-ai-powered-public-access-social-listening-tool.

Edelman, R. 2020. Trust Barometer Special Report: Brand Trust and the Coronavirus Pandemic. *Edelman*. www.edelman.com/research/covid-19-brand-trust-report.

Eysenbach, G. 2020. How to Fight an Infodemic: The Four Pillars of Infodemic Management. *Journal of Medical Internet Research* 22, no. 6.

Feis, A. 2021. 'Damning' Science Shows Covid-19 Likely Engineered in Lab: Experts. *New York Post*. https://nypost.com/2021/06/06/damning-science-shows-covid-19-likely-engineered-in-lab/.

Galhardi, C.P., N.P. Freire, M.C. Minayo, and M.C. Fagundes. 2020. Fato Ou Fake? Uma Análise Da Desinformação Frente à Pandemia Da Covid-19 No Brasil. *Ciência & Saúde Coletiva* 25, no. suppl 2: 4201–4210.

Gallotti, R., F. Valle, N. Castaldo, P. Sacco, and M. De Domenico. 2020. Assessing the Risks of "Infodemics" in Response to Covid-19 Epidemics, *Nature Human Behaviour* 4, no. 12: 1285–1293. http://doi.org/10.1038/s41562-020-00994-6.

Gao, J., P. Zheng, Y. Jia, H. Chen, Y. Mao, S. Chen, Y. Wang, H. Fu, and J. Dai. 2020. Mental Health Problems and Social Media Exposure during COVID-19 Outbreak. *PLoS ONE* 15, no. 4.

Geirdal, A.Ø., M. Ruffolo, J. Leung, H. Thygesen, D. Price, T. Bonsaksen, and M. Schoultz. 2021. Mental Health, Quality of Life, Wellbeing, Loneliness and Use of Social Media in a Time of Social Distancing during the COVID-19 Outbreak. A Cross-Country Comparative Study. *Journal of Mental Health*: 1–8.

Goel, A., and L. Gupta. 2020. Social Media in the Times of Covid-19. *JCR: Journal of Clinical Rheumatology* 26, no. 6: 220–223.

Golder, S., A.Z. Klein, A. Magge, K. O'Connor, H. Cai, D. Weissenbacher, and G. Gonzalez-Hernandez. 2020. Extending a Chronological and Geographical Analysis of Personal Reports of COVID-19 on Twitter to England, UK, *medRxiv* [Preprint]. http://doi.org/10.1101/2020.05.05.20083436

González-Padilla, D.A., and L. Tortolero-Blanco. 2020. Social Media Influence in the COVID-19 Pandemic. *International Braz j Urol* 46, no. suppl 1: 120–124.

Gozzi, N., M. Tizzani, M. Starnini, F. Ciulla, D. Paolotti, A. Panisson, and N. Perra. 2020. Collective Response to Media Coverage of the COVID-19 Pandemic on Reddit and Wikipedia: Mixed-Methods Analysis. *Journal of Medical Internet Research* 22, no. 10.

Haddad, J.M., C. Macenski, A. Mosier-Mills, A. Hibara, K. Kester, M. Schneider, R.C. Conrad, and C.H. Liu. 2021. The Impact of Social Media on College Mental Health during the COVID-19 Pandemic: A Multinational Review of the Existing Literature. *Current Psychiatry Reports* 23, no. 11.

Hanlon, A., and L. Bullock. 2021. Global Social Media Statistics Research Summary 2022. *Smart Insights*. www.smartinsights.com/social-media-marketing/social-media-strategy/new-global-social-media-research/.

Hidayati, A., and M. Yansi. 2020. Role of Social Media in Marketing of Micro, Small, and Medium Enterprises (Msmes) Product during COVID 19 Pandemic. *Jurnal Ilmiah Teunuleh* 1, no. 2: 239–249.

Huang, C., X. Xu, Y. Cai, Q. Ge, G. Zeng, X. Li, W. Zhang, C. Ji, and L. Yang. 2020. Mining the Characteristics of COVID-19 Patients in China: Analysis of Social Media Posts. *Journal of Medical Internet Research* 22, no. 5.

Islam, M.S., T. Sarkar, S.H. Khan, A.-H. Mostofa Kamal, S.M. Hasan, A. Kabir, D. Yeasmin, et al. 2020. Covid-19–Related Infodemic and Its Impact on Public Health: A Global Social Media Analysis. *The American Journal of Tropical Medicine and Hygiene* 103, no. 4: 1621–1629.

Islam, T., A.H. Pitafi, V. Arya, Y. Wang, N. Akhtar, S. Mubarik, and L. Xiaobei. 2021. Panic Buying in the COVID-19 Pandemic: A Multi-Country Examination. *Journal of Retailing and Consumer Services* 59: 102357.

Jelodar, H., Y. Wang, R. Orji, and S. Huang. 2020. Deep Sentiment Classification and Topic Discovery on Novel Coronavirus or COVID-19 Online Discussions: NLP Using LSTM Recurrent Neural Network Approach. *IEEE Journal of Biomedical and Health Informatics* 24, no. 10: 2733–2742.

Jogezai, N.A., F.A. Baloch, M. Jaffar, T. Shah, G.K. Khilji, and S. Bashir. 2021. Teachers' Attitudes towards Social Media (SM) Use in Online Learning amid the COVID-19 Pandemic: The Effects of SM Use by Teachers and Religious Scholars during Physical Distancing. *Heliyon* 7, no. 4.

Jones, M.O. 2020. Disinformation Superspreaders: The Weaponisation of Covid-19 Fake News in the Persian Gulf and Beyond. *Global Discourse* 10, no. 4: 431–437.

K, D. 2020. Analysing Covid-19 News Impact on Social Media Aggregation. *International Journal of Advanced Trends in Computer Science and Engineering* 9, no. 3: 2848–2855.

Karabela, Ş.N., F. Coşkun, and H. Hoşgör. 2021. Investigation of the Relationships between Perceived Causes of COVID-19, Attitudes towards Vaccine and Level of Trust in Information Sources from the Perspective of Infodemic: The Case of Turkey. *BMC Public Health* 21, no. 1.

Katz, M., and N. Nandi. 2021. Social Media and Medical Education in the Context of the COVID-19 Pandemic: Scoping Review. *JMIR Medical Education* 7, no. 2.

Kemp, S. July 2020. Digital 2020: July Global Statshot—Datareportal—Global Digital Insights. *DataReportal. DataReportal—Global Digital Insights.* https://datareportal.com/reports/digital-2020-july-global-statshot.

Kemp, S. July 2021. Digital 2021 July Global Statshot Report—Datareportal—Global Digital Insights. *DataReportal. DataReportal—Global Digital Insights.* https://datareportal.com/reports/digital-2021-july-global-statshot.

Kemp, S. Oct 2021. Digital 2021 October Global Statshot Report—Datareportal—Global Digital Insights. *DataReportal. DataReportal—Global Digital Insights.* https://datareportal.com/reports/digital-2021-october-global-statshot.

Khan, K.S., M.A. Mamun, M.D. Griffiths, and I. Ullah. 2020. The Mental Health Impact of the COVID-19 Pandemic across Different Cohorts. *International Journal of Mental Health and Addiction* 20, no. 1: 380–386. http://doi.org/10.1007/s11469-020-00367-0

Khan, M.N., M.A. Ashraf, D. Seinen, K.U. Khan, and R.A. Laar. 2021. Social Media for Knowledge Acquisition and Dissemination: The Impact of the COVID-19 Pandemic on Collaborative Learning Driven Social Media Adoption. *Frontiers in Psychology* 12.

Khan, T.M. 2020. Use of Social Media and WhatsApp to Conduct Teaching Activities during the COVID-19 Lockdown in Pakistan. *International Journal of Pharmacy Practice* 29, no. 1: 90–90.

Klein, A.Z., A. Magge, K. O'Connor, H. Cai, D. Weissenbacher, and G. Gonzalez-Hernandez. 2020. A Chronological and Geographical Analysis of Personal Reports of Covid-19 on Twitter. *Digital Health.* http://doi.org/10.1177/20552076221097508

Kouzy, R., J. Abi Jaoude, A. Kraitem, M.B. El Alam, B. Karam, E. Adib, J. Zarka, C. Traboulsi, E. Akl, and K. Baddour. 2020. Coronavirus Goes Viral: Quantifying the Covid-19 Misinformation Epidemic on Twitter. *Cureus* 12, no. 3: e7255. http://doi.org/10.7759/cureus.7255

Li, C., L.J. Chen, X. Chen, M. Zhang, C.P. Pang, and H. Chen. 2020. Retrospective Analysis of the Possibility of Predicting the Covid-19 Outbreak from Internet Searches and Social Media Data, China, 2020. *Eurosurveillance* 25, no. 10.

Li, L., Q. Zhang, X. Wang, J. Zhang, T. Wang, T.-L. Gao, W. Duan, K.K.-Fai Tsoi, and F.-Y. Wang. 2020. Characterizing the Propagation of Situational Information in Social Media during COVID-19 Epidemic: A Case Study on Weibo. *IEEE Transactions on Computational Social Systems* 7, no. 2: 556–562.

Li, S., Y. Wang, J. Xue, N. Zhao, and T. Zhu. 2020. The Impact of Covid-19 Epidemic Declaration on Psychological Consequences: A Study on Active Weibo Users. *International Journal of Environmental Research and Public Health* 17, no. 6: 2032.

Lim, L.J.H., L.M. Fong, J. Hariram, Y.W. Lee, and P.-C. Tor. 2020. Covid-19, a Pandemic That Affects More than Just Physical Health: Two Case Reports. *Asian Journal of Psychiatry* 53: 102200.

Lisitsa, E., K.S. Benjamin, S.K. Chun, J. Skalisky, L.E. Hammond, and A.H. Mezulis. 2020. Loneliness among Young Adults during COVID-19 Pandemic: The Mediational Roles of Social Media Use and Social Support Seeking. *Journal of Social and Clinical Psychology* 39, no. 8: 708–726.

Liu, D., Y. Wang, J. Wang, J. Liu, Y. Yue, W. Liu, F. Zhang, and Z. Wang. 2020. Characteristics and Outcomes of a Sample of Patients with COVID-19 Identified through Social Media in Wuhan, China: Observational Study. *Journal of Medical Internet Research* 22, no. 8.

Loomba, S., A. de Figueiredo, S.J. Piatek, K. de Graaf, and H.J. Larson. 2021. Measuring the Impact of COVID-19 Vaccine Misinformation on Vaccination Intent in the UK and USA. *Nature Human Behaviour* 5, no. 3: 337–348.

López Seguí, F., J. Vidal-Alaball, and M.S. Katz. 2020. Covid-19 and the "Film Your Hospital" Conspiracy Theory: Social Network Analysis of Twitter Data. *Journal of Medical Internet Research* 22, no. 10.

Lwin, M.O., J. Lu, A. Sheldenkar, P.J. Schulz, W. Shin, R. Gupta, and Y. Yang. 2020. Global Sentiments Surrounding the COVID-19 Pandemic on Twitter: Analysis of Twitter Trends. *JMIR Public Health and Surveillance* 6, no. 2.

Mackey, T., V. Purushothaman, J. Li, N. Shah, M. Nali, C. Bardier, B. Liang, M. Cai, and R. Cuomo. 2020. Machine Learning to Detect Self-Reporting of Symptoms, Testing Access, and Recovery Associated with Covid-19 on Twitter: Retrospective Big Data Infoveillance Study. *JMIR Public Health and Surveillance* 6, no. 2.

Mason, A.N., J. Narcum, and K. Mason. 2021. Social Media Marketing Gains Importance after Covid-19. *Cogent Business & Management* 8, no. 1.

Merkley, E., A. Bridgman, D. Ruths, and O. Zhilin. 2020. A Rare Moment of Cross-Partisan Consensus: Elite and Public Response to the COVID-19 Pandemic in Canada. *Canadian Journal of Political Science* 53, no. 2: 311–318.

Mohammed, R., T.M. Nguse, B.M. Habte, A.M. Fentie, and G.B. Gebretekle. 2021. COVID-19 Vaccine Hesitancy among Ethiopian Healthcare Workers. *PLoS ONE* 16, no. 12.

Moscadelli, A., G. Albora, M.A. Biamonte, D. Giorgetti, M. Innocenzio, S. Paoli, C. Lorini, P. Bonanni, and G. Bonaccorsi. 2020. Fake News and COVID-19 in Italy: Results of a Quantitative Observational Study. *International Journal of Environmental Research and Public Health* 17, no. 16: 5850.

Muric, G., Y. Wu, and E. Ferrara. 2021. COVID-19 Vaccine Hesitancy on Social Media: Building a Public Twitter Data Set of Antivaccine Content, Vaccine Misinformation, and Conspiracies. *JMIR Public Health and Surveillance* 7, no. 11.

NewIndianXpress. 2020. Suicide Cases on the Rise in Nepal during COVID-19 Lockdown. *The New Indian Express*. www.newindianexpress.com/world/2020/jul/07/suicide-cases-on-the-rise-in-nepal-during-covid-19-lockdown-2166528.html.

Novitasari, A.T. 2021. Digital Media Marketing Strategies for MSMES during the COVID-19 Pandemic. *Focus* 2, no. 2: 72–80.

OECD, Anon. 2021. Enhancing Public Trust in COVID-19 Vaccination: The Role of Governments. *OECD*. www.oecd.org/coronavirus/policy-responses/enhancing-public-trust-in-covid-19-vaccination-the-role-of-governments-eae0ec5a/.

O'Leary, D.E., and V.C. Storey. 2020. A Google–Wikipedia–Twitter Model as a Leading Indicator of the Numbers of Coronavirus Deaths. *Intelligent Systems in Accounting, Finance and Management* 27, no. 3: 151–158.

Our World in Data, Anon. 2022. Covid-19 Data Explorer. Our World in Data. Accessed January 1. https://ourworldindata.org/explorers/coronavirus-data-explorer?tab=map&facet=none&Metric=Confirmed%2Bcases&Interval=Cumulative&Relative%2Bto%2BPopulation=true&Align%2Boutbreaks=false&country=USA~ITA~CAN~DEU~GBR~FRA.

Pathare, S., L. Vijayakumar, T.N. Fernandes, M. Shastri, A. Kapoor, D. Pandit, I. Lohumi, S. Ray, A. Kulkarni, and P. Korde. 2020. Analysis of News Media Reports of Suicides and Attempted Suicides during the COVID-19 Lockdown in India. *International Journal of Mental Health Systems* 14, no. 1.

Patma, T.S., L.W. Wardana, A. Wibowo, B.S. Narmaditya, and F. Akbarina. 2021. The Impact of Social Media Marketing for Indonesian Smes Sustainability: Lesson from COVID-19 Pandemic. *Cogent Business & Management* 8, no. 1.

Peng, Y., C. Li, Y. Rong, C.P. Pang, X. Chen, and H. Chen. 2021. Real-Time Prediction of the Daily Incidence of COVID-19 in 215 Countries and Territories Using Machine Learning: Model Development and Validation. *Journal of Medical Internet Research* 23, no. 6.

Peng, Z., R. Wang, L. Liu, and H. Wu. 2020. Exploring Urban Spatial Features of COVID-19 Transmission in Wuhan Based on Social Media Data. *ISPRS International Journal of Geo-Information* 9, no. 6: 402.

Plus, Anon., T.T.O.I. 2021. Covid's Uncounted Death? A Big Increase in Suicide Cases—Times of India. *The Times of India*. https://timesofindia.indiatimes.com/india/covids-uncounted-death-a-big-increase-in-suicide-cases/articleshow/87391278.cms.

Qin, L., Q. Sun, Y. Wang, K.-F. Wu, M. Chen, B.-C. Shia, and S.-Y. Wu. 2020. Prediction of Number of Cases of 2019 Novel Coronavirus (COVID-19) Using Social Media Search Index. *International Journal of Environmental Research and Public Health* 17, no. 7: 2365.

Rana, U. 2020. Elderly Suicides in India: An Emerging Concern during COVID-19 Pandemic. *International Psychogeriatrics* 32, no. 10: 1251–1252.

Recive News, Anon. 2020. The Coronavirus 'Infodemic' Is Real. We Rated the Websites Responsible for It. *Receive News—USA and World News.* https://receive.news/02/28/2020/the-coronavirus-infodemic-is-real-we-rated-the-websites-responsible-for-it/.

Reger, M.A., I.H. Stanley, and T.E. Joiner. 2020. Suicide Mortality and Coronavirus Disease 2019—A Perfect Storm? *JAMA Psychiatry* 77, no. 11: 1093.

Relias Media, Anon. 2021. Social Media Fuels COVID-19 Vaccine Fear. *Relias Media—Continuing Medical Education Publishing.* Accessed December 26. www.reliasmedia.com/articles/147885-social-media-fuels-covid-19-vaccine-fear.

Rovetta, A., and A.S. Bhagavathula. 2020. Global Infodemiology of COVID-19: Analysis of Google Web Searches and Instagram Hashtags. *Journal of Medical Internet Research* 22, no. 8.

Rufai, S.R., and C. Bunce. 2020. World Leaders' Usage of Twitter in Response to the COVID-19 Pandemic: A Content Analysis. *Journal of Public Health* 42, no. 3: 510–516.

Saha, K., J. Torous, E.D. Caine, and M. De Choudhury. 2020. Psychosocial Effects of the COVID-19 Pandemic: Large-Scale Quasi-Experimental Study on Social Media. *Journal of Medical Internet Research* 22, no. 11.

Sahoo, S., S. Rani, S. Parveen, A. Pal Singh, A. Mehra, S. Chakrabarti, S. Grover, and C. Tandup. 2020. Self-Harm and COVID-19 Pandemic: An Emerging Concern—a Report of 2 Cases from India. *Asian Journal of Psychiatry* 51: 102104.

Salrzman, L.Y., T.C. Hansel, and P.S. Bordnick. 2020. Loneliness, Isolation, and Social Support Factors in Post-Covid-19 Mental Health. *Psychological Trauma: Theory, Research, Practice, and Policy* 12, no. S1.

Saluja, R. 2021. Social Media Provided a Lifeline to a Desperate India at COVID-19's Peak. *Foreign Policy.* https://foreignpolicy.com/2021/06/28/social-media-covid-19-india-resources/.

Sandford, A. 2020. Coronavirus: Half of Humanity on Lockdown in 90 Countries. *Euronews.* www.euronews.com/2020/04/02/coronavirus-in-europe-spain-s-death-toll-hits-10-000-after-record-950-new-deaths-in-24-hou.

Sear, R.F., N. Velasquez, R. Leahy, N.J. Restrepo, S.E. Oud, N. Gabriel, Y. Lupu, and N.F. Johnson. 2020. Quantifying COVID-19 Content in the Online Health Opinion War Using Machine Learning. *IEEE Access* 8: 91886–91893.

Share Your Story, Anon. 2021. Coronavirus May Have Originated in Lab Linked to China's Biowarfare Program · Covid-19 Archive. *Share Your Story · A Journal of the Plague Year · Covid-19 Archive.* Accessed December 25. https://covid-19archive.org/s/archive/item/12429.

Shen, C., A. Chen, C. Luo, J. Zhang, B. Feng, and W. Liao. 2020. Using Reports of Symptoms and Diagnoses on Social Media to Predict COVID-19 Case Counts in Mainland China: Observational Infoveillance Study. *Journal of Medical Internet Research* 22, no. 5.

Sobaih, A.E., A.M. Hasanein, and A.E. Abu Elnasr. 2020. Responses to COVID-19 in Higher Education: Social Media Usage for Sustaining Formal Academic Communication in Developing Countries. *Sustainability* 12, no. 16: 6520.

Statista, Anon. 2021. Social Media. *Statista.* Accessed December 11. www.statista.com/topics/1164/social-networks/#dossierKeyfigures.

Sujarwoto, R.A. Saputri, and T. Yumarni. 2021. Social Media Addiction and Mental Health among University Students during the COVID-19 Pandemic in Indonesia. *International Journal of Mental Health and Addiction*, 1–15. http://doi.org/10.1007/s11469-021-00582-3

Sutton, J., S.L. Renshaw, and C.T. Butts. 2020. COVID-19: Retransmission of Official Communications in an Emerging Pandemic. *PLoS ONE* 15, no. 9.

Syaifullah, J., M. Syaifudin, M.A. Sukendar, and J. Junaedi. 2021. Social Media Marketing and Business Performance of MSMEs During the COVID-19 Pandemic. *The Journal of Asian Finance, Economics and Business* 8, no. 2: 523–531. http://doi.org/10.13106/JAFEB.2021.VOL8.NO2.0523.

TOI, Anon. 2021. Infodemic Management Key to Fight COVID-19 Pandemic. *Times of India Blog.* https://timesofindia.indiatimes.com/blogs/development-chaupal/infodemic-management-key-to-fight-covid-19-pandemic/.

Tsao, S.-F., H. Chen, T. Tisseverasinghe, Y. Yang, L. Li, and Z.A. Butt. 2021. What Social Media Told Us in the Time of COVID-19: A Scoping Review. *The Lancet Digital Health* 3, no. 3.

Uyheng, J., and K.M. Carley. 2020. Bots and Online Hate during the COVID-19 Pandemic: Case Studies in the United States and the Philippines. *Journal of Computational Social Science* 3, no. 2: 445–468.

Valdez, D., M. ten Thij, K. Bathina, L.A. Rutter, and J. Bollen. 2020. Social Media Insights into US Mental Health during the COVID-19 Pandemic: Longitudinal Analysis of Twitter Data. *Journal of Medical Internet Research* 22, no. 12.

Volkmer, I. 2021. *Social Media and COVID-19: A Global Study of Digital Crisis Interaction among Gen Z and Millennials.* https://www.who.int/news-room/feature-stories/detail/social-media-covid-19-a-global-study-of-digital-crisis-interaction-among-gen-z-and-millennials

Wajahat, Hussain. 2020. Role of Social Media in Covid-19 Pandemic. *The International Journal of Frontier Sciences* 4, no. 2: 59–60.

Wang, Y., H. Hao, and L.S. Platt. 2021. Examining Risk and Crisis Communications of Government Agencies and Stakeholders during Early-Stages of COVID-19 on Twitter. *Computers in Human Behavior* 114: 106568.

WHO, Anon. 2021. Infodemic. *World Health Organization.* Accessed December 24. www.who.int/health-topics/infodemic#tab=tab_1.

Wikipedia, Anon. 2021. Protests over Responses to the COVID-19 Pandemic. *Wikipedia.* Wikimedia Foundation. https://en.wikipedia.org/wiki/Protests_over_responses_to_the_COVID-19_pandemic.

Wilson, S.L., and C. Wiysonge. 2020. Social Media and Vaccine Hesitancy. *BMJ Global Health* 5, no. 10.

World Health Organization, Anon. 2021. Who Director-General's Opening Remarks at the Media Briefing on COVID-19–12 November 2021. *World Health Organization.* Accessed December 29. www.who.int/director-general/speeches/detail/who-director-general-s-opening-remarks-at-the-media-briefing-on-covid-19-12-november-2021.

Worldometer, Anon. 2022. Coronavirus Cases. *Worldometer.* Accessed January 1. www.worldometers.info/coronavirus/.

Yin, F., J. Lv, X. Zhang, X. Xia, and J. Wu. 2020. COVID-19 Information Propagation Dynamics in the Chinese Sina-Microblog. *Mathematical Biosciences and Engineering* 17, no. 3: 2676–2692.

Yousefinaghani, S., R. Dara, S. Mubareka, and S. Sharif. 2021. Prediction of COVID-19 Waves Using Social Media and Google Search: A Case Study of the US and Canada. *Frontiers in Public Health* 9.

Zarzycka, E., J. Krasodomska, A. Mazurczak-Mąka, and M. Turek-Radwan. 2021. Distance Learning during the COVID-19 Pandemic: Students' Communication and Collaboration and the Role of Social Media. *Cogent Arts & Humanities* 8, no. 1.

Zhong, B., Y. Huang, and Q. Liu. 2021. Mental Health Toll from the Coronavirus: Social Media Usage Reveals Wuhan Residents' Depression and Secondary Trauma in the COVID-19 Outbreak. *Computers in Human Behavior* 114: 106524.

Zhong, B., Z. Jiang, W. Xie, and X. Qin. 2020. Association of Social Media Use with Mental Health Conditions of Nonpatients during the COVID-19 Outbreak: Insights from a National Survey Study. *Journal of Medical Internet Research* 22, no. 12.

Zhu, Y., J. Xie, Y. Yu, and A. Chen. 2020. Using Social Media Data to Assess the Impact of COVID-19 on Mental Health in China. *Psychological Medicine* 20: 1–8. http://doi.org/10.1017/S0033291721001598

Index